Rounding the Bases

Sports and Religion

A SERIES EDITED
BY JOSEPH L. PRICE

Books in the series:

Robert J. Higgs and Michael C. Braswell, *An Unholy Alliance: The Sacred and Modern Sports* (2004)

Allen E. Hye, *The Great God Baseball: Religion in Modern Baseball Fiction* (2004)

Marc A. Jolley, *Safe at Home: A Memoir on God, Baseball, and Family* (2005)

Joseph L. Price, ed., *From Season to Season: Sports as American Religion* (2001; 2004)

Joseph L. Price, *Rounding the Bases: Baseball and Religion in America*

Forthcoming:

Eric Bain-Selbo, *Game Day and God: Football, Religion, and Politics in the South*

Craig Forney, *The Holy Trinity of American Sports*

W. David Hall, *Faith and Religion in the Big Blue Nation: The Cultural and Religious Sensibilities of the Kentucky Basketball Faithful*

Rounding the Bases

Baseball and Religion in America

Joseph L. Price

Mercer University Press
Macon, Georgia
2006

ISBN 978-0-86554-999-9
MUP/H708

First Edition.

∞The paper used in this publication meets the minimum requirements of American
National Standard for Information Sciences—Permanence of Paper for Printed Library
Materials, ANSI Z39.48-1992.

Library of Congress Cataloging-in-Publication Data

Price, Joseph L., 1949-
Rounding the bases : baseball and religion in America /
by Joseph L. Price. -- 1st ed.
p. cm.
Includes bibliographical references and index.
ISBN-13: 978-0-86554-999-9 (hardback : alk. paper)
ISBN-10: 0-86554-999-0 (hardback : alk. paper)
1. Baseball—Social aspects—United States. 2. Sports—United
States—Religious aspects. 3. Civil religion—United States.
I. Title.
GV867.6.P75 2006
796.3570973--dc22
2006013604

For the good friends

with whom I have embraced

the great game of baseball—

especially Don Musser

Contents

Acknowledgments

Baseball is a game for friends. It's tough to enjoy playing the game alone—although I tried on many afternoons as a child when I would toss the ball up and swing through its descent or when I'd try to play catch with a brick wall, hoping to carom a tennis ball off the wall in such a way that it might bounce awry or at least far enough away to make me lunge for it backhanded. Whiffle-ball homerun derby games with Bubba Tatum or George Ferguson were far more satisfying because baseball is more fun with friends.

So, too, I might add, are thinking and writing about baseball. For this book would not have been conceivable without the conversations with friends who have stimulated my imagination, who have offered research suggestions and support, and who have provided critical feedback. To my good baseball-loving friends I owe much of this book.

The project itself has developed in response to queries and encouragement by Marc Jolley. Of all of the sports and religion books that I had imagined, this one had not come to mind until Marc prompted me to pull together a few previous pieces, recasting some and melding them together with additional chapters conceived specifically for this work.

My initial soiree into thinking about sports as religion was provoked by my grad school friend and colleague Jamie Price in 1980. Late one evening in my Chicago apartment, he mused with me about organizing a conference in Atlanta on "Braves, Falcons, and Other Deities." When I got to Whittier College a couple of years later, my colleague Hilmi Ibrahim asked me at a faculty sack lunch one day what course I'd like to teach. Without hesitating, I quipped, "Braves, Falcons, and Other Deities," and then described the project to him. Miraculously, it seemed to me at that time, he said that if I would agree to team-teach the class with him during the following year, he would guide the proposal through the necessary academic committees. And so we taught "Sport, Play, and Ritual" in January 1984. Now I offer the course every other year.

During the summer before teaching the course, I attended a marvelous Dodgers-Phillies game with my departmental colleague and mentor Glenn

Yocum. As we watched Steve Carlton best Fernando Valenzuela from our perch behind home plate in the fifth deck of Dodger Stadium, we looked down on the field and began to talk about its cosmology and rituals. And shortly thereafter I began to work on an essay that, now expanded and revised, appears as Chapter 3—"The Pitcher's Mound as Cosmic Mountain."

In subsequent years, I have attended games and conferences with numerous friends, family, and colleagues, several of whom have made distinct contributions to my work. At Whittier, Charles Adams and Mike McBride consistently support my work—as well as being great friends with whom I enjoy watching games. Among their multiple contributions, Charles first alerted me to the phenomenon of "Faith Nights" at Minor League ballparks (a topic addressed in Chapter 1), and Mike has frequently directed resources my way that deal with the sacred character of ballparks and the virtual canonization of baseball's stars. Correspondingly, my compatriot Dallas Rhodes has listened attentively and quizzically to my ideas while we have attended games in cities throughout the country. Annually at meetings of the Popular Culture Association, I have benefited from the encouragement and feedback provided by Doug Noverr, Larry Ziewacz, Allen Hye, and Pete Williams, among the frequent participants in the sports sessions of that multi-disciplinary organization. And Fred Bergerson and Warren Hanson, friendly competitors in the Whittier College Fantasy Baseball League that has entered its third decade, have contributed much to my understanding of devotion to teams and a love for the game.

Throughout the past quarter-century, however, no one has exerted more influence and support on this work than Don Musser. He has attended games with me in Chicago, where in box seats provided by Don's friend and former church member Art Howe, we witnessed Rennie Stennett go 7 for 7 in John Candelaria's record-setting 22-0 shut out of the Cubs; in Atlanta, where Don re-introduced me to Howe, then managing the Astros; in Denver, where we were hosted by former Hezbollah hostage Tom Sutherland, who taught us theologians about living the power and compassion of forgiveness; and in Tampa Bay, where Don and his wife Ruth drove me to Tropicana Field so that I could sing the National Anthem for a Devil Rays' rare come-from-behind victory.

Probably more remarkable than the influence that Don has exercised in sharing his passion for baseball, conversations at the ballpark, and reflections on my writing is the fact that he has prompted me to overcome one of the traumas of my childhood: Bill Mazeroski's home run. Not only have I now forgiven Maz for ruining my October in 1960, I have even done penance, making pilgrimage to the portion of wall, now preserved as a memorial, where the ball crossed above Yogi Berra's head at old Forbes Field and ended the dramatic World Series that year.

Earlier versions, often abbreviated, of a few of the following chapters have appeared in other works; and I also want to express my appreciation for the support that previous editors and publishers, in working with these editions, have provided. "The Pitcher's Mound as Cosmic Mountain," has been updated as Chapter 3; initially, it appeared in the first volume of the Mercer Series on Sports and Religion: *From Season to Season: Sports as American Religion* (2001), edited by Joseph L. Price. A pre-tribulation version of Chapter 4, "Conjuring Curses and Supplicating Spirits: Baseball's Culture of Superstitions," appeared on-line as the featured essay in September 2004 in "The Religion and Culture Web Form" of the Martin Marty Center at The University of Chicago Divinity School. Portions of Chapter 6, "Fusing the Spirits: The Sacramental Power of Baseball," appeared in an extensive review, "Fusing the Spirits: Baseball, Religion, and *The Brothers K*," in *Nine: A Journal of Baseball History and Social Policy Perspectives* 2/2 (Spring 1994). And an abridged version of Chapter 8, "Here I Cheer: Conversion Narratives of Baseball Fans," appeared in *Criterion* (Spring 2003).

Finally, although my wife Bonnie could hardly be called a true believer in the church of baseball, she has attended many of its services with me, and more importantly, she has accepted my love for the game. To her and to my adult sons Jared and David, with whom attending games still provides an enduring experience of the bonding of family, faith, and friendship, I owe the greatest appreciation for their stimulation and support.

Introduction

On Deck

To a certain extent I've always associated baseball with church and faith. The final chapter in this book relates the story of my baseball conversion and my enduring commitment to the game, and it expresses my theological understanding of my decision to begin my allegiance to the Yankees. In the days before T-ball teams for first graders, I became a devout fan of the game, and I yearned to play it like my heroes who played in places far from my hometown in Mississippi. Daily, I would take practice swings with a heavy wooden bat with a swollen barrel, one so large that I imagined that only a sleeveless Ted Kluszewski could swoop it through the strike zone. Seeing an imaginary pitch from Yankee killer Frank Lary, I'd swing low, looping an arc in slow motion that I would identify as being like that of Mickey Mantle or Enos "Country" Slaughter, a fellow Southerner with whom I could remotely identify. I could see the sweet spot on the bat crush the ball so hard that the ball itself bore a deep, ugly bruise. Even before the video technology was invented, I could watch the ball in super slow-motion as it would rise, soaring farther and higher than I had ever seen a real baseball hit.

Or I would invite Bubba Tatum or George Ferguson to join me for a game of front-yard baseball, with a broken bay-window behind the sofa in the living room of the parsonage attesting to my opposite-field line-drive potential, or we would play a game of back-yard Wiffle-ball homerun derby. There the protrusion of the sunroom roof provided a short-field porch for left-handed batters like at Yankee Stadium. So I decided to become a switch-hitter, relying on my youngest sister Fan (Really, that's her name in some providential baseball way!) to toss pitches underhanded while I learned to make contact from the left side.

As a pre-adolescent I desperately wanted to play *real* baseball: to play on an organized team and to try out for the Little League in west Jackson. The official Little League field near Calvary Baptist Church had dugouts, white foul lines, and a fence around the outfield. At age nine or ten, I thought that it was certainly a field of dreams, a realm of pretend to which my play was regrettably relegated. Since Little League practices and games were scheduled on late Wednesday afternoons and early evenings, it was not possible for me, as the preacher's kid, to miss junior choir practice, Wednesday night church suppers, and prayer meetings, all of which were scheduled late on Wednesdays.

In place of the tutoring and supervision offered by Little League coaches, I did enjoy baseball bonding with my father. Almost like a golden retriever awaiting the return of its master, having fetched the leash and pawing its loose end, I virtually straddled the threshold of our home each afternoon, bat leaning against the door frame and fielding glove sweating on my left hand while I thwapped the ball as rhythmically as possible (at least as rhythmically as possible for a non-dancing Baptist) into the pocket of my black glove, supple with hope. Many afternoons after his return from sermon preparation, hospital visitation, or pastoral counseling, my father would hit one-armed grounders and line drives to me, allowing me to dive like Clete Boyer to my right, stabbing the ball and throwing from me knees to nip an imaginary Luis Aparacio by an eyelash at first. On more frequent occasions, my stab at the ball would send it glancing away, with me lunging after it and throwing again to my father's other hand, mitt-covered, imagining that this time it was, mercifully, Sherm Lollar or Gus Triandos lumbering toward first and permitting my throw to beat him by a step and a half. During these afternoons of late pre-adolescence, the chance to field grounders with my father hardly supplanted my desire to play Little League, despite the incredible bond that I continued to build with my father. Instead, the afternoon fielding exercises whetted my appetite all the more to display my fielding agility to friends and to claim the social status accorded to baseball stars.

In my case the baseball alternative to Little League was to play on the less competitive church league team for the Royal Ambassadors (RA's), a Southern Baptist response to Boy Scouts. Usually, the church fields where we played were level, although the infields were pocked with about as many rocks and pebbles as scrawny blades of grass and the dugouts were open benches in foul territory. Not surprisingly, a sense of enthusiasm engulfed a group of us RA's when a local landowner allowed a church field to be built near the intersection of Ellis Avenue and Lynch Street. A short bike ride from the parsonage where I lived, the field was fitted with fences and uncovered but enclosed dugout benches for church youths to use for games.

Among the items that I retrieved from my mother's attic a few years ago was a folder of materials related to my participation in the Royal Ambassadors. I found a small business-card sized permit for me to play in the Royal Ambassador League. The card, which I carried dutifully in my wallet at all times, identified both my name and my church, Parkway Baptist Church. Having seen the card now fifty years later, I'm prompted to recall my sense of urgency in keeping the card in my pocket during my play for the RA team. I guess that I thought that it was an identification card that I should produce, like driver's license or car registration, when demanded by the police, an umpire, or the opposing coach to certify my eligibility. Or in case of the rapture, I guess, I could have used the card to verify my approved status among the elect. The most intriguing feature of the card is the pledge that appears on the reverse side of the card: "In order to play baseball on a Royal Ambassador team, each boy must make and live up to the following pledge: I will: Live pure. Speak truth. Right wrong. Follow Christ the King."

The last line of this pledge shifts its focus from behavior, which might be subject to discipline, to beliefs, which might orient behavior. Little did I realize at the time that playing in the league basically required a profession of faith, even though I had made that public expression a few years earlier. In essence, however, the affirmation of accepting Jesus as one's savior was required for players. Yet it was never clear to me that the team from rival Calvary Baptist Church actually had professing believers on its team. Instead, Calvary's line-up seemed to be filled with hard-hitting heathens from the real Little League whose field lay near its rear doors.

Like my love of playing baseball, my fondness for watching baseball games is also tied closely to piety. I think that my first television exposure to baseball was at the home of Nancy McKeller, a childhood friend whose father was a deacon in the church where my father was minister. In part because we did not have a television in my home until I was almost a teenager, I was lured to the Saturday afternoon telecast of the *Game of the Week*, featuring Dizzy Dean and Pee Wee Reese as the announcers. The timbre and pace of their Southern accents made the distant games seem immediately familiar. Exuding a love of the game itself, they literally sounded like my Mississippi neighbors. Dizzy hailed from the Delta, and Pee

Wee had grown up in Louisville. I understood their cadence and their hominess, even though I had not heard others sing Dizzy's favorite song, "The Wabash Cannonball." Issues of piety are written as large in my memory as Dizzy's crooning, for I recall how Mr. McKeller came into his living room, saw me riveted to the game and its advertisements, and instructed me to turn my attention away from the telecast when the advertisements for Falstaff Beer, with its delightful cartoon characters who playfully promoted the brew, appeared between innings.

The other early memory of watching baseball is more directly associated with church, not merely the moral imperatives that deacons sought to extend to me. Particularly, I connect baseball—its network telecast—with the lounge in the children's education and recreation building, which was constructed in the late 1950s, at the Parkway Baptist Church. Because my father was the pastor, he provided access for me to watch the games by myself on Saturday afternoons. Even the presence and the placement of the television there had a distinct family feel. My maternal grandfather died about the time of the completion of Parkway's children's building (which was renamed for my father two decades later), and my mother was designated as the recipient of Granddaddy's television since each of her siblings already owned television sets. Although she thought that television itself might be an intrusion on family time, my mother would not condemn its appropriate, designated use for social situations or for providing some companionship for the elderly since my compassionate grandfather, whom she adored, had served as a minister in rural Mississippi churches for more than half a century. And he, of course, had regularly enjoyed the company of voices and smiles from the remote actors and audiences transmitted into his home. Thus in a quandary about the destiny of the television, my mother decided to give it to the church for rare use in the youth lounge that was being designed as part of the new children's building. In that way it could serve a social function for the youth, it could respect my grandfather's love of Baptist churches and young people, and it would not infect our household.

Because my father shared, in part, my passion for baseball and because he accepted my obsession with the Yankees, who were a frequent feature on the Saturday afternoon *Game of the Week* telecasts by CBS, he occasionally provided access for me to watch the Yankees' games in the church's lounge. Baptists, of course, do not have liturgical acolytes, children who assist ministers during worship, working in the secret places behind the altar. Although I didn't associate the new youth lounge in that way at the time, it was located in the room behind the chapel, and access to the room was often controlled by the minister's key.

Thus in this secret, somewhat sacred place on Saturday or sometimes Sunday afternoons while no one else was around, I could see the house that the Babe had built. From my perch on the sofa near the TV provided by my late grandfather, I imagined the Bronx ballpark like heaven—other, remote, perfect, a place of destiny for the faithful. While I prayed for Kubek and Richardson to turn a double play, for Berra to loft a pitch in the dirt over the right-field fence, or for Mantle to launch a homer off the façade above the third deck, I associated this field of dreams with the spirit of my heaven-abiding "Granddaddy" and the inner sanctum of the lounge space to which I, by ministerial invitation, had access. Images of this televised field of dreams, where monuments studded the centerfield frontier of Yankee Stadium, were associated with the basement lounge area of the new building.

Add to these early associations of watching baseball my intense desire to see Major League games in person—a hope that seemed as remote as the fulfillment of pilgrimage directives—and you can begin to understand the thrill that I experienced when Bob "What a *Friend* We Have in Jesus" (as Chris Berman might have dubbed him) pitched a game against the Cardinals, seemingly a Catholic team, from *Saint* Louis, and with a priestly hierarchical name at that. For my first Major League game in the summer of 1960, my father, my mother, and I sat in the upper deck of the left-field stands where I expected Ken Boyer to hit a home run. He didn't. But Stan Musial did line a home run to right, Roberto Clemente did throw a runner out at home, and Ernie Broglio (then still a Cardinals' All Star) did beat the Pirates 2-1. At least that's how my memory mythologizes the game, whose precise data appear on the framed scorecard kept in pencil with my best fifth-grade penmanship. Now the scorecard hangs among the souvenirs that threaten to crowd out the books in my study, and among the baseball treasures that stand tall on my bookcases and cabinets is the Cardinals' concession popcorn megaphone whose contents I devoured in early innings so that I could cheer for Boyer to hit one to me. Although the megaphone is now an artifact that shares space with various religious souvenirs garnered throughout my travels and studies, my voice has continued for more than forty years to cheer for players to hit one to me, which they have done on several occasions.

Baseball, family, and faith: this trinity fused in my childhood experience in ways that have prompted me in years since to work through the distinctions, convergences, and conflicts related to these multiple affections and allegiances. The chapters in this book, many of which were initially conceived as discreet presentations, have emerged out of my ongoing desire to deal with these passions and to reflect on them in various ways—confessionally, historically, sociologically, mythically, journalistically, and literarily, but always theologically, always exploring the worldviews of persons and how their pursuit of meaningful lives fits within their cosmologies.

The first chapter provides a journalistic survey—a kind of "rounding the bases"—of the intersections between baseball and religion in the past century and a half of American life. One of the points of intersection involves the early twentieth-century barnstorming baseball team sponsored by the House of David, a millenarian community in southern Michigan. A historical and spiritual examination of that religious community and its team furnish the focus for the second chapter. In chapter 3, attention shifts to possible meanings of the game itself with a mythic analysis of the rituals associated with the *omphalos*, the Greek word for the navel of the earth, the center of reality. Quite differently, myths are also featured in chapter 4, wherein I quite playfully explore the culture of superstition and curses that underlie Major League play. I must admit that I had quite a bit of fun writing, revising, and reading the chapter because of the frequency of word play that takes place. But the humor and playfulness of the chapter should not detract from its analysis of the ways in which beliefs and rituals undergird players' performances.

To a great degree, chapter 5 functions as the heart of the book because it develops a sociological analysis of baseball as an American civil religion. If baseball were not experienced as having the power to shape worldviews, the other essays in the book would be merely a string of occasional reports and confessions rather than an argument about the religious power of baseball. In chapters 6 and 7, theological themes and concepts—of sacramentalism, soteriology, and eschatology—

are drawn out of recent literary works by David James Duncan and W. P. Kinsella. And the final chapter presents my own confession while providing a literary analysis of the worldview-shaping power of baseball for many who have become its passionate fans.

As baseball and faith have occasionally come into conflict in my own experience, I should relate one anecdote that will identify the depth of my passions and the location of my faith. In October 2003 I left home despondent on a Thursday evening for a choir rehearsal with orchestra for a performance of Faure's *Requiem*. The Yankees were down by three runs, and Pedro Martinez had kept the Yankees' offense off-balance. During the drive to the church, the Yankees rallied. As I parked the car, Jorge Posada blooped his hit to short right-centerfield, scoring the tying run. I could hear the crowd going wild while Grady Little was making his way to the mound, gesturing for the relief pitcher to come in. For me, at that moment, I knew where my deepest faith truly lay, for I turned off the engine and the radio, went in to the choir rehearsal, and did not sneak a cell-phone update of the score. Instead, after an amazing rehearsal of that incredible piece with the choir and orchestra, I returned apprehensively to my car, turned on the radio, and learned in the post-game broadcasters' sign-off that Aaron had hit his dramatic home run. Then I shrieked and bellowed that this time it had been Aaron who had led the chosen ones to the Promised Land.

1

Rounding the Bases:
Baseball Intersecting Religion

Surveying the Field

Throughout the past century and a half in America, baseball
and religion have intertwined in multiple ways. During baseball's earliest days, religious leaders began to take opposing
views about the threats and virtues of the game. Among the
initial critics of baseball, some ministers enjoined faithful followers to avoid playing baseball on Sunday since the Sabbath
was prescribed in biblical laws to be a day of rest and worship
rather than one of recreation or competition. Often the pious
advocates also sought to subject baseball to civic blue laws or
Sabbatarian statutes, especially when games required admission
fees, promoted corollary enterprises, or featured teams com-
prised of co-workers from the same workplace.[1] Meanwhile,
other devout Christians and religious leaders advocated ban-
ning baseball entirely because of its perceived detrimental
influence on character development.

In diametrical contrast to these popular restrictions
against baseball, other religious leaders and groups embraced
baseball as a desirable means for muscular Christianity to
nurture faith in a physical way. Not only did some ministers

---

[1] Robert Lee, *Religion and Leisure in America: A Study in Four
Dimensions* (Nashville: Abindgon Press, 1964) 151–95.

espouse the virtues of exercise in baseball, one turn-of-the-century utopian religious community even determined that the game itself offered opportunities to express the nature of its faith, not merely by providing a means for increasing the evangelism that is germane to Christianity, but also by displaying its principles and values. In the following chapter, we will examine how and why, during the early decades of the twentieth century, the House of David (a Protestant, millenarian community in southwestern Michigan) sponsored a baseball team as an expression of its own spiritual orientation.

In addition to these religious proscriptions against baseball and the apparent baptism of baseball by others, baseball has also intersected religion when its fields and stadiums have been used for religious ceremonies, and its interface with religion has been tested as religious services have been held for players in the clubhouse and for fans in the grandstands. This fusion of the character and purpose of a religious organization with the play of baseball suggests that at times baseball itself has functioned as a form of faith, not merely providing an expression of faith, but actually becoming one of the distinct denominations in America's civil religions (the focus of chapter 5).

Although a comprehensive survey of the intersections between religion and baseball exceeds the scope of this introductory chapter, it is possible for us to survey the field of their interplay by examining samples of the multifarious ways that the two have become entangled in America since the middle of the nineteenth century.

Religious Proscriptions against Baseball

At its inception in 1876 the National League forbad games to be played on Sunday, yet in 1882 when the American Association was founded, one of the ways that it distinguished itself from the initial league was by permitting Sunday play. At about the time that the National League was being formed, police in Brooklyn were issued orders to arrest anyone playing baseball on a Sunday. And within a few years the friction between baseball and established religions flared throughout other urban areas when members of the Cincinnati and Indianapolis teams in the American Association were arrested for desecrating the Sabbath in days following their play of a game in Indianapolis on Sunday, 18 May 1884. About a month later in another American Association game at Columbus, Ohio, the players in a Sunday game were arrested on the field. But because a riot threatened to break out among the 3,000 fans who attended the game, an agreement was reached that the game could continue if the players would present themselves at the constable's office following its conclusion, which they did.[2]

Two years later St. Louis officially dropped out of the National League because of the league's ban on Sunday play, although a judge in Missouri had already ruled that playing baseball on Sunday did not violate the law. In 1892 when the American Association was consolidated into the National League, an agreement was reached that Sunday play would not be forbidden by league rules. Not long thereafter, the first National League game to be played on a Sunday, 17 April 1892, saw Cincinnati, the home team, defeat St. Louis by a score of 5-1.

Not only were there formal rules and agreements prohibiting Sunday play in the National League, ministerial associations throughout the Northeast and Midwest advocated bans against baseball's recreational play on Sundays.

---

[2] Charlie Bevis, *Sunday Baseball: The Major League's Struggle to Play Baseball on the Lord's Day, 1876–1934* (Jefferson NC: McFarland and Company, 2003) 5–6.

Throughout the closing decades of the nineteenth century, Protestant ministers who were affiliated with an organization called "The Good Citizen's League" started to attend Sunday ballgames for the purpose of taking roll of the spectators whom they knew. However, because they disrupted the fans' appreciation for the game, the ministers were apparently escorted out of the ballparks.

Although ministers were prevented from raising a Sunday ruckus at the ballpark, they continued to decry the desecration of Sunday by playing baseball. In 1878 in Brooklyn, for instance, one minister insisted that unless the evil of Sunday baseball were stopped, the city's churches would be rendered "useless and the rights of a large proportion of the community [would] be wrested from them."[3] About a decade later, *The Sporting News* commented on the growing national trend in allowing Sunday baseball: "Sunday is getting to be the great day for sports in America, which if present trends continued would make the Sabbath remembered only as a tradition of the past."[4] Trying to break that trend toward sports co-opting the Sabbath, ministers in New York City over the next few years lobbied to prohibit Sunday baseball. With their strong support, the Raines Law was passed in March 1897, and it specifically outlawed playing baseball on Sunday.

Almost immediately, the application of the Raines Law was restricted to professional games where an admission fee was charged. In the early twentieth century, however, Charles Ebbets, the owner of the Dodgers, attempted to circumvent

---

[3] *Brooklyn Eagle*, 24 August 1878, 2, quoted in Charles DeMotte, "Baseball and the Battle against Sunday Observance in New York" (manuscript presented at the St. Olaf Conference on Sport and Religion, 28 October 2005) 8.

[4] *The Sporting News*, 17 January 1891, 4, quoted in DeMotte, "Baseball and the Battle against Sunday Observance in New York," 9.

the statute by offering free admission to Sunday games in Brooklyn. To compensate for the loss of admission fees for those games, he charged more for scorecards whose customary price was a nickel. Color-coordinated with the sections of the grandstand, the cards ranged in price from a quarter to a dollar. Although no players were arrested in the dozens of Dodgers' Sunday games, in court proceedings Ebbets lost on appeal. In a manner similar to Ebbets's tactic, the Yankees played an exhibition game on a Sunday in 1909: While they opened the gates for the fans, they also had strategically placed donation boxes at the entrances, expecting voluntary contributions by those who attended the Sunday game. On that occasion, too, the teams distributed flyers, requesting that the fans refrain from cheering in order to minimize possible community disruption. Taking a different tack to New York's Sabbatarian restrictions, the Giants scheduled their first Sunday "home game" in 1898 to be played in nearby Weehauken, New Jersey, where the Raines Law did not apply.[5]

As late as 1918, the Giants were still being prosecuted for playing Sunday games. During that season, the Giants also sponsored a pre-game concert whose ostensible purpose was to raise money to assist in the war effort. Both managers John McGraw of the Giants and Cincinnati's Christy Mathewson, who had refused during his playing career to pitch on Sunday but who frequently managed on that day during his three years at the helm of the Reds, were arrested as representatives of their respective teams. Before their cases were heard, however, magistrate Francis X. McQuade became one of the Giants' administrative officers for the following season and dismissed the charges. By spring of 1919 former New York Mayor Jimmy

---

[5] Jonathan Fraser Light, *The Cultural Encyclopedia of Baseball* (Jefferson NC: McFarland and Company, 1997) 709–10.

Walker introduced state legislation authorizing Sunday games throughout the state, and following the bill's passage, the Dodgers, Giants, and Yankees held Sunday home games on the first two Sundays in May. In response to concerns that were still raised by religious leaders, Walker remarked, "I defy anyone to say that the morals of New York have been lowered since Sunday baseball was given to the people."[6]

In a number of cities throughout the Midwest, Sunday games had been permitted following the merger of the American Association and the National League. Yet although St. Louis had allowed Sunday games as early as any of the National League cities, neither the Browns nor the Cardinals permitted the airing of Sunday games on radio during the early years of baseball broadcasts.

Throughout the half-century between the Civil War and World War I, religious concerns about baseball's play on Sundays were not restricted to cities where professional teams might play. As pioneers pressed westward across the prairie, "the profanation of the Sabbath became a symbol of the evil the early [frontier] churches sought to confront," Jack Higgs notes, "and frontier sports and rough amusements figured prominently in such profanation, along with drunkenness, which had reached epidemic proportions."[7] By contrast, the issue of Sunday baseball in Utah did not arise, in large part because of the comprehensive reverence of Mormons for the Sabbath. Yet baseball demonstrated the American character of Mormons to their neighboring states, even while their religious differences were being scrutinized. In 1903 when the "Salt Lake City Mormons, Elders and Bishops" joined the Pacific Northern League, the team was celebrated by both the

---

[6] Quoted in ibid., 710.

[7] Robert J. Higgs, *God in the Stadium: Sports and Religion in America* (Lexington: University Press of Kentucky, 1995) 55.

religious and secular press in Utah. Jim Warnock notes, "While baseball in other Western cities often served to legitimize claims to civic status and to give peaceful voice to regional rivalries, in Utah the sport offered a vehicle to unite Mormons, members of a formerly and now accommodating religious sect, with their 'gentile' neighbors."[8]

While civic statutes regulated Sunday games throughout the other regions of the country, particularly the Northeast and Midwest, in the late nineteenth and early twentieth centuries, many Southern Protestant leaders feared, as one Disciple Minister put it, that any and all "base ball [*sic*] playing is apt to lead to Sunday base ball playing," and the editor of the Arkansas Baptist paper in the early 1890s decried that baseball players often would "execute more deviltry, use more profanity, and make idiots of themselves in more ways" than other men. Similarly, a decade later, the editor of the Mississippi Baptist paper castigated baseball fans because the "murderous" game is, as he put it, "more brutal than a bull-fight, more reprehensible than a prize-fight, and more deadly than modern warfare."[9] Underlying most of the accusations about baseball's violence were assumptions that leisure and play inherently tempted players to exercise evil. Historian Clifford Putney concludes, "But exercising one's muscles for no particular end except [physical] health struck many Protestants in the mid-nineteenth century as an immoral waste

---

[8] Jim Warnock, "The Mormon Game: The Religious Uses of Baseball in Early Utah," *Nine: A Journal of Baseball History and Social Policy Perspectives* 6/1 (Fall 1997): 1–2.

[9] Quoted in William R. Hogan, "Sin and Sports," in *Motivations in Play, Games, and Sports*, ed. Ralph Slovenko and James Knight (Springfield IL: Charles C. Thomas, Publisher, 1967) 129.

of time."[10] Although denominations differed in the degree of their proscription against baseball on weekdays, they uniformly endorsed the Sabbath ban.

Concerns about the moral threats posed by baseball were expressed not only by ministers in established churches, they also redirected the career of Billy Sunday, the former major league outfielder turned full-time evangelist. In his view the schedules and demands of professional sport and religion could not be reconciled, especially when baseball consistently contested the application of the Sabbath commandment to daily life by insisting on Sunday play. Even while he shirked professional baseball for its excesses and temptations, he adopted its images and language in his sermons and revival promotions, featuring his baseball past in advertisements for his crusades and often dramatizing baseball plays in the pulpit. For example, one illustrated announcement in an Indiana newspaper in 1897 lauded the success of his three-week series of revival services with the title "Scoring Runs off Satan's Delivery."[11]

In four decades of evangelistic ministry, it is likely that Sunday preached to almost 100 million people, initially in the Midwest and then throughout the nation.[12] Although Sunday often utilized baseball illustrations and gestures in his sermons, he "never developed a conceptual framework for a twentieth-

---

[10] Clifford Putney, *Muscular Christianity: Manhood and Sports in Protestant America, 1880–1920* (Cambridge: Harvard University Press, 2001) 24.

[11] W. A. Firstenberger, *In Rare Form: A Pictorial History of Baseball Evangelist Billy Sunday* (Iowa City: University of Iowa Press, 2005) 27.

[12] Robert F. Martin, foreword to *The Sawdust Trail: Billy Sunday in His Own Words*, by William A. "Billy" Sunday (Iowa City: University of Iowa Press, 2005) vii.

century muscular Christianity."[13] In fact, Sunday seemed to undermine or contravene the formation of a conceptual framework for muscular Christianity because he perceived a fundamental conflict between the competitive orientation of sports and the formation and nurture of Christian character. Seemingly to contrast baseball with a faith built on the Ten Commandments, he published a list of ten reasons why he had turned his back on his professional baseball career:

1. Because [baseball] is a life which has an undesirable future.
2. Because it develops a spirit of jealousy and selfishness; one's whole desires are for personal success regardless of what befalls others.
3. Because it tends to indolence as shown by the fact that few use the five months of unemployed time for study and self-improvement and preparation for future pursuit.
4. Because it is better to benefit mankind than simply to amuse them.
5. Because, after one attains to a certain standard of efficiency, there is no more room for development.
6. Because it does not develop one for future usefulness, as illustrated by the fact that many ex-ball players are engaged in the saloon business.
7. Because it is a life in which morality is not an essential to success; one might be a consummate rogue and a first class ball player.
8. Because reflections in the past "grand stand catches," "great slides to the plate," "stolen bases,"

---

[13] Tony Ladd and James A. Mathisen, *Muscular Christianity: Evangelical Protestants and the Development of American Sport* (Grand Rapids: Baker Books, 1999) 82.

and the echo of applauding multitudes are very poor
food for consolation.

9. Because I felt called of God to do His service.
10. Because of the anticipated contentment (now
    realized) which comes to any man who finds himself
    in the right place.[14]

Although Sunday offers his reasons in this enumerated
manner, they are often redundant, focusing primarily on the
non-utilitarian nature of the game, on the unwillingness of
players to use their free time for self-improvement and social
service, and on his perception of a divine call to him to become
a minister. However, they consistently manifest his acceptance
of general religious proscriptions against baseball, and they
specify his reservations about the question of whether baseball
might serve as one of the exercises in muscular Christianity.

In the months following his conversion and before he gave
up the base paths in Pittsburgh for the sawdust trail of
evangelists, Billy Sunday participated in "Athletic Sundays,"
whose goal was to reach un-churched men in the Northeast. In
those days, he later recalled, the local YMCA where his team
had played on Saturday would arrange for him to preach on
Sunday since the team was not scheduled to play ball. And he
also insisted that, in those days of daylight baseball, he would
regularly go to Wednesday night prayer meetings.[15]

With other notable athletes and coaches at the turn of the
century, he regularly spoke about the manliness of Christianity
while denouncing the evils associated with Sunday sports
competition, drinking alcohol, and gambling. So prominent
was he among prohibitionist advocates that in 1917 the *Atlanta*

---

[14] Billy Sunday, "Why I Left Professional Baseball, *Young Men's Era* 19/20 (27 July 1893): 1, quoted in Ladd and Mathisen, *Muscular Christianity*, 80.

[15] Sunday, *The Sawdust Trail*, 45.

Constitution ran a front-page editorial cartoon depicting him driving out a booze-soaked devil, and the popular song "John Barleycorn—Goodbye!" credited him with having made the state of Colorado dry.[16]

Muscular Faith and Baseball

Although specific religious proscriptions against baseball multiplied in the last quarter of the nineteenth century, they were preceded by an initial affirmation of baseball by ministers and religious leaders who had advocated its importance in the development of muscular Christians. As early as the Civil War, Horace Bushnell, a liberal Congregationalist minister, and Henry Ward Beecher, son of Lyman Beecher and minister at the Plymouth Church in Brooklyn, had begun to extol the desirable features of play. In the revised version (1861) of his collection of sermonic essays titled *Christian Nurture*, Bushnell praises children's play as being a symbol of Christian freedom, and he suggests that since "play is the forerunner of religion, so religion should be the friend of play."[17] Extending the appreciation for play to organized games, Beecher lauds the virtues of physical exercise, discipline, and teamwork in sports.

Noting Beecher's passion for sports, including his pride of his grandson who quarterbacked the Yale football team toward the end of the century, Tony Ladd and James A. Mathisen suggest that Beecher was the first national minister for muscular faith. In general, Beecher believed that Christian associations would share the "very gospel" by extending opportunities for young men to engage in physical activities promoting "vigor and health" in contrast to the temptations afforded by leisure and urban living. Writing during the

---

[16] Firstenberger, *In Rare Form*, 70, 73.

[17] Horace Bushnell, *Christian Nurture* (New York: Scribners, 1861) 341.

middle of the Civil War, Beecher commended the expansion and popularization of sport. Specifically, he expressed appreciation for baseball, judging it to be "comparatively inexpensive, and open to all," as well as noting that one could "hardly conceive of better exercise."[18] Within a few years following Beecher's endorsement of sports, another devout Christian asserted in a popular New England periodical that the recreation and competition in baseball should be encouraged in part because games, like baseball, had not been "expressly discountenanced in the Bible."[19]

During this period the YMCA began to stimulate Protestants to accept the idea that men should refresh and repair their bodies along with their souls. While the YMCA added baseball to its athletic programs, the Northfield conference, which in 1885 had been initiated by Dwight Moody to support Protestant missions, also featured baseball among the athletic activities for the hundreds of collegians who attended. In part, the inclusion of baseball in the programs of the YMCA and the College of Colleges, which was the outgrowth of the Northfield conference, was facilitated by the acceptance of baseball by Beecher and other ministers two decades earlier.[20]

Although Billy Sunday generally endorsed the ministries of the YMCA, having been employed by the organization following his retirement from baseball, he did not fully embrace baseball as a means to prompt conversion or to

---

[18] Henry Ward Beecher, *Eyes and Ears* (Boston: Ticknor and Fields, 1863) 205–206, quoted in Ladd and Mathisen, *Muscular Christianity*, 31.

[19] Quoted in Ladd and Mathisen, *Muscular Christianity*, 32.

[20] Putney, *Muscular Christianity: Manhood and Sports in Protestant America*, 2, 68. Ladd and Mathisen identify 1886 as the year of the initial Northfield conference.

nurture piety. While Sunday was withdrawing from baseball because of his perception that its focus on competition deflected the energy and attention of players away from their participation in the desired conquest by Christian faith, others found opportunities to exemplify their faith within the game itself. At an amateur level, Amos Alonzo Stagg pitched the Yale University team to five championships before entering seminary and discovering that his talents lay not in preaching but in coaching football. Despite the shift from baseball to football as his primary sport, Stagg became one of the stalwart proponents for muscular Christianity at the turn of the century. Notable among professional baseball's exemplars of faith at that time were Branch Rickey and Christy Mathewson, both of whom refused to play on Sundays. Remaining faithful to a promise that he had made to his mother not to play baseball on Sundays, Rickey was fired by the Cincinnati Reds in 1904. To a certain extent, however, both Mathewson and Rickey competed on Sundays later in their careers, with Mathewson managing the Reds on Sundays and Rickey hiring players to compete on the Sabbath.

As blue laws became less restrictive during the period between the World Wars, Sunday baseball increasingly became accepted, especially after Pennsylvania laws were amended to allow professional play on Sundays in Pittsburgh and Philadelphia, the last cities to permit major league play on that day. Following the repeal of blue laws, ecclesiastical expectations also began to shift about Sunday restrictions, with requirements for strict adherence to Sabbath regulations dwindling among American Christian denominations. But in the latter part of the twentieth century, Sabbath play again became an issue when Edwin Correa, a Seventh Day Adventist pitcher for the Texas Rangers, refused to pitch on the Sabbath itself—Friday night games and those on Saturdays before sunset.

By the middle of the twentieth century, players had begun to increase the number of ways that they expressed muscular Christianity. Not only did players continue to demonstrate their faith by their display of character, their style of play, and their adherence to biblical commands, their public testimonies also became more common, in part because they were featured speakers in the Billy Graham Crusades. Utilizing a different forum, Norman Vincent Peale, the pastor of the Marble Collegiate Church in New York City for half a century, supervised the publication of *Faith Made Them Champions*.[21] The book is a collection of various celebrity inspirational stories that had appeared in *Guideposts*, a weekly newsletter that he edited for business leaders. Among the contributors were several prominent baseball players and officials: Bob Feller, Mickey Mantle, Babe Ruth, Jackie Robinson, and Branch Rickey, the former general manager of the Brooklyn Dodgers whose faith had inspired him to break the color line in professional baseball by signing and guiding Robinson. Although many of the stories in the volume do not articulate specific Christian doctrines or espouse distinct Christian practices, they inspire success by affirming the effectiveness of disciplined work, the significance of loyal friendship, and the creative possibilities of courageous action.

The interplay of sports and religion in mid-century, however, was not restricted to evangelical Protestants. Notable among other star athletes of faith, of course, was Hank Greenberg, the Hall of Fame slugger for the Detroit Tigers who was dubbed by sportswriters as "the Hebrew star."

---

[21] Norman Vincent Peale, ed., *Faith Made Them Champions* (Carmel NY: Guideposts Associates, Inc., 1954).

Although at times he heard anti-Semitic epithets hurled at him by fans and opposing players, he later indicated that such attempted derision only motivated him all the more to excel. And excel he did: in 1934, for example, he clubbed 26 homeruns, garnered 139 RBIs, and batted .339.

During the height of the Tigers' pennant race that season, concerns about the possible conflicts between his faith and baseball were raised by sportswriters, fans, and Jewish communities throughout the country when it became apparent that Rosh Hashanah and Yom Kippur fell on game days. Having consulted rabbis and devout Jews about his predicament of whether to sacrifice his personal allegiance for possible public good by symbolically melding Jews into the national pastime, Greenberg opted to play on Rosh Hashanah, belting two homeruns for the only Tigers' tallies in a 2-1 victory over the rival Red Sox. For the most part, to his relief, the public supported his decision to play, as did most of the Jewish community. But much less public attention was paid to his decision not to play several days later on Yom Kippur, the Day of Atonement.

More recently other Jewish ballplayers have continued to affirm their faith and devotion in dramatic ways that affected their baseball play. Notably, Sandy Koufax refused to pitch the opening game of the 1965 World Series because it conflicted with the Yom Kippur, the holiest day in the Jewish year. Several years later Ken Holtzman similarly affirmed his faith while the Yankees pursued a pennant in the late 1970s. At that time his refusal to pitch so mired him in manager Billy Martin's disfavor that Holtzman's career never recovered the luster that it had enjoyed only a short time earlier.

During the height of the National League Western Division playoff run in 2001, Dodgers' outfielder Shawn Green opted to sit out the Wednesday night game against arch-rival

Giants in late September. Already having set a franchise record for homeruns in a season, Green also interrupted his major league leading streak of consecutive games played in order to observe the holy day, which began at sundown. "There is nothing I would rather do than play against the Giants in a pennant race," he told a sportswriter, "but some things take precedence over that. I think it's important as a Jewish athlete to set an example for kids, even kids who are not Jewish, to show them that there are certain priorities in life. To put my religion before [the game] is a good example to set. Whether we like it or not, we as athletes are role models."[22] Enthusiastically endorsing Green's stance, Rabbi Richard Camras of the suburban Los Angeles synagogue Shomrei Torah remarked that since "sports is the religion in America" the actions that Green took exert an impressive cultural power. Furthermore, he added, true heroes are not merely athletic all-stars. True heroes are persons who take right actions; and in that regard, Rabbi Camras concluded, Green is a true hero as well as being an all-star athlete.[23]

Much less well known but equally as principled an action as those taken by Greenberg, Koufax, and Green was the debut-delaying observance of Yom Kippur by Larry Yellen. Scheduled to make his first major league start for the Houston Colt 45s on that day in the fall of 1963, Yellen received a called from his mother reminding him about his need to observe the Day of Atonement. He informed the team's manager and general manger that he would not pitch on that day, and he sat

---

[22] Quoted in Steve Springer, "Dodgers' Green Keeps the Faith," *Los Angeles Times*, 26 September 2001, D5.
  [23] Ibid.

out the game. The following year, he pitched in only fourteen games before his career ended.[24]

As one fan's response to the Jewish heritage of these and other major league players, Martin Abramowitz founded Jewish Major Leaguers, Inc., a not-for-profit organization whose mission is to document the Jewish players in "America's game." In tribute to many of these players who often competed in obscurity, Abramowitz created a limited edition baseball card set of the 141 Jewish players who had been in the major leagues. He started the project because he felt that someone owed it to the forty-one Jewish ballplayers for whom a baseball card had never been issued. Of those, he further notes, a dozen enjoyed a single-game cup of coffee in the major leagues. Among the statistical totals that he tallied were proportionately higher batting averages for Jewish players than the major league composite, as well as a lower ERA than the overall average. Yet, according to Meir Ribalow, author of *Jewish Baseball Stars*, the cumulative averages matter less than the symbolic achievements of Greenberg and Koufax. Ribalow avers, "Hank Greenberg could slug with *anyone*, and was a physically huge (for the time), powerful symbol of athletic strength that made him so important to the American Jewish community." Similarly, he notes that Sandy Koufax compares favorably with the greatest pitchers of the game. The symbolic power provided by the character and accomplishments of Greenberg and Koufax, Ribalow concludes, "is hard to overestimate," especially "in a fair-minded democracy that

---

[24] Peter Ephross, "Hall of Fame Celebrates Jewish Major Leaguers," *Canadian Jewish News* 34/36 (9 September 2004): 70.

looks to individuals as 'champions' of those [whom] they represent."[25]

Although Jewish expressions of religious devotion have become more prominent in baseball as players and fans have followed the leading roles taken by Greenberg, Koufax, and Green, muscular faith in America has been dominated by evangelical Protestants, in part because of their mission to share their faith but also to a significant degree because of the swelling number of players since mid-century who have been willing to write and talk about their religious experiences. About a decade after Peale's publication of *Faith Made Them Champions*, Bobby Richardson, Alvin Dark, Felipe Alou, Carl Erskine, Vernon Law, and Brooks Robinson teamed together with other baseball players and prominent sports figures to produce a collection of their Christian testimonies in *The Goal and the Glory: America's Athletes Speak Their Faith*.[26] Among the testimonies and meditations, Alou tells about his conversion experience, Robinson reflects on the numerous and powerful temptations that professional baseball players encounter, and Richardson ponders the enduring, covenantal character of his commitment to Christ. In a somewhat different manner of sharing one's faith, former St. Louis Cardinals' pitcher Lindy McDaniel, an ordained minister in the Church of Christ, wrote and distributed a monthly newsletter entitled *Pitching for the Master*.

In addition to the written testimonies that players have published in *The Goal and the Glory*, denominational perio-

---

[25] Quoted in Martin Abramowitz, "The Making of a Card Set: American Jews in America's Game," *Heritage: Newsletter of the American Jewish Historical Society* [1/2] (Fall/Winter 2003): 11.

[26] Ted Simonson, ed., *The Goal and the Glory: America's Athletes Speak Their Faith* (Westwood NJ: Fleming H. Revell Company, 1962).

dicals, or *Sports Spectrum* (which is a glossy magazine in the style of *Sports Illustrated* that is published in conjunction with *Christianity Today*), they also found new ways to express their faith in non-ecclesiastical ways. For one, Gary Gaetti, the former all-star third baseman for the Minnesota Twins, taped an evangelical message to his glove, which he flashed to the television cameras during the 1989 All Star Game introductions. Or before each game in which he pitches, Pedro Martinez inscribes the instep of his shoes with the phrase "*Dios camina comigo*," meaning "God walks with me," because, as he testifies, "I believe that with every step I take, here or on the baseball field, I have got to thank God."[27] Other expressions of faith include the way that John Wetteland, former closer for the Expos, Yankees, and Rangers, added a scripture reference (Titus 3:3) to autographs that he signed, and distinct, affirming gestures, such as Barry Bonds wearing a dangling cross earring or his routine pointing one finger to the heavens after circling the bases in his home-run trot.

More typical than these visible displays of faith are the verbal testimonies offered frequently in post-game interviews. During the postseason play of Major League Baseball in early October 1997, for instance, there were several distinct examples of athletes affirming their faith or attributing their sports success to divine intervention. Following the Cleveland Indians' pennant winning game, Bip Roberts and Tony Fernandez credited their extra-inning victory to divine intervention. Roberts had been scheduled to start in, as he put it, "the biggest game of my life," but he was scratched from the line-up after getting injured during pre-game warm-ups.[28] His replacement, Tony Fernandez, hit a solo home run for the the

---

[27] Quoted in Steve Hubbard, *Faith in Sports: Athletes and Their Religion on and off the Field* (New York: Doubleday, 1998) 24.

[28] ESPN postgame interview, telecast, 15 October 1997.

game's only run, and in the post-game, locker-room interview he credited God with helping him to see to the pitch well.

With a different tenor, the Indians' teammate Orel Hershiser affirmed his faith even following their defeat in the first game of the World Series. Talking with a reporter for the *Los Angeles Times*, Hershiser remarked on his manner of praying before games: "People are surprised, I suppose, because I really haven't had a bad outing in the postseason. But when I pray before a game and think about the game, it's not that I'm supposed to win or do well because it's the postseason, but it's that I'm thankful I'm here and able to pitch, and hopeful I do my best."[29] Hershiser, of course, had already taken testimonies to a new level a decade earlier when on *The Tonight Show* he spontaneously sang "The Doxology" while talking with Johnny Carson.[30]

To a great extent players have been emboldened to offer their public testimonies or to express their faith in interviews by the support that they have received from other devout Christian players, especially through a program known as Baseball Chapel. Bobby Richardson is often credited with having started clubhouse worship services when he broke into the Yankees' line-up in the late 1950s. Shortly thereafter, players on the Chicago Cubs and Minnesota Twins began to hold informal worship services in the team hotel when they were on road trips. Recognizing the beneficent effects on their public behavior that these brief meetings for worship and Bible study exerted on players, Commissioner Bowie Kuhn a few years later entertained a proposal from Watson Spoelstra, a Detroit sportswriter, to organize religious services for each

---

[29] Ross Newhan, "Hershiser Isn't Overly Perturbed by Defeat," *Los Angeles Times*, 19 October 1997, C14.

[30] Orel Hershiser with Jerry B. Jenkins, *Out of the Blue* (Brentwood TN: Wolgemuth and Hyatt, 1989).

major league team. A devout man of faith who often spoke to Catholic men's groups and spiritual workshops following his retirement, Kuhn approved the proposal to create Baseball Chapel, a non-denominational Christian ministry that held its first services in ballparks during the 1974 playoffs. By the start of the following season, all of the major league teams had organized a chapel program.

In 1978 the program was expanded to include all minor league teams and the winter ball league in Latin America. By the beginning of the twenty-first century, more than 200 professional teams participated in Baseball Chapel, whose services were attended by about 3,000 players, managers, umpires, and team staff each Sunday. Every week, Baseball Chapel provides a standard Bible study curriculum, and it also secures and supervises the services provided by the chapel leaders. Before games, the chapel leader is responsible for procuring the space for the players to gather on a Sunday for about fifteen minutes after batting practice. Former Rockies reliever Todd Jones, a frequent participant and supporter of Baseball Chapel, recalls that sites for the meetings have varied from bathrooms in Milwaukee to sequestered areas under the grandstands in San Diego to shower stalls in Boston. He notes that since it is so easy for players to become self-absorbed, the brief time for Bible reading and prayer enables them "to take a step back from the game and focus on things that really matter."[31]

In its first few decades Baseball Chapel operated with little public fanfare because it was oriented exclusively to players and team personnel, but it gained a great deal of notoriety toward the end of the 2005 major league season. Then, Washington

---

[31] Todd Jones, "Religion Serves Great Purpose in Baseball," *The Sporting News*, 26 December 2002.

Nationals' outfielder Ryan Church attended his team's regular Sunday ballpark Bible study, and he asked Jon Moeller, an FBI agent who volunteered as a chapel leader, about whether his former girlfriend, a Jew, would be doomed to hell. Moeller confirmed that, because of her lack of faith in Jesus, she would not go to heaven.

In the days following the exchange, *The Washington Post* reported the brief story, and all hell broke loose in a subsequent exchange of remarks from religious leaders in Jewish and Christian groups. Initially, Orthodox Rabbi Shmuel Herzfeld complained to Tony Tavares, Nationals' team president, that "the locker room of the Nationals is being used to preach hatred," and he urged the team to separate itself from such a position. Church himself responded that he regretted the situation since the quote attributed to him in the *Post*'s article had not been uttered in disrespect for "the religious beliefs of others."[32] Two months after the initial controversy, Church was still addressing issues related to his queries and remarks. Writing a letter to *USA Today* in response to an article by Tom Krattenmaker,[33] Church acknowledges that Krattenmaker's overall premise was on target—that "promoting religion in sports and life is good" and that "promoting it to the point of denigrating other religions is not." Church goes on to specify that his "biggest mistake" was in thinking that, by asking the question of the chaplain in the context of the regular meeting of Baseball Chapel, he had been "attending a chapel meeting where asking questions, learning,

---

[32] Alan Cooperman, "Nats" Church Apologizes for Remarks about Jews, *Washington Post*, 21 September 2005, E6.

[33] Tom Krattenmaker, "Does Proselytizing Cross the Line in Pro Sports?" *USA Today*, 7 November 2005, 13A.

expressing and sharing thoughts on religion were not only appropriate, but also encouraged and private."[34]

When the initial response became public, some evangelical leaders, such as the Rev. Richard Land, a Southern Baptist minister who heads up his denomination's Ethics and Religious Liberty Commission, came to the defense of Church and Moeller and indicated that Moeller had merely been re-restating a traditional Christian belief drawn from the Gospel of John, wherein Jesus is identified as saying: "I am the way and the truth and the life; no one comes to the Father, but by me" (14:6). Meanwhile, the Rev. Christopher M. Leighton, a Presbyterian minister who directs the Institute for Christian and Jewish Studies in Baltimore, expressed dismay over the fact that Church's comment about Moeller's affirmation had been criticized initially by a rabbi rather than by one of the Christian leaders who understood salvation in a more inclusive way than conservative Christians accept.[35]

Baseball's responses to the incident were also swift. The Nationals suspended the credentials of Jon Moeller and notified the commissioner's office, which immediately began a review of the relationship between Major League Baseball and Baseball Chapel. Among other concerns, some rabbis raised questions to Commissioner Bud Selig about why Baseball Chapel was "the sole Christian ministry granted access" to all major league teams and their organizations. By contrast, the American Family Association, a conservative Christian

---

[34] Ryan Church, "No Intent to Disparage Others' Religions," *USA Today*, 18 November 2005, 12A.

[35] Quoted and reported in Cooperman, "Nats' Church Apologizes for Remarks about Jews," E6. See also "Minister Tells Players that Jews Go to Hell," *Canadian Jewish News* 35/39 (29 September 2005): 86.

enterprise headquartered in Tupelo, Mississippi, began to circulate a petition in defense of Church and Moeller.[36]

Unrelated to the reports of the fiasco swelling out of Church's questions and Moeller's gestures, two stories on Baseball Chapel appeared at the same time in newspapers serving the regions of recent World Champions—the Angels and the Red Sox. Both were quite different in tone and character from the debate that developed out of the Nationals' incident. One focused on the contributions of chaplain Chuck Obremski, the inspirational pastor to the Angels who had recently succumbed to a two-year battle with cancer. Only three years earlier, the Angels had considered him so crucial to their team that they voted to give him a World Series ring, the first ever for the franchise. On 18 September 2005 Paul Byrd started for the Angels, and thinking that Obremski would be watching the game from his death-bed, Byrd completed his warm-up throws each inning by turning to the centerfield camera, extending his arms over his head, and making a sign of "O" to encourage Obremski to continue to fight. Even though he learned in the fifth inning of Obremski's death, Byrd gestured one final "O" as he left the mound with a secure lead in the seventh inning. Then he handed the ball to a teammate to put away so that he could give it to Obremski's widow.[37]

The other story relates to the Red Sox. In the season following their first world championship in almost ninety years, they typically enjoyed having a dozen players attend meetings of Baseball Chapel. In spirit, their motto seemed to echo the mantra that Barry Bonds had issued a few years earlier

---

[36] Quoted and reported in Alan Cooperman, "MLB Is Reviewing Baseball Chapel; Evangelical Group Concerns Selig," *The Washington Post*, 1 October 2005, E9.

[37] Kevin Modesti, "Byrd Draws Inspiration from Pastor's Battle," *The Daily News of Los Angeles*, 20 September 2005, S1.

when the Giants improbably had won the Western Division title. "I'm just glad all those other teams gave up on the players we got," Bonds said about his teammates who had just won their first title in a decade. "Nobody thought we could do anything, but we played together and prayed together."[38] The dozen Red Sox players who gathered for worship and prayer with Chaplain Walt Day exuded the same kind of camaraderie that Bonds had identified with his championship group.

The news report that appeared in the *Boston Globe* about two weeks before the Nationals' controversy erupted even featured a comment by Jewish teammate Gabe Kapler, who said: "Everyone is very respectful of one another and what they choose to believe in. The guys in this clubhouse live in harmony when it comes to that kind of stuff."[39] Kapler is one among half the team who are not evangelicals yet who commend the attendees of Baseball Chapel for their inclusiveness.

The Red Sox, however, were distinct because they represent the largest group of players who gather for weekly services, an observation confirmed by participant John Olerud whose career had included stints with four other major league teams. By contrast, minutes before the dozen Red Sox "apostles" (as they were playfully nicknamed) convened, the Rev. Day had met in a storage room with five players from the visiting Detroit Tigers to conduct their service. Several of the Boston players who gathered had played significant roles in their conquest of the Yankees and their sweep of the Cardinals ten months earlier. Reflecting on his dramatic performance

---

[38] Ross Newhan, "San Francisco Gets to Heart of Matter by Clinching First Title Since 1989," *Los Angeles Times*, 28 September 1997, C1.

[39] Bob Hohler, "Faith Binds Many of Sox—Evangelicals Give Sport a Spiritual Context," *The Boston Globe*, 31 August 2005, A1.

while the incision from an experimental surgical procedure (to hold his dislocated ankle tendon in place) bled through his sock, Curt Schilling proclaimed that "when all was said and done" he really wanted "to be able to glorify God's name."[40]

Resonating with Schilling and with the mission of Baseball Chapel, relief pitcher Mike Timlin said, "This is our platform, our place to speak our faith and live our faith. This is a special gift from God, to play baseball, and if we can spread God's word by doing that, then we've almost fulfilled our calling." As focused as Timlin's remarks are, perhaps even more impressive are the thoughts of Tim Wakefield. In the playoff against the Yankees a year before the Red Sox's miraculous win over their arch rival, he had given up the pennant defeating homerun to Aaron Boone. He said, "It's so easy to be thankful when you're on top of your game and everything is going right, but when I gave up the homerun to Aaron, I had to be thankful for that, too. It may have been God's plan to make me stronger for 2004."[41]

Certainly, one of the reasons why personal testimonies by baseball players have become more common at the turn of the new millennium has been the communal support provided to them by Baseball Chapel. Another is probably the burgeoning number of opportunities afforded players to comment on live camera following victories and defeats. With the expansion of cable and satellite networks in the last two decades of the twentieth century, more players have begun to enjoy opportunities to make immediate expressions of faith, often beginning a post-game interview with a brief tribute to God that would get ignored by a newspaper reporter or edited out of a new clip for telecast later. While some players have

---

[40] Ibid.
[41] Ibid.

consistently made efforts to share their faith in interviews, sportswriters for some major newspapers like the *Los Angeles Times* have operated with specific instructions to omit such references to faith and to focus on reporting the sports story itself.

In line with the rise of electronic media, Athletes in Action produced a DVD titled "Reversing the Curse." Released in 2005, the video features testimonies of many of the Red Sox players from their World Championship run. Shifting from print to video, the DVD duplicates efforts of earlier works like *The Goal and the Glory* to present the testimonies of all star athletes. Other new forums for muscular messages include the publication of the print and on-line periodicals *Sports Spectrum* (which features stories of three or four athletes and their Christian message in each issue), *Sharing the Victory* (the official magazine of the Fellowship of Christian Athletes), *Christian Sports Flash*, and the *Jewish Sports News* (a newsletter featuring Jewish perspectives and athletes). Expanding its outreach into broadcast media, *Sports Spectrum* magazine initiated a syndicated radio show in 1991. An hour-long program broadcast nationally on more than two hundred outlets during its first few years, *Sports Spectrum* radio featured conversations with athletes about their Christian experience as well as a sports trivia segment to appeal to other sports junkie listeners.

These excursions into producing target-specific periodicals and electronic publications represent religious groups' continuing efforts to utilize the appeal of baseball to express and expand their faith.

The Fusion of Baseball and Religion

A third cluster of connections between baseball and religion in America has developed primarily in the last half century as baseball and religion have often fused their facilities and their functions. This third set of connections features the use of ballparks and the baseball field itself as sanctuaries for traditional religious ceremonies, and it includes the recent marketing of minor league baseball games as "Faith Nights."

The blending of sports events with sacred spaces goes back in history as far as the original Olympic events in ancient Greece or the Mayan game of ball in the temple compounds of the Yucatan peninsula. For baseball and religion, the mutual respect, if not early fusion, of their spaces became apparent with the construction of the Cathedral of St. John the Divine in New York City in 1920. Prior to the building of Yankee Stadium, the cathedral enjoyed the installation of a sports bay window, which featured a baseball player taking his place among the row of apostolic windows. In a correlated manner, the expansive cover on the fiftieth anniversary issue of *Sports Illustrated* featured an artistic redeployment of Michelangelo's work on the ceiling of the Sistine Chapel. At the center of the cover, the figure replacing Adam in the creative touch from God is baseball's archangel, Babe Ruth. In auxiliary positions the cover also portrays other legends of the game, with Jackie Robinson, Hank Aaron, Willie Mays, Ted Williams, Mickey Mantle, Yogi Berra, Casey Stengel, Sparky Anderson, Joe Morgan, and Leo Durocher among stars from baseball and other sports reflecting the good and hopeful, while positions of error, threat, and evil are depicted in part with likenesses of Bill Buckner, Shoeless Joe Jackson, and Pete Rose.

Complementing this placement of baseball images in religious sites is the temporary consecration of ballparks and diamonds for the purpose of saying masses, holding revivals, convening prayer services, or performing weddings and memorial services. At Yankee Stadium, for instance, the largest crowds in its history eclipsed the record sporting event crowd of 88,150 who attended the championship boxing match between Joe Louis and Max Baer in 1935. In 1965 Pope Paul VI attracted a crowd of more than 90,000 to Yankee Stadium to celebrate a mass; yet a throng of more than 100,000 gathered there for the final service of Billy Graham's Manhattan Crusade in the mid 1950s. Although this single service record was not surpassed by Pope John Paul II during his 1987 visit to the United States, he did fill every possible seat, not only in the fixed grandstand gallery but also in the temporary seats placed on the field itself, for the mass that he delivered at Dodger Stadium on September 16. Even without the marquis names of Billy Graham or one of the Popes, the annual Harvest Crusade in Anaheim each July draws more than 100,000 weekend attendees to Angels Stadium where the revival services are held.

A more intimate religious service at a ballpark is the saying of Orthodox Jewish prayers at the Oriole Park at Camden Yards in Baltimore. Following the fifth inning of home games except those on Sabbath, as many as thirty Orthodox males gather in a pantry area near baseball's first kosher food stand. With aromas of potato knishes and kosher hot dogs wafting through the area, the men convene for the afternoon prayer known as *mincha*. Although the prayer at the ballpark is not consensually endorsed by Orthodox rabbis, Saul Newman, a professor of political science and an Orthodox Jew, enjoys having the chance to pray among a quorum of ten or more adult Jewish males. He notes that the Talmud does not specifically forbid such a ritual at the ballpark, and he admits that, as needy as the Orioles might be for a rally during their next at bat, the ten-minute prayer session maintains focus on fulfilling the obligations of prayer rather than petitioning God for intervention in the Orioles' offense.[42]

A more common religious ceremony at ballparks is the celebration of a wedding. Made popular in part by the cinematic marriage between utility infielder Jimmy and the townie Millie in *Bull Durham*, marriage ceremonies at ballparks have become much more routine, but still expensive, in recent years. Although many of the newer major league ballparks now feature wedding ceremonies among the special services for which the diamond, outfield, or other spaces might be rented, not all ballparks—particularly Yankee Stadium—have embraced this auxiliary enterprise. Couples who get married at the ballpark often do so because of the importance of baseball in their lives or because the ballpark itself is the place where they first met, had a date, or proposed marriage. Some desire to have a traditional church wedding but to use the ballpark—rather than a ballroom—for the reception. That was the case with Susie and Brad Byers, a Los Angeles couple who met at Dodger Stadium on a blind date. Although they described themselves as being more in the jeans and T-shirt set rather than tuxedo and formal dress, they wanted a church wedding in November, after which they had the reception at Dodger Stadium's Dugout Club. There, guests enjoyed Dodger Dogs along side more standard wedding fare, but the cake was decorated with small bats and gloves atop the icing. The baseball theme for the wedding was completed with music as they took the floor for their first dance as husband and wife, waltzing to the accompaniment of "Take Me Out to the Ball Game."[43]

---

[42] Peter Maas, "A Gathering Place for Faithful Fans," *Washington Post*, 16 May 1996, B1, B5.

[43] Christine Frey, "Eat, Drink, and Be Married at the Ballpark," *Los Angeles Times*, 21 April 2002, E1, E4.

The aura of a ballpark itself—the mysterious perception of Otherness that one can experience there—is spiritually akin to the sensation that one has in a grand sanctuary or cathedral. Recognizing this possibility, the monthly photo-essay on "Real Weddings" in *Modern Bride* promoted a traditional wedding ceremony and reception at the Minute Maid Park in Houston. Among the expenses that the featured couple Casey and Chris Johnson incurred while sticking to their budget of $20,000 were the rental of the facility, ballpark tours for ninety guests, hats and jerseys for their photos, and catering costs (including the distinct ball-glove cake), as well as the standing costs for wedding paraphernalia.[44]

The use of ballparks as the site for weddings is not restricted to the new or famous stadiums in major league cities. On its official website, the city of Mesa, Arizona, for instance, markets the opportunity for couples to be married at home plate in Hohokam Stadium, followed by a reception at either the Third Base Patio or the one along the first base line. For Ruben Lardizabal, a former Oakland Athletics' pitching prospect who stayed in the majors for about a month, the Isotopes' ballpark in Albuquerque was an appropriate place for his wedding to Darlene McDuffie. Initially, they had met when Lardizabal coached McDuffie's oldest son on the freshman baseball team at the high school where he teaches. Baseball indeed connected them. But for Darlene especially, the idea of marrying on the pitcher's mound was quite attractive since it meant that she would be at the center of the largest diamond in the world at the time of their nuptial exchange.[45]

---

[44] Lambeth Hochwald, "A Ballpark Blast," *Modern Bride*, December 2003.

[45] Jan Jonas, "His Big Pitch Leads to Ballpark Wedding," *Albuquerque Tribune*, 25 July 2003.

In addition to the worship services and marriage ceremonies that signify the religious character of the ballpark and playing field, baseball stadiums also facilitate spiritual experiences when they serve as memorial sites. For various civic figures and baseball personnel, ballparks have been used as the venues for memorial services, with Yankee Stadium having served as the place where a memorial tribute was held in New York on 20 September 2001 to honor and remember the lives of the victims in the terrorist attacks on the World Trade Center. Following the deaths of former players and current teammates, such as Thurman Munson, times of silence before games often transformed the cheering crowd and the baseball field itself into a reverential audience and hallowed space where the spirit of the deceased could be embraced. And the public memorial service for *Los Angeles Times* sports columnist and Hall of Fame journalist Jim Murray was held along the first base line and in the lower box seats at Dodger Stadium. Although not a funeral or a memorial service, the ceremony honoring Lou Gerhig on "his day" following his retirement from baseball bore all of the mournful marks of a wake, with friends and fans delivering a permanent farewell—a kind of eulogy—to a beloved, steady friend, despite Gerhig's own heroic statement about considering himself to be "the luckiest man on the face of the earth." The monument memorializing Gerhig in centerfield was installed four days after his death in early July 1941.

Before the renovation of Yankee Stadium in the 1970s, the great reaches of centerfield had provided space for the erection of monuments within the field of play that served as memorial tributes to Yankee greats: Gerhig, Ruth, and Miller Huggins. Expanded and moved beyond the outfield fence at the time of the renovation of the ballpark, the gallery of plaques now includes tributes to almost twenty former Yankee greats. The new memorial park within the stadium functions like a graveyard adjacent to an old community church or like memorial crypts in cathedrals.

Following the death of at least one life-long Yankee fan, Yankee Stadium served as more than a place for memorial; it literally provided a final resting place. The late grandmother of Eddie Ellner, a California author, wanted to express her ultimate devotion to the Yankees. So fervent in her love of the Yankees that she taught her parakeet to squawk "Go Mickey, go Yankees," she had requested on her deathbed that if the Yankees ever won the pennant again, she wanted Eddie to scatter her ashes across the field of Yankee Stadium. So Ellner flew across the country in late October 1996 and dusted her ashes on home plate, along the first base line, across the infield, and in the on-deck circle. Although Ellner would not confirm how he had gotten access to the field, he did remark: "It is serendipity. Somehow my grandmother arranged it," hinting that even in death her spirit might prevail.[46]

The fusion of baseball and religion has also been manifest in a new way for minor league teams in recent years. The attendance promotion known as "Faith Nights," initiated by the Nashville Sounds, has been so entrepreneurial and successful that ABC's *World News Tonight* featured one of the events in late summer 2005. "It's Friday night and many Americans are on their way to the ballpark tonight," Terry Moran read as the newscast began. "Players have always offered up prayers before, after, and during the game. And so have fans. But now baseball team owners are turning to prayer as a marketing opportunity."[47] Because there are more than 3,000 churches within a two-hour drive of Nashville's Greer

---

[46] "Morning Briefing," *Los Angeles Times*, 4 November 1996, C2.

[47] Terry Moran, "Faith Night, Baseball, and the Bible," ABC-TV World News Tonight (26 August 2005).

Stadium, Nashville Sounds Vice President Brent High and sports marketer Mike Snider came up with the idea of promoting the game not merely to a single church youth group or another church's men's organization, but to as many churches a possible. Like hundreds of other organizations in the Nashville area, churches had often been offered the chance to purchase group tickets at discount. Faith Night, however, takes the marketing initiative and incentives to a new level. Not merely content with providing cheaper tickets to the game, High and Snider added promotional campaigns to the pitches, offering to provide Christian musical acts and faith-based activities oriented to the attendees, such as quiz questions about biblical trivia.

At the pre-game celebrations at the ballpark or in the parking lot, church-going fans can enjoy live musical performances by contemporary Christian rock groups like Bid Daddy Weave, a chart-climbing band who performed at the Greensboro Hoppers Faith Night event in early August 2005.[48] Or at one of the Sounds' games, faithful fans might join Nate Sallie, a Gospel Music Award nominee, in singing, as he put it, "to the same person…[since] we all have one common goal."[49]

In 2001, the Sounds featured three Faith Nights and expanded the number to five in each of the following two years. And for three of the seven Faith Nights in 2004 High added an additional promotional reward—bobble-head figures of Samson, Noah, and Moses. That season, attendance at Faith Nights almost doubled the average attendance of non-Faith Nights. During the 2005 season, new bobble heads were added—of Queen Esther, Daniel and the Lions, and John the

---

[48] Nancy H. McLaughlin, "Christian Band Helps Fill the Ballpark," *News and Record* (Greensboro NC), 4 August 2005, B1.

[49] Reid Cherner, "If You Billed it around Faith, They will Certainly Come," *USA Today*, 22 July 2005, 1A.

Baptist, whose representation apparently preceded his disfigurement following the request of Herod's daughter. Also in 2005 Snider took the promotion on the road beyond the Bible Belt; he found that attendance at the Hagerstown (Maryland) Suns' game in mid July drew 50 percent more fans than average. In addition to the gate give-away items, which obviously have nothing to do with baseball itself, Snider also began to feature guest appearances of VeggieTale characters. Because they were added to the lineup of stars and events in the promotion, one family drove 600 miles so that they could see Larry and Bob, a seven-foot tall cucumber and a round tomato who are characters in the VeggieTales pantheon.[50]

Often, faith nights have been planned to be as unobtrusive as possible by having a number of the acts and pre-game events staged in the parking lot and by continuing to sell beer at the concessions, even if the beer is offered in fewer of the food and drink stalls. But in some of the Faith Night promotions, the display of muscular Christianity returns with power. For one, at the West Tenn Diamond Jaxx game in Jackson, Tennessee in June 2005, outfielder Matt Murton, who played for the Chicago Cubs later in the season, provided a pre-game testimony before taking the field for the Jaxx. "There are a lot of similarities between life and baseball. A lot of ups and downs," he said. "You know the Lord controls your steps. I know how difficult it would be going through baseball without knowing he was in control." Also exercising a voice in muscular evangelism, Turner Ward, a former major league player in a dozen seasons, served in 2005 as one of the ministers at the First Baptist Church of Satsuma in Mobile, Alabama. When he accompanied church members and their friends on the trek to Nashville for Faith Night festivities at a Sounds' game, he

---

[50] Ibid.

usually delivered devotional messages lasting fifteen minutes or so. Repeatedly in his remarks, he connected baseball and faith, emphasizing that "the greatest thing in baseball was scoring a run," reaching home safely, and that a great thing in "Faith Night is coming home to your faith."[51]

Conclusion

Throughout the past 150 years, baseball and religion have intersected in various ways, trying to pick each other off base during periods of protest against Sabbath restrictions or rounding the bases together in muscular expressions of faith. One of the early twentieth-century religious groups that exercised faith while playing baseball was the millenarian community known as the House of David, which provides the focus for the next chapter. But before turning to an exploration of that group's fusion of baseball and faith a century ago, let me identify a current, playful intersection between baseball and faith.

One of the humorous lists circulating through the Internet features an alignment of baseball with religion. The reversal or double play of this list is that rather than suggesting that baseball resembles religion in some respect, the quips depict religious groups using baseball terms and themes. Certainly, the list is playful, but its characterizations also express theological, ritual, and moral distinctions of the religious groups. Here are a few:

Calvinists believe the game is fixed.
Quakers won't swing.
Unitarians can catch anything.
Amish walk a lot.

---

[51] Ibid.

Televangelists get caught stealing.
Fundamentalists balk.
Baptists want to play hardball.
Adventists have a seventh-inning stretch.

And my favorite is the one that is reminiscent of the undefiled days at Wrigley Field before the installation of lights: "Premillennialists expect the game to be called soon on account of darkness."

For years, the idea of applying baseball metaphors to Christian denominations would have seemed sacrilegious to many devout believers, especially in the early years of baseball as it began to become the National Pastime during the decades following the Civil War. By the turn of the twentieth century, Billy Sunday had accelerated the acceptance of baseball allusions to explain the Christian faith to audiences frequently unfamiliar with ecclesiastical practices and church dogma. And now, in an era when marriage ceremonies at ballparks are marketed to prospective brides, when memorial services are held on the diamond, and when Faith Nights feature bobble-head dolls of biblical heroes, we sense that baseball and faith are rounding the bases together.

2
Exercising Faith:
Baseball and Faith for the
House of David

In the early spring of 1903, former itinerant preachers Benjamin Purnell and his wife Mary led a few members of a small millenarian community to relocate from Ohio to Benton Harbor, Michigan. There they purchased property for a developing sect called "The Seventh Church at the Latter-Day, the Israelite House of David, Church of the New Eve, Body of Christ." A decade later, the community would found a local baseball team that would grow into one of the most successful barnstorming franchises—a description applied wisely since by the 1930s there were at least three House of David barnstorming teams competing simultaneously in various regions of the country during the height of their sporting prowess. During their heyday in the 1920s and 1930s, the David teams regularly won two-thirds to three-fourths of their games against minor league teams, Negro league teams, and local all-star teams. An impressive feature connected to their record is that in some years they played 200 games, often two in a day in different cities, and the team traveled in cars and vans for more than 25,000 miles in a summer.

Self-described as a Christian Israelite community whose purpose was to gather the lost tribes of Israel in preparation for the advent of the Millennium, the House of David team distinguished itself from many Protestant utopian communities by soliciting Jewish players from synagogues in southern Michigan and northern Indiana to join their team. While sporting beards and hair styles that made the players look like they had just stepped out of the Old Testament, the team did provide aspiring Jewish baseball players a chance to play professionally in the earliest decades of the twentieth century.

In terms of scholarly studies about the House of David and its baseball ventures, little has been produced. In the last half century, giants of American religious historical study have been Martin Marty, Sidney Ahlstrom, Winthrop Hudson, Robert T. Handy, and E. Scott Gaustad.[1] Routinely, their works ignore the House of David. Even Ahlstrom's magisterial *History of American Religious People* and Marty's more recent three-volume study of modern American religion, the first volume of which focuses on the period of 1893–1919 and bears title *The Irony of It All*, ironically fail to identify the millenarian movement of the House of David or the leadership—even the entrepreneurial ventures—of the Purnells. Not surprisingly,

---

[1] Martin E. Marty, *Pilgrims in Their Own Land: 500 Years of Religion in America* (New York: Little, Brown and Company, Inc., 1984); Martin E. Marty, *Protestantism in the United States: Righteous Empire*, 2nd ed. (New York: Charles Scribner's Sons, 1986); Martin E. Marty, *The Irony of It All, 1893–1919*, vol. 1 of *Modern American Religion* (Chicago: The University of Chicago Press, 1986); Sidney E. Ahlstrom, *A Religious History of the American People* (New Haven: Yale University Press, 1972); Winthrop Hudson, *Religion in America* (New York: Charles Scribner's Sons, 1965); Robert T. Handy, *A Christian America: Protestant Hopes and Historical Realities*, 2nd ed. (New York: Oxford University Press, 1984); Edwin Scott Gaustad, *A Religious History of America*, rev. ed. (San Francisco: Harper & Row, Publishers, 1990).

Catherine Albanese, Peter Williams, and John Corrigan,[2] who are collaborators with and former students of Marty, Ahlstrom, and Hudson, also ignore the House of David. And somewhat similarly, Lawrence Foster's revealing examination of the distinct sexual styles of nineteenth-century millenarian communities,[3] Robert Fuller's imaginative exploration of the Mesmeristic healing initiatives and religious diets of the same period,[4] Donald Dayton's explanation of the roots of charismatic movements,[5] and the chorus of feminist historians and theologians (featuring Rosemary Reuther, Ann Braude, and Anne Taves)[6]—who have exhumed the records of women

---

[2] Catherine L. Albanese, *America: Religion and Religions* (Belmont CA: Wadsworth, 1981); Catherine L. Albanese, ed., *American Spiritualities: A Reader* (Bloomington: Indiana University Press, 2001); Peter W. Williams, *America's Religions: Traditions and Cultures* (Urbana: University of Illinois Press, 1998); Winthrop S. Hudson and John Corrigan, *Religion in America*, 7th ed. (Upper Saddle River NJ: Pearson/Prentice Hall, 2004).

[3] Lawrence Foster, *Religion and Sexuality: The Shakers, the Mormons, and the Oneida Community* (New York: Oxford University Press, 1981).

[4] Robert C. Fuller, *Mesmerism and the American Cure of Souls* (Philadelphia: University of Pennsylvania Press, 1982).

[5] M. Darrol Bryant and Donald W. Dayton, eds., *The Coming Kingdom: Essays in American Millennialism and Eschatology* (Barrytown NY: New Era Books, 1983). Cf. Charles Nordoff, *The Communistic Societies of the United States, from Personal Visit and Observation*, with new introduction by Mark Holloway (New York: Dover Publications, 1966), and Mark Holloway, *Heavens on Earth: Utopian Communities in America, 1680–1880*, 2nd ed. (New York: Dover Publications, 1966).

[6] Rosemary Radford Ruether and Rosemary Skinner Keller, *The Nineteenth Century*, vol. 1 of *Women and Religion in America* (San Francisco: Harper and Row, Publishers, 1981); Ann Braude, *Radical Spirits: Spiritualism and Women's Rights in 19th Century America* (Boston: Beacon Press, 1991); Ann Taves, *Fits, Trances, and Visions:*

ministers and religious leaders in the last two centuries of American religious history—all have ignored the House of David. Even Robert Ellwood and William M. Kephart,[7] both of whom have produced exquisite studies of the formation of "extraordinary" religious groups in America, do not include the study of the House of David in their comprehensive works. One dissertation has been published about the history of the community, but its account is heavily dependent on archives in the State Historical Commission and the Michigan Attorney General's office because Colony records, including manuscripts and diaries, remain closed. But little attention is devoted to baseball in that work.[8] Despite its neglect by leading historians of American Christianity, the House of David is, in fact, the third oldest continuing American religious community, having been formed only after the Sabbath Lake Shakers in Maine and the Hutterite community in Montana.

Experiencing Religion and Explaining Experience from Wesley to James (Princeton: Princeton University Press, 1999). Cf. Martha Banta, *Imaging American Women: Idea and Ideals in Cultural History* (New York: Columbia University Press, 1987).

[7] Robert S. Ellwood, Jr., *Alternative Altars: Unconventional and Eastern Spirituality in America* (Chicago: The University of Chicago Press, 1979); Robert S. Ellwood and Harry B. Partin, *Religious and Spiritual Groups in Modern America*, 2nd ed. (Englewood Cliffs NJ: Prentice-Hall, 1988); William M. Kephart and William W. Zellner, *Extraordinary Groups: An Examination of Unconventional Life-Styles*, 5th ed. (New York: St. Martin's Press, 1994).

[8] Robert S. Fogerty, *The Righteous Remnant: The House of David* (Kent: Kent State University Press, 1981) x-xi. A more popular history of the community similarly pays only passing attention to baseball. Cf. Clare E. Adkin, *Brother Benjamin: A History of the Israelite House of David* (Berrien Springs MI: Andrews University Press, 1990) 240–46.

Even though several popular and polemical works deal with the history of the House of David community or with the rosters and records of the baseball teams that the community sponsored,[9] I want to turn our attention to several larger issues that are not the primary concerns of the popular works: (1) identifying the roots of the religious movement; (2) specifying distinct religious beliefs and practices of the House of David; (3) locating its place in the larger cultural, religious, and utopian movements at the end of the nineteenth and beginning of the twentieth century; and (4) speculating about the significance of baseball as an exercise of faith for the community.

The Roots of the Religious Movement

In 1792 in England, Joanna Southcott received a series of revelations that she was the first of the Seven Messengers whom God would send to save the world before the establishment of the millennial kingdom. In the book of

---

[9] Much of the following information about the community and its teams comes from promotional information distributed by the museum arm of the community itself. Other information is derived from Joel Hawkins and Terry Bertolino, *Images of America: The House of David Baseball Team* (Chicago: Arcadia Publishing, 2000). The text garnered the 2000 baseball research award from *The Sporting News* and the Society of American Baseball Research. The book is primarily an annotated photograph album that features the teams' players, their brief biographies, and their baseball highlights—like a sepia-toned set of Topps baseball cards. Thus, apologetic documents and captioned scrapbook photographs provide much of the following information about the House of David religious community, its practices, or the leadership of the Purnells in most of the authoritative histories of American religious life. Unless otherwise indicated, the information in this chapter about the House of David and Mary's City of David can be found on their websites, http://www.maryscityofdavid.org and http://www.israelitehouseofdavid.org.

Revelation, she noted, the seven messengers are identified as "seven angels" to the seven churches. The movement that Joanna Southcott initiated developed into the House of David community a little more than a century later. During her lifetime, her influence extended to about 150,000 followers, including British nobles and bishops in the Church of England. The next two messengers would overlap her ministry, and two others would begin their proclamations of prophecies within a decade following her death. The first six messengers, each of whom claimed their place in the sequence of their lineage, were British. The sixth, James Jezreel, founded the New and Latter House of Israel and wrote the pamphlet "Extracts from the Flying Roll," which, decades later, proved to be a significant text for the House of David. He also made a world tour and sent missionaries to America. In the late 1880s a Richmond, Indiana couple, Mary and Benjamin Purnell, became followers of Jezreel.

Regarding the transition of the movement from England to America and Australia, conflicting reports exist. Some suggest that the expansion was the result of evangelistic efforts; others indicate that the movement was expelled from England because of a controversial sexual initiation rite for cleansing of sins.[10] Prior to the Purnells' becoming followers of Jezreel, Benjamin had served as an itinerant Campbellite (or Disciples of Christ) preacher at county fairs and on street corners in small communities near his Kentucky birthplace. Although details about their joining with Jezreel are not known, in the early 1890s the Purnells affiliated with the Detroit commune of Michael Mills who, before his conviction on morals charges, claimed to be the seventh messenger. Almost immediately after joining the commune, the Purnells were commissioned as

---

[10] Cf. Fogarty, *Righteous Remnant*, 25-26.

traveling preachers. In 1894 Jezreel announced that all of the married women in the community would become the shared wives of the group. According to at least one account,[11] it was Benjamin Purnell who encouraged Mills's wife to sue for divorce and who then assumed leadership of the group when Mills was convicted and sentenced for "the blood-cleansing rite."

In 1902 the Purnells and several members of the group relocated to Fostoria, Ohio, and in 1903, following the death of the Purnells' daughter, whom Benjamin reportedly refused to bring back to life (as might expected of "the younger brother of Christ," an appellation that he applied to himself), some from the group migrated again under the Purnells' leadership to Benton Harbor, Michigan, where there were already gathered perhaps as many as 200 "Flying Rollers"—or followers of the sixth church identified with Jezreel. There the Purnells founded the Israelite House of David, which, they believed, would be the self-proclaimed seventh and final church before the establishment of the millennial kingdom of God.

Distinct Religious Beliefs and Practices

As the Purnells established the commune, they did not forbid interaction with the citizens of Benton Harbor although the male members of the community distinguished themselves with their full beards and long hair, which occasionally grew below their belt lines. Although Ben Purnell's beard never reached the incredible lengths of several of the more dramatic ballplayers, he sought to grow his beard and shape his hair like Jesus; but sporting a western style hat, he looked quite a bit like Wild Bill Hickok. Even though members of the House of

---

[11] Cf. Adkins, *Brother Benjamin*, 79–115.

David were prohibited from owning any personal property, they were encouraged to work in the community and in local industry and services. In fact, at one point when the local cable car company discriminated against some of the House of David members because of their long hair, the commune purchased controlling interest in the company, thus allowing all of the conductors to sport long hair. For the House of David, the biblical directive for leaving hair uncut does not have to do with Samson and his strength, but with the vows taken for the Nazarite order, which (according to Num 6) required that hair be left uncut during the Nazarite covenant and the followers' pursuit of the "pure holiness of God."

Other rituals that distinguished the House of David were its dietary proscriptions, its endorsement of non-Sabbatarian practices, its support of women in leadership roles, its encouragement of modest form of dress, and its celibate lifestyle. Like Seventh Day Adventists, the House of David prescribed a vegetarian diet because of biblical injunctions against killing and because it was presumed that the diet in Eden—the primeval paradise after which their amusement park was named—had been without meat. In addition, it called for abstinence from caffeine, alcohol, and tobacco because of the messenger's teaching that "one seeking for the life of the body should be careful to do his part for the proper preservation of his health, in a meek and unobtrusive [or temperate] way."[12] Members of the House of David also distinguished themselves by conducting business on Sundays, thus failing—according to local residents—to set aside the Sabbath as a day for worship and rest. Although the members of the House of David observed a modest Sunday worship service, they regarded each

---

[12] Unless otherwise noted, the brief quotations throughout the following pages can be located on the website of Mary's House of David, http://www.maryscityofdavid.org.

day as providing the same opportunities for worship, and much like the Shakers, they attempted to infuse their spirituality into the ordinary work, routines, and recreation of life.

With Mary Purnell having assisted in the writing of *The Star of Bethlehem*, it is not surprising that the text indicates that women could assume roles of leadership in the community. And in terms of the elections that took place within the community itself, women were given the right to vote from the time of the community's inception in 1903, almost two decades before the passage of the Nineteenth Amendment. Equal opportunities for women also seemed to extend to the sponsorship of baseball teams. By 1919 the colony sponsored women's teams, and in that year the House of David Girls Baseball Team went undefeated, including victories again the Chicago Colored Girls Team and the Chicago All-American Ladies Team. Yet the perfect record was invalidated because at least six of the players on the women Davids were men who shaved in order to play on the team and who used their long hair as a deceitful disguise rather than as a testimony of their faith.

In terms of dress, outside observers noted how the members wore simple, plain clothing; the community's general guidelines for dress called for attire that would not be sexually attractive. The men were often photographed in three-piece suits, while Ben Purnell also sported an elegant cowboy hat. Although no specific dress restrictions applied to women, sisters were encouraged to avoid make-up, perfume, and jewelry. They did, however, wear long flowing robes that were thought, like uncut hair, to be in line with the "simple frock of the Nazarite order." And although celibacy was officially espoused within the commune, local residents often complained about sexual activities in the House of David until police raided the private facilities of Purnell and found him coordinating an orgy.

Certainly these rituals separated members of the community from other residents in Benton Harbor. But the House of David also distinguished itself by several of its inventions and entrepreneurial accomplishments. By 1908 the community had opened an amusement park that bore the theologically significant name of the Park Springs of Eden, or Eden Springs Park, a name recalling the primeval innocence, pleasure, and play that characterized the biblical Eden. Ben Purnell had selected Benton Harbor as the ingathering place for the remnant of the faithful because, as he put it, Benton Harbor lies at the "heart of the most healthful summer resorts in America." A few years after its founding, a Chicago periodical identified Eden Springs as a place "where thousands of people seeking rest and recreation find Israel's faith more attractive than worldly pleasures." Among its features were a movie theater, various nature paths, a mineral spring, a zoo, and a "pygmy railway," as it was playfully called. Years later, one of the mini-steam locomotives from the miniature railway was purchased by Walt Disney before he opened his California theme park.

During the first week of its operation in the summer of 1908, Eden Springs Park sold more than 5,000 admissions, and almost one-fourth of the visitors rode the miniature steam railroad with each car bearing the insignia of B & M (for Ben and Mary Purnell). In addition, in an era before significant interfaith dialogues, the House of David served as a resort for Jewish vacationers, especially from nearby Chicago, and in 1938 it constructed and dedicated a synagogue for use by vacationers.

Not only did the community sponsor the barnstorming baseball team, it also sponsored a basketball team that conducted an exhibition tour throughout Europe with the Harlem Globetrotters. It established several touring bands, especially a highly successful jazz band and a marching band that enjoyed having John Philip Sousa as its guest conductor on one tour. The House of David also takes credit for having invented the automatic pin-setting equipment for bowling and the waffle cone or sugar cone that is featured in ice cream parlors.

The most popular distinction of the House of David, however, was its baseball team. In part because Benjamin Purnell was an avid baseball fan, the community erected a baseball stadium in 1910, primarily for the local semi-pro team, the Speed Boys. When the Speed Boys were playing games on the road, the Israelite community would field a team for after-school entertainment for children supervised in daycare. In addition, the games became popular among the patrons of the amusement park, especially since the players looked so unorthodox.

As the popularity of the team grew, the House of David began to charge a separate admission for the games. By 1914 the community fielded a competitive team, and the following year the House of David team qualified for the local league's championship games, which the Davids won. In 1916 colony secretary Francis Thorpe, who as the team's first manager had been instrumental in introducing baseball as an adult sport, set up a competitive tour for the team to play in Indiana, Illinois, and Wisconsin. By 1920 the House of David team had begun its barnstorming trips throughout the country. Yet about that time, the team realized its need for greater talent and expanded its roster beyond the members of the community. It began to recruit Jewish ballplayers from area synagogues, and in 1924 it also began to hire players who, as part of the requirement for playing with the team, would grow their beards and refuse to cut their hair. According to some outsider accounts, the ringers were exposed when it was discovered that they were wearing beard masks and wigs rather than allowing their own hair to grow. At the very least, however, the publicity photos of the team are quite striking since the players often posed in ways that displayed their unshorn locks rivaling Godiva's or Samson's full sweep of hair.

Despite their appearance, the House of David teams performed at an extraordinarily high level. According to stories passed on to family members of players who had competed against the House of David, the high winning percentage resulted in part from the ease with which the Davids pitchers could "grease the ball" by stroking their beards before delivering "spitters" to opposing batters. During the decade of the 1920s, the team's success was remarkable, even if spit-balling pitchers regularly tossed for the Davids, who won three-fourths of their games. Similarly, in 1935 the City of David ended its season in early October with a victory over a Paris, Texas team. That season's record stood a 146-50, with the team having traveled about 30,000 miles, crossing twenty states, Canada, and Mexico. The following year, the team won 144 games (how millennially symbolic and convenient!), lost forty-six, and tied five.

In addition to their excellent play and striking appearance on the field, they were known for several innovations associated with the game. The House of David was the first team to play a baseball game at night—in Independence, Kansas, in April 1930. Because the team had portable lights, it was able to draw large night-time crowds to the novelty of night games wherever they played. Although already accustomed to the challenges of playing under the lights, the House of David team lost a 1931 exhibition game to the St. Louis Cardinals in the first night game ever played at

Sportsman's Park; and the Davids also played the first night game in Ebbets Field.

Among the other entertaining promotions conceived by House of David promoter Ray Doan were Donkey Baseball and the token use of women players. The House of David was the first professional male team to sign a woman to a permanent contract. In the 1933 season, curve-balling pitcher Jackie Mitchell, the first female player in professional baseball, started in a number of the Davids' games, including a late September appearance against Dizzy Dean and the St. Louis Cardinals. Two seasons earlier, she had signed a contract with the Chattanooga Lookouts (Class AA). Then as a seventeen-year-old rookie, she had pitched to the heart of the Yankees' lineup in an exhibition game. Facing her first batter, she disposed of Babe Ruth on four pitches, followed by her second strikeout—of Lou Gehrig on three pitches. Within a matter of days, however, Baseball Commissioner Judge Kennesaw Mountain Landis voided her contract on the pretense that baseball would be too strenuous for women. In her 1933 appearance at Sportsman's Park, the Davids defeated the National League champions by a score of 8-6. After pitching a single inning, Miss Mitchell retired to the dugout, leaving the mound with a 4-0 lead. And in her only plate appearance, she popped up to Leo Durocher, who was playing shortstop for the Cardinals.

Although the House of David never hired an African American player, Satchell Paige was loaned to their promoter by the Pittsburgh Crawfords in time for him to pitch for them during their championship pursuit in the 1934 Denver Post Tournament, which he did. Paige was no stranger to the Davids since he frequently played against them as they barnstormed against teams from the Negro leagues, especially the Kansas City Monarchs and Paige's own team of all-stars. In fact, it was Satchel who nicknamed them "Jesus' Boys."

In 1930 when the schism occurred between the House of David colony and the newly formed City of David group who followed Mary Purnell, three of the four most gifted athletes on the House of David team walked out with Mary. One was John Tucker, who set a nine-inning game record by recording twenty-three putouts at first base in the Davids' 13-3 defeat of the Refugio (Texas) Firemen on 20 April 1935. Because of his prominence and prowess on the original Davids' team, Tucker commanded attention and accorded respect, even off the field. Resonating with the advice given by his friend Satchel Paige,[13] Tucker followed four rules that he thought characterized great players: (1) "You can't take your work home with you"; (2) "Go to bed the same day you get up"; (3) "Never go on a liquid diet"; (4) "Last, but not least, you got to be able to hit that curveball."[14] "Doc" Tally, who along with Tucker and Faust had invented the "Pepper Game," went with Thorpe and Tucker to the new team. And joining them was George Anderson. Meanwhile "Dutch" Faust remained with Judge Dewhirst and the House of David team. Four years earlier, Faust had become the only devout member of the House of

---

[13] In his autobiography, Paige emphasized six rules for staying young: "[1] Avoid fried meats which angry up the blood. [2] If your stomach disputes you, lie down and pacify it with cool thoughts. [3] Keep the juices flowing by jangling around gently as you move. [4] Go very light on the vices, such as carrying on in society—the social ramble ain't restful. [5] Avoid running at all times. [6] And don't look back. Something might be gaining on you." LeRoy Satchel Paige, as told to David Lipman, *Maybe I'll Pitch Forever: A Great Baseball Player Tells the Hilarious Story behind the Legend* (New York: Doubleday and Company, 1962) 227.

[14] Hawkins and Bertolino, *Images of America: The House of David*, 63.

David to play for a minor league team. Initially playing for the Dallas Steers in the Texas Association, Faust never advanced beyond A-level play.

There are records of other long-term players who were recruited to play for the Davids and who got tryouts and contract offers from major and minor league teams. For example, Holman "Pee Wee" Bass pitched for the City of David team during the decade of the 1930s, winning thirty-four games during the 1935 season and at one point winning twenty-four games in a row. Later in his career he pitched two no-hitters for the Corpus Christi team in the Texas League. And Al Nusser, who pitched for the City of David in both 1934 and 1936, signed a contract with the Cubs and even enjoyed playing a few games in the major leagues. During the 1930s, both of the competing David communities began to rely more and more on players for hire, some of whom from season to season would shift back and forth between the Israelite House of David and Mary's City of David sponsors.

It was also in the 1930s that promoter Ray Doan hired Chief Bender as a pitcher and Grover Cleveland Alexander as a pitcher/manager. The future Hall of Famer, however, had several stipulations in his contract. One was that he would pitch an inning each game; but since he was the manager, he often scheduled himself to pitch the eighth or ninth inning, hoping for rain before the end of the game. In addition, he was not required to let his hair grow, and he was allowed to shave, even receiving an extra thirty-five cents a day for a razor fee. But, not surprisingly, he spent much of his shaving money on sherry. By the mid-1930s, many of the players on the David teams did not retain the strictures of the Nazarite covenant for letting their hair grow, and most of them trimmed their beards to a modest length.[15]

During World War II, both communities suspended their barnstorming play, and following the war, Mary's City of David team resumed play for a decade while relying primarily on hired players to fill the rosters. Pictures of the barnstorming team during the final years of its existence show that the players look like almost any other team, clean shaven with regular length hair.[16] One of the initial vaudevillian attractions to the team was gone: No longer could the House of David team be easily recognized as "Jesus' Boys," the bearded barnstormers.

Other distinctions of the House of David teams were that they offered Babe Ruth a contract to join them in the barnstorming tour, but he never responded, other than having his picture taken with the Davids' touring team in the East. The House of David was more successful in securing the services of other stars, such as Babe Didrickson, who played for the House of David team touring the East in 1934.

The Religious and Cultural Context

Although baseball gave the House of David its most widespread fame, the community thrived because of the coherence and demands of its doctrines and rituals, which were set forth in a four-volume treatise written by the Purnells primarily during their itinerant preaching years. The work, titled *The Star of Bethlehem, the Living Roll of Life*, provided the covenant that bound the members together.

In several respects, the beliefs and practices of the House of David resembled those of other utopian communities and Adventist groups in the late Victorian period. Like the

---

[15] Ibid., 104.
[16] Ibid., 110.

Mormons, members of the House of David accepted as a central scriptural authority a text not known before modern times. For Mormons, the Book of Mormon had been revealed verbatim on golden tablets discovered in the 1820s on a hill near Cumorah, New York. While members of the House of David affirmed the primary authority of the King James translation of the Bible, they also depended upon several other texts, including the Purnells' massive treatise *The Star of Bethlehem* and a work called *Nazarites*, which they used as hermeneutical guides. According to the House of David's own accounts, the text of the *Nazarites*, which had been lost for centuries, had been transported aboard Noah's ark. Somewhat similar to the method of discovery of the tablets containing the Book of Mormon, *Nazarites* was "found by an expedition led by Stanhope Bruce, a Bishop of the Church of England and a follower of Joanna Southcott."[17]

The House of David shared distinct practices and beliefs with other utopian and millenarian movements. Like the Shakers, the House of David was celibate. Like Seventh Day Adventists, they were vegetarians, teetotalers, and abstainers from caffeine and tobacco. Like the Oneida community, they manifest entrepreneurial inventiveness. Like the Shakers, they provided retreat support for persons on various spiritual quests. And again like the Shakers, who attributed the status of divine incarnation to Mother Ann Lee, their founder, the House of David accepted female leadership and conceived a significant role of the feminine in the Divine. Specifically, the House of David regarded the Holy Ghost as feminine, as the Mother of Christ since, they reasoned, it would not be possible for the

---

[17] http://www.maryscityofdavid.ord/html/teachings.html. Accessed on 13 September 2002.

divine Father to sire a son without having a woman to give birth to the child.

Local, public response to the actions of the House of David was similar to that of the press reports about the Oneida community in upstate New York or the residents reacting to the Mormon kingdom established in Nauvoo, Illinois. Like the accusations leveled against John Humphrey Noyes and Joseph Smith, morals accusations were repeatedly directed toward Ben Purnell by local residents for reported sexual orgies with virgins whose religious rite of initiation into the House of David supposedly included sexual intercourse with Ben Purnell himself.[18] By 1923 a series of feature stories in the *Detroit Free Press* brought greater public attention to Purnell and the commune at Benton Harbor. Like Noyes a half century earlier, Purnell was arrested in 1926 and convicted the following year. But while appealing the conviction, he died in 1927 within two weeks of receiving the verdicts. Without dealing with the specific morals conviction of the deceased, the Michigan Supreme Court set aside several other verdicts—for fraud, perjury, and obstruction of justice—against the members and corporation of the House of David.

Following the court's reversals in 1929, attention in the House of David turned to the issue of leadership. For a three-year period beginning with the arrest of Ben Purnell, a bitter struggle developed between Mary Purnell, who was co-founder of the community and co-author of the *Star of Bethlehem*, and Judge H. T. Dewhirst, one of the directors on the House of David's governing board. The sequence of events resembles the struggles for leadership at Nauvoo following the death of Joseph Smith. There, Brigham Young, as one of the apostles, led the majority of Mormons on the trek to the Utah

---

[18] Adkin, *Brother Benjamin*, 79ff.

settlement, while Emma Smith led a smaller group, which did not endorse polygamy, back to Missouri where the Reorganized Church of Latter Day Saints was established. In the schism at Benton Harbor, Mary dissolved her holdings in the House of David, ceding its leadership to Judge Dewhirst. However, she did have a loyal following of 217 members, including most of the star players from the Benton Harbor House of David baseball teams, and they walked with her to a new site less than half a mile from the original headquarters of the House of David. At the new site in March 1930, the Israelite House of David as reorganized by Mary Purnell was incorporated.

Speculations about the Significance of Baseball for the House of David

In the latter half of the nineteenth century, religious attitudes about recreation and sport began to shift. Several trends and factors converged during the final decades of the century to increase the prospects for aligning recreation and sport with spiritual health: the emergence of phenomena called "muscular Christianity,"[19] the expansion of YMCA facilities and programs throughout the country,[20] the appreciation of football among Christian soldiers,[21] the growth of alternative spiritualities that

---

[19] Tony Ladd and James A. Mathisen, *Muscular Christianity: Evangelical Protestants and the Development of American Sport* (Grand Rapids: Baker Books, 1999).

[20] Clifford Putney, *Muscular Christianity: Manhood and Sports in Protestant America, 1880–1920* (Cambridge: Harvard University Press, 2001).

[21] Robert J. Higgs, *God in the Stadium: Sports and Religion in America* (Lexington: The University Press of Kentucky, 1995).

respected the body, and the creation of sports—basketball and volleyball—for use as evangelistic tools.[22]

By the turn of the twentieth century mainline ministers, theologians, and church leaders had begun to express appreciation for the spiritual roles that recreation and sport could play for religious groups. In 1914, for instance, the periodical *Current Opinion* reported that "if the church wishes to hold its young people...it cannot ignore the recreation of its young people." Theologian Charles Gordon Gilkey put it succinctly for an article in *Playground*: "Religion and recreation belong together." And the Reverend William R. Taylor, a Presbyterian minister, agreed that sports' exercise and recreation could produce "healthier, stronger, lither, more efficient purer bodies" while simultaneously "increas[ing] interest in, and devotion to, the church and Sunday school."[23]

At about the same time that the House of David was beginning to play baseball, other religious communities and traditions throughout the country were turning attention to sports, and in many cases particularly baseball. In Utah at the turn of the century, professional baseball play by the Salt Lake City Mormons, Elders of Bishops, a team in the Pacific Northern League, helped the Mormon territory prove its American character to its nearby states, who recognized in the Mormons' appreciation of baseball their common character with American ideals.[24] Similarly, for the House of David and City of David colonies, baseball also served as a cultural tool

---

[22] Putney, *Muscular Christianity*, and Joseph L. Price, ed., *From Season to Season: Sports as American Religion* (Macon GA: Mercer University Press, 2001).

[23] Quoted in Putney, *Muscular Christianity*, 55, 61, 63.

[24] Jim Warnock, "The Mormon Game: The Religious Uses of Baseball in Early Utah," *Nine: A Journal of Baseball History and Social Policy Perspectives* 6/1 (Fall 1997): 1–14.

for assuring nearby residents of the American spirit and values of the communes. Yet for the Davids' colonies, baseball also served as an exercise of their religious beliefs and distinct identity in several specific ways: as evangelism, as entertainment, as exercise, and as an entrepreneurial affirmation of the success of their eschatological vision.

Evangelism. Building upon the apologetic emphasis of the muscular Christianity movement, the Israelite House of David used baseball as an evangelistic tool for sharing the Word, not so much about the particular millenarian beliefs of the colony members, but about the religious acceptability of the commune itself. By competing against the all-star teams of communities throughout the Midwest, the barnstorming Davids teams proved their American character even while resembling refugees from the lost tribes of Israel. In addition, their willingness to travel, to be seen as migrant players, and to be adventuresome excursionists identified them with a frontier or pioneering spirit still romantically enjoyed by early-twentieth-century Americans. And these perceptions reduced the prospects for misunderstanding them as a reclusive, separatist group that condemned American society as a whole. Furthermore, by making some improvements or expansions on the game—introducing night games, for instance—the Davids provided a progressive model that invited others to join with them, both in terms of playing baseball and accepting the beliefs in prophecy that they enjoyed.

Entertainment. In the wake of the first major wave of industrialism's success in American economy, leisure and entertainment became more available and more desirable to workers at the beginning of the twentieth century. The House of David colony early determined that entertainment was not evil, although its religious texts do not seem to be either entertaining themselves or endorsing entertainment. But unlike the Puritan spirit that had dominated much of American religious life in preceding centuries, the House of David did not condemn entertainment as a distraction from doing good works or practicing piety. Within the House of David it is likely that the openness to the entertainment provided by baseball was developed out of the positive reception of the amusement park at Eden Springs.

Exercise. In the same way that various millenarian and utopian communities began to focus on the body as the temple of God, and in concert with the affirmations afforded by muscular Christianity (with its appreciation for building strong bodies for Christian service), the House of David was able to utilize the physical play of baseball for building strong bodies among the faithful of its community. Additionally, by requiring players publicly to practice the dietary restrictions of the community (at least at the time of the formation of the team) and by having them display beards and long hair, which were ritual distinctions of the community, the House of David team also exercised or exemplified the faith of the community.

Entrepreneurial Success. As the barnstorming efforts began to yield profits for the community, the House of David sought ways to increase the profit, thereby supporting the members of the community and assuring the continuation of its mission and vision. The barnstorming teams often traveled in packs of three cars, driven by staffers who filled in at various jobs on the field, setting up lights and also selling souvenirs in the stands during the games. One of the more profitable ventures, apparently, was the sale of posed postcards of Davids players. Adapting the model of baseball cards and capitalizing on their popularity, the distinct cards featured players with flowing beards and wavy streams of hair draped over their shoulders and descending to their belts; the cards became collectible souvenirs of the unusual team.

Although the entrepreneurial success of the teams prompted several secondary or supportive ventures, the lure of success on the field and in the accounts office also proved somewhat destructive, or in their mindset "demonic," for the Davids teams. Starting in 1924, the House of David began to hire players who were not colony members or believers. Increasingly, the hired players were not subject to the same regulations that were required of member players. Although some of the hired players grew beards, others wore fake beards, and several did not allow their hair to grow long. By the time of the hiring of Grover Cleveland Alexander, exceptions to the facial hair rule were beginning. And within a decade, one of the traveling teams could be photographed clean shaven. Although the permission to shave might not seem like a significant accommodation on the part of the Davids, it undermined the consistent application of rules that the community also derived from the Bible. In short, the shift to shaving suggests a loss of the theological center of the team and the community.

A second way that the loss of the theological center of the team can be seen is the acceptance of alcohol use by some of the hired players, particularly Chief Bender and Grover Cleveland Alexander, whose alcohol consumption was well known. In addition, although believing Davids could not imbibe, hired players began to bet kegs of beer on the outcome of games, especially when they were playing the team from Blatz Brewery. As with the reduction of restrictions on growing long hair and beards, the acceptance of the use of alcohol by contracted players annulled the evangelistic effectiveness of the team in displaying the practices of the House of David community.

A third indication of the loss of spiritual underpinnings for their play can be identified with the establishment of the women's team in 1919. Promoters for the team allowed their desire for victory (a common aspiration among millenarian groups) to dominate their play by having at least six men play on the women's team. In short, when the purpose of the team shifted to winning rather than being entertaining and displaying the distinctions of the House of David community, deception became commonplace, not only infecting the "women's" team but also contaminating the men's team by allowing contracted players to wear wigs of long hair and masks of beards.

Although the introduction of baseball to the House of David community seems to have been an expression of the religious ideals and playful spirit of the community, the lure of success for its teams seems to have seduced the community into compromising its theological character in favor of public appeal and the pursuit of winning on the diamond.

3

The Pitcher's Mound as Cosmic Mountain: Baseball and Religious Myths

During a Wrigley Field rain delay in the summer of 1986, several theologians and historians of religion overheard a conversation between two teenage boys in the bleachers. One asked the other: "Why is the pitcher's mound higher than home plate? Why is it the only part of the field that is raised?" His friend responded with technical data about the exact height of the mound and the historical observation that the height of the mound had been reduced two decades earlier in order to give the batters a better chance to hit against such overpowering pitchers as Bob Gibson. Despite the correct and seemingly sufficient information reported by his friend, the first boy then mused, "No, that's not it. There must be some *real* reason why the pitcher's mound is higher."[1]

This story advocates my turn to religious studies in an effort to understand the lure and sufficiency of baseball for millions of Americans. It should not be surprising that some philosophical or academic framework is applied to the game in order to understand its compelling attraction. Attempts have

---

[1] Knowing of my previous work on baseball and religious myth, Professor Frank Reynolds of the University of Chicago Divinity School noted this conversation and reported it to me.

been made to interpret the game of baseball by looking at the physics of the phenomena, such as the difficulty of hitting a ninety-mile-per-hour fastball released only sixty feet away. With the ball traveling at a speed of 132 feet per second, it is easy to calculate that the batter has less than half a second to judge the angle of approach, speed, and altering rotation on the ball in order to swing a bat that weighs a little more than two pounds quickly enough to make solid contact with the pitch.

Other academic interpretations of the game have been summarized and offered by Roland Garrett, who finally opts for the sufficiency of a metaphysical approach. Among other options he considers how both mathematical and psychological models have been proposed for analyzing the appeal of the game. In terms of mathematical options, Garrett suggests that intuitive trigonometric calculations enable an outfielder to time the speed of his approach to the point of a fly ball's descent. And he notes the psychological—in this case certainly Freudian—attempt to explain the fascination with the game:

> In baseball, it might be said, the competition of pitcher and batter represents the age-old conflict between father and son. The pitcher-father attempts to reach home with a thrown ball, representing semen, while the batter-son uses his bat, a phallus, to deflect and scatter the semen-ball. The pitcher-father gains success when a pitched ball either enters the strike zone or (after being hit) enters a glove of his teammates. The batter may be put out either way. But if, by getting a hit, the batter-son can prevent the pitcher-father from attaining sexual union at home, he can himself attain it by rounding the bases and reaching home again.[2]

_____

[2] Roland Garrett, "The Metaphysics of Baseball," *Sport Inside Out: Readings in Literature and Philosophy* (Fort Worth: Texas Christian University Press, 1985) 645.

Another set of reasons that provoke my religious interpretation of the game comes from the extensive attention and allegiance given to the game. Because this latter set of reasons can be dealt with more quickly, I will turn attention to it first. In this regard, an appeal to statistical computations (which are one of the fascinations of baseball fans) identifies the inordinate attention commanded by the game. After examining the extensive appeal of baseball, I will explore then the mysterious, if not mystical, dimensions of the teenage fan's curiosity.

Fascination and Fanaticism

During the 2005 season—one during which Barry Bonds was absent from the Giants' lineup until their elimination from pennant hopes, but one that enjoyed tight pennant and playoff races until the final weekend of the season—approximately 74 million fans walked through the turnstiles at major league baseball games, eclipsing the attendance record that had been set in the previous season. In other words, about a half-million fans attended major league games each day of the season between the beginning of April and October. According to these attendance statistics, the most popular team, the New York Yankees, drew more than 4 million fans to Yankee Stadium; and five other teams—the Dodgers, the Cardinals, the Angels, the Giants, and the Cubs—attracted more than 3 million fans to their home games. In fact, attendance at major league games has doubled in the past twenty-five years. While Major League Baseball was setting attendance records during the 2005 season, minor league attendance also surged to new levels. The rise in attendance is credited variously to increased media coverage (with regional and national sports networks heightening public awareness about games), the introduction of fantasy baseball games for fans, the construction of new fan-friendly stadiums in a dozen cities throughout the county, the improvement of attendance promotion packages, and the introduction of inter-league play.[3]

Although the attendance at these professional games in 2005 exceeded previous tallies, the mediated audiences via telecast and broadcast made baseball an even more popular phenomenon. The Fox network featured a prominent game each Saturday during the season, and ESPN regularly telecast multiple games throughout the week. Meanwhile, devout fans also subscribed to cable and satellite packages for the Baseball Extra Innings programming that featured regional Fox telecasts as well as the Yankees on the national YES (Yankees Entertainment and Sports) network and the Red Sox on NESN (New England Sports Network). Add to these regular telecasts the special features of the All-Star Game, playoffs, and World Series (which did see a decrease in viewership from the previous year when the Red Sox broke their 85-year drought and became World Champions). It is reasonable to project that Major League Baseball's attendance—those whose attention was directed to the games during the game—approximated 4 billion viewers during the 2005 season. This seemingly astronomical figure of those who, in one way or another, viewed the games does not take into account the hundreds of millions of others who daily "attended" the games via radio broadcasts. These figures can be extended even further when one considers that the minor league teams—about 150 of which are somehow affiliated with the major league teams—command local radio audiences, and occasional television audiences, for the faithful following of their games.

---

[3] Attendance data and analysis can easily be tracked at www.espn.com, the web site of sports and media magnet ESPN, and www.mlb.com, the official site of Major League Baseball.

In addition to the kind of religious devotion to Major League Baseball that is evinced through attendance statistics, the trappings of the game also bear remarkable similarities to the styles of reverence and rituals associated with established religious traditions. Like many religions, baseball has a binding creed, as Jim Murray, sports columnist for the *Los Angeles Times*, has described its nearly inexorable set of traditional rules: "Baseball is a game that revels in its predictability.... It's not a sport, it's a religion. It takes on new beliefs with the greatest of reluctance." By contrast, he continues, "Football changes its rules, its concepts, as nonchalantly as a debutante changes her wardrobe."[4]

Along somewhat the same line of comparison, Murray Ross compares the attraction that fans have to sports like baseball and football. Classifying sport as some sort of popular theater (since it has a sort of rudimentary drama shaped by the heroic or comic actions of various characters), he goes on to muse about the activity of sports viewing, which, he says, "involves something more than the vicarious pleasures of identifying with athletic prowess. I suspect," he admits, "that each sport contains a fundamental myth which it elaborates for its fans, and that our pleasure in watching such games derives in part from belonging briefly to the mythical world which the game and players bring to life."[5]

In addition to its religious affection for rules, baseball has its temples—its stadiums—where the rites are performed, and its shrines—like the Hall of Fame, the commemorative plaques on the centerfield fence in Yankee Stadium, and the bronzed

---

[4] Jim Murray, "Wanted: Playoff Memories," *Los Angeles Times*, 9 October 1983, III:1:1.

[5] Murray Ross, "Football Red and Baseball Green," *Sport Inside Out: Readings in Literature and Philosophy* (Fort Worth: Texas Christian University Press, 1985) 716.

shoes of Johnny Bench at Cincinnati's Great American Ballpark—where the players and games are commemorated. Baseball has its cult of saints, its superheroes of bygone years now "enshrined" (as avid enthusiasts put it) in the Hall of Fame. Baseball, like religions, also has its relics, its tangible artifacts that help to call to mind the journeys to the games and the contact with the heroes. For the fan, the relics are called game balls, players' autographs, and memorabilia—officially licensed souvenirs—that can be purchased at stadium souvenir stands. Like many religions, baseball has its sacred texts—the official tables of statistics and the official publications ranging from yearbooks to the fans' weekly tract, *The Sporting News*, which for years bore the subtitle, "The Baseball Bible." Baseball also has its high priests, like all-star pitchers and Cy Young Award winners, and its true believers, like the most faithful fans who, typified by Cubs' devotees, never give up even when hope has become unreasonable. Like some religions, baseball identifies its sins by calculating and tabulating errors for fielders; strike outs for batters; and walks, balks, and hit batters for pitchers. And finally, baseball has its own liturgical calendar—its own list of holy days or holidays that begins with the festive "new year" celebrations of opening day; includes national holidays like Memorial Day, July 4th, and Labor Day; features the All-Star Game; and concludes with the high holidays of the divisional playoffs and World Series.

The ability of baseball to establish a cohesive identity as a community—like that of an avid fan immediately and fully establishing communion with other fans who otherwise are strangers—and to evoke a sense of personal wholeness is neither fully derived from the public veneration of the game and its heroes nor from the personal thrill generated by great plays. By way of comparison, the fundamental character of religion is not fully located in its appeal (expressed in popular devotion and apotheosis) or in its power to evoke a peak experience. Including these appealing and powerful elements, a religion establishes its essential character with its ability to generate, orient, and sustain an identity in community, and a religion accomplishes this process by means of its structure of symbols—its mythology—both in explicit and implicit ways.

Although a functional analysis of baseball as religion provides a useful index of the prominence of baseball in the life of Americans, I suggest that baseball, as America's national pastime, not only commands religious respect but that because of the mythology that it implies and exemplifies, its rituals and symbols manifest an underlying mythology that should be called religious. And the mythology of baseball is manifest most clearly in its cosmology, its ritual action, and its dramatization of a kind of cosmic dualism.

The Cosmos of Baseball

The most significant, inherent reason that baseball can provide religious coherence for many Americans is that the game has a cosmology of its own. It has its own sense of order. And, as the philosopher Alfred North Whitehead once noted, "Whatever suggests a cosmology, suggests a religion."[6] Historian of religion Peter Gardella specifically extends this cosmological connection to baseball. Writing in the periodical *Books and Religion*, he proposes that indeed there is a cosmic sort of reason that the field and game are the way that they are: "Baseball diamonds organize space in the same way as the basilica of St. Peter at Rome, the altar of heaven at Peking and the great mosque in Mecca. What happens on baseball diamonds may seem to be only a sport, but the pattern of the

---

[6] Alfred North Whitehead, *Religion in the Making* (New York: The Macmillan Company, 1926) 141.

field and the rules of the game also form a ritual. Understanding baseball requires the analytic tools of psychology and comparative religion."[7] Although I differ with Gardella in determining the kind of mythic or ritual structures that underlie the game, I do agree that the lure and love of baseball can be explained most adequately (but certainly not exclusively) by appeal to the methods and insights of religious studies. Baseball claims the devotion, allegiance, and fanaticism of millions of persons, and it serves as a center of meaning and hope for many players and fans who look to its order to provide a semblance of significance and order in their perhaps otherwise mundane, unfocused, or disorganized lives.

In baseball, the cosmos is structured in terms of the myth of the center. The game itself—the field and the rituals of its play—has a sacred center and a highly developed cosmology that is connected to the pitcher's mound, the mythical center of the field. In mythological terms, it does not matter that the pitcher's mound is not the geographic center of the field, for the sacred center does not connote geographic or geometric centrality—a unique, exclusive kind of centrality—but mythological and metaphysical centrality—one of meaning and being.[8]

Baseball is structured by such a mythical and metaphysical center, one that signifies the cosmology of the game. This is not, however, to say that Abner Doubleday[9] or Casey Stengel

---

[7] Peter Gardella, "Baseball Samadhi: A Yankee Way of Knowledge," *Books and Religion* 14/3 (September 1986): 15.

[8] Mircea Eliade, *Patterns in Comparative Religion*, trans. Rosemary Sheed (New York: Sheed and Ward, 1961) 231.

[9] The established tradition (oral tradition) of baseball has long recognized Abner Doubleday as the creator of the game. But in recent years, the process of demythologization has been applied to this *textus receptus*. See, for instance, Victor Salvatore, "The Man

comprehended the significance or even consciously appre-
hended the presence of the myth of the center in the structure
of the game. For a myth does not have to be articulated,
understood, or even recognized in order to manifest power and
exert dominance in the shaping of an identity. There are some
claims by Buddhist enthusiasts, however, that Doubleday, who
was a member of the Theosophical Society, intentionally
infused the game, as Helen Tworkov notes, "with mystical
Buddhist numbers—nine (innings, players, yanas), three
(strikes, jewels, vehicles), and four (balls, bases, noble truths)."[10]
And although modern baseball historians have questioned the
historicity of Doubleday's influence on the game, some of the
enthusiasts have considered the shape of the baseball field as an
oblique reference to the *Diamond Sutra*. One further
coincidence, which Buddhologists often disregard since the
mysteries of the universe underlie and eventually explain all
such unusual convergences, merits mention: "The 108 stitches
(as in suture of 'sutra') on the hardball. This is the total of 9 x 3
x 4: the same number of Buddhist prayer beads on a sacred
mala as well as the number used ritually and repeatedly
throughout Buddhist cultures."[11]

The dominant myth in the game of baseball, however, is
one that transcends the particularities of Buddhism and bears
remarkable similarity to the myth of the center, or as it was
first known at Delphi, the *omphalos* myth.[12] For ancient Greeks,

---

Who Didn't Invent Baseball" *American Heritage* 34 (June–July 1983):
65–67.

[10] Helen Tworkov, "The Baseball Diamond Sutra," *Tricycle: The
Buddhist Review* 2/3 (Summer 1993): 4.

[11] Ibid.

[12] For an alternate application of the *omphalos* myth to baseball,
see A. Bartlett Giamatti, *Take Time for Paradise: Americans and Their
Games* (New York: Summit Books, 1989) 86ff. Former Commissioner

the idea that the *omphalos*, or navel, was the center of the earth indicated that the rock also manifested a biological connection with the rest of the world; that is, it was the point from which creation began. In the ancient world, the summit of the cosmic mountain often was identified with the navel of the earth, for at the highest point in the world (not necessarily the highest geographic point on the planet earth but the highest mythical point for a people, their place of peak experiences) the gods first touched the earth and began the process of creation.

Because of its relative height and its nearness to the heavenly arena of the gods, the cosmic mountain was thought to be the place of divine activity, the place of the world's beginning, and the place for efficacious sacrifice to the gods. The myth of the center, as expressed in the designation of cosmic mountains, was not restricted to the Greeks or to cultures that embraced multiple deities. Native Americans in the San Francisco Bay region regarded Mt. Diablo as the dwelling place of the gods, and in the history of Israel's religions, for example, mounts Tabor, Hebron, Zion, and Sinai were thought at one time or another to be the center of the world, the place whether God both began the creation of the world and the nation of Israel.[13]

---

of Major League Baseball Giamatti identifies home plate as the center, which distorts a number of the mythical directions that prove to be significant for a cosmogony of the game. Giamatti's work, which appeared posthumously, does not make reference to my earliest published account connecting baseball and the *omphalos* myth. See my "'The Momentary Grace of Order': Religious Aspects of a Sport," *Journal and Times of the California Association of Health, Physical Education, Recreation and Dance* (March 1987) 16–19ff.

[13] Samuel Terrien, "The Omphalos Myth and Hebrew Religion," *Vetus Testamentum* 20:319. For further comment on the general identification of the cosmic mountain with the *omphalos*, see

As the place of the origin of creation, the *omphalos* represents the point of intersection of the cosmic spheres. At the rock of the center, heaven, hell, and earth come together. As this point of cosmic intersection, the *omphalos* is the place where the axis from the center of heaven to the center of hell penetrates the earth. The *omphalos* thus provides the point of entry into earth from both the heavenly and chthonic realms. As such, the *omphalos* becomes the ideal location for duals between cosmic forces, between the creative powers associated with the heavenly gods and the destructive forces connected to the chthonic spirits. In addition to its concentration on creation mythology, the *omphalos* myth has several other motifs that are often found in conjunction with the sacred stone and the cosmic mountain. Some of these are snake worship, sun worship, chthonic rituals, and bisexual rituals.[14] Although all of these motifs are not found in baseball, elements of some of them appear in the structure of the game, and their presence confirms the similarity of the implicit mythology of baseball with that of the *omphalos* myth.

For the *omphalos* myth and its exemplification in the game of baseball, the most important point of correspondence is the identification of the *omphalos*—the central, sacred stone—with the cosmic mountain. In the world of baseball, the cosmic center is the sacred "stone" that is atop the sacred mountain. The pitcher's rubber is located at the top of the pitcher's mound, a twelve-inch-high rise that provides the only topographical elevation in the field.[15] Rising above the level

---

Mircea Eliade, *Images and Symbols: Studies in Religious Symbolism,* trans. Philip Mairet (New York: Sheed and Ward, 1961) 43.

[14] Terrien, "The Omphalos Myth and Hebrew Religion," 320.

[15] At this point, I recognize the one intentional aberration that occurred at the old Crosley Field in Cincinnati, where the warning track (normally a band of bare dirt or cinders that provides a liminal

contour of the field, the pitcher's mound corresponds to the cosmic mountains of old and its stature as such is reinforced by the presence of the rubber at its crest.

In the world or cosmos of baseball, the *omphalos* is located at the top of the cosmic mountain. As the mythical center of the field, the pitcher's mound is the point at which creation of the game begins. The pitcher, who starts play by throwing the ball to the batter, must stand on top of the pitcher's mound and must keep his foot on the rubber until he has released the ball. There is, then, an umbilical connection between the creative activity of the pitcher (as a high priest) and the *omphalos* itself.

The cosmic structure of the game is not limited to the centrality of the pitcher's mound and the creativity that begins there. Among the essays that have been written on sports as one form of American folk religion,[16] there has been little mention of the significance of baseball's bases, each of which lies at one of the cardinal direction points, thus forming the four corners of the world.[17] It is also interesting to note that the base runners can find safety and security only at the four corners of the world and that in line with the *omphalo*-mythic

---

area between the outfield grass and the home run fence) was replaced by an upward sloping area of grass; and in Houston's new Minute Maid Park, the deep centerfield is a rising terrace. In addition, the bases, which represent the geographic extremes of the cardinal directions, are artificially elevated, although only slightly. It is not insignificant that the slightly elevated portions of the base paths are the only points of safety for a runner.

[16] See, for example, James Mathisen, "From Civil Religion to Folk Religion: The Case of American Sport," in *Sport and Religion*, ed. Shirl J. Hoffman (Champaign IL: Human Kinetics, 1992) 17–33.

[17] The notable exception is Michael Novak's metaphysically oriented essays in his book *The Joy of Sports: End Zones, Bases, Baskets, Balls and the Consecration of the American Spirit* (New York: Basic Books, Inc., 1976) especially chapters 2–4 and 7.

practice of sun worship, the base runners must follow the apparent course of the sun in its relation to the world. Like the apparent direction of the sun's motion, base runners move in a counterclockwise fashion, from home to first to second to third and back to home. (Correspondingly, when a batter stands at home plate [the southernmost point of the diamond—its place of warmth and safety], he perceives the sun's movement from right to left, with east lying to the right and west to the left.)

The cosmological correspondence between the *omphalos* myth and the structure of baseball extends beyond the points in the infield to the outfield reaches at the foul poles, which seem to be misnamed since they stand in fair territory. Lying in a direct line from home plate (the southernmost corner of baseball's world) to first and third bases (the eastern and western corners of the world), the foul poles correspond to the sun and moon. Like the two astral bodies that in ancient times were thought to lie at the edge of the sky, the foul poles are found at the farthest reaches of the outfield, baseball's expansive northern territory. According to the mythic astral cosmologies, the sun and moon were thought to determine the course of events on earth, and similarly in baseball, the play of balls as fair or foul is determined by their relation to these two poles.

Ritual Activity

Although the baseball diamond can be understood in *omphalo-mythic* terms, it also achieves its status as sacred space by the particular ritual of consecration that occurs at the beginning of each season and before each contest. The consecration ritual is not conducted by the players but by the grounds crew who are, so to speak, "the custodians of the temple." Their responsibilities include the care of the field between games, the immediate pre-game preparation of the field, and the restoration of the field during the middle innings or after rain delays.

Baseball is the only team sport that, at the professional level of play, requires that the infield be covered with a tarpaulin between games in order to protect it from the possibility of saturation with rain. In addition, baseball is the only team sport that can be postponed or halted during play because of rain. What this relationship to rain suggests is that the world of the baseball game can be threatened by the destructive waters of the mythic flood or the primeval waters of chaos, both of which are intimated or conjured up by the waters of rain. The grounds crew bears the responsibility for protecting the game from such threat of destruction, from such chaos.

Before the players begin their pre-game practice, the grounds crew removes the protective covering, and the fore-taste of order is brought to the field as the players throw and hit the ball. After the players on the opposing teams have taken batting and fielding practice, the grounds crew continues the ritual of preparing the field for play. Failure to adhere to the details of the ritual provides either team with "grounds" for protesting the validity of the contest. The grounds crew chalks the batter's box and the foul lines between home plate and first and third bases. The crew rakes the pitcher's mound, smoothing it off and filling in indentations. Members of the crew then drag the dirt portion of the infield, using screens to sweep the dirt. After smoothing the dirt portions of the infield, the crew finally sprinkles water on the dirt to settle the dust.[18]

---

[18] In some of the "cookie cutter" ballparks that were erected in the early 1970s, such as Cincinnati's Riverfront Stadium and Pittsburgh's Three Rivers Stadium, there was an artificial playing surface that covered most of the area normally known as the dirt portion of the infield. At stadiums such as these, there were dirt

At this point the correspondence of the waters with cosmic forces switches from the destructive threat of rain and chaos to the fructifying force of water as the bearer of life. The use of water in the final purification rites at the pitcher's mound signals the dual orientation of water rituals with baseball and connects the creative forces—those associated with birth and growth—with the center itself. Perhaps coincidentally, at Dodger Stadium the spigot that supplies water for the settling of dust is located on the back side of the pitcher's mound.

The final portion of the consecration ritual by the grounds crew is the placing of freshly whitened bases at the corners of the infield. Yet with the full preparation of the field, there is one final act that remains necessary to complete the consecration process—the fusing of the mythical with the political. By singing the national anthem, public sanction and political approval of the game are secured. The chaos that existed prior to batting and fielding practice is transformed into a cosmos ready for contest between two forces, the home team and the visiting team.

Just as the baseball diamond undergoes ritual consecration before it is made ready for play, so too does the ball require proper ritual preparation for admission into the game. Before a ball can be used in play, it must also be introduced into the game by the home plate umpire. Not just any ball, however, is acceptable, for before each game the home plate umpire rubs each ball with a substance of Delaware River mud, taking the sheen off the ball by physically introducing it to the earth. And when the pitcher receives the ball, he rubs it down, adding the particularity of his "priesthood" to the sacred object itself. If for some reason, such as intentionally scuffing or wetting the

---

portions around the bases that received comparable ritual care by the grounds crew before, during, and after each game.

ball (as Joe Niekro and Gaylord Perry were accused of doing) or inadvertently getting marred after being hit, the ball becomes contaminated and gets thrown out of play by the umpire. Although the home plate umpire is the only one who can introduce a ball into play, on the "holy days" of the baseball season the ceremonial first ball of the game will be introduced by a cultural or political celebrity, who performs the ritual of "tossing out the first pitch."

As in the ball games and religious rituals of the Oglala Sioux, so too in baseball is the field itself identified with the world. Yet the *ball* also represents the world. There is no contradiction or duplication here, however, between the world represented by the ball and the world constituted by the diamond. They are mythical worlds, not exclusive or contradictory worlds but merely multiple worlds, each with its own realm of significance.[19] The ball itself is covered with horsehide, and it has a single row of stitching that, always appearing as if it were two rows of stitches, ties together two symmetrical, identical, reversed pieces, somewhat like the yin and the yang, whereby dualistic forces are bound together in a unified whole. The ball is white, signifying the undefiled purity of creation,[20] and the stitching is red, the color of blood, suggesting the possibilities of both birth and death. The ball itself manifests the clear dualism of the game, consummately expressed in the conflict between the forces of creation (the

---

[19] Eliade, *Images and Symbols*, 39.

[20] Several years ago Charles Finley, the former maverick owner of the Oakland Athletics, experimented with orange colored baseballs during spring training. Although he claimed that the fans enjoyed the color and that the hitters enjoyed seeing the ball better, no serious thought was given by the commissioner of Major League Baseball or by the rules committee of the owners to making a change from the traditional white baseball.

pitcher delivering the pitch) and the forces of destruction (the batter swatting the ball).

Even as there are rituals of consecration for the field in order to distinguish it from ordinary space and even as there are rituals that govern the introduction of a ball into play, so too are there rituals that a pitcher must follow in order for a pitch to be valid. For instance, a pitcher must take the sign from his catcher while his foot is in contact with the rubber. On the other hand, the pitcher cannot touch his mouth while he is on the pitcher's mound for fear that his own sputum will pollute the ball. The pitcher as high priest cannot allow that which is earthly to defile the purity of a new world in the process of creation unless, of course, the pitcher himself is perverse.

These two rituals of prohibition prevent contamination of the ball while within the area of the cosmic mountain. When runners are on base, most pitchers use a motion called "the stretch" rather than the full wind-up. In this way they hope to prevent base runners from taking a large lead and stealing a base. But rules govern also the ritual of the stretch. The pitcher must bring his hands to a complete stop at or above his belt before resuming his motion to deliver the pitch. And the pitcher must stride toward home plate when pitching to the batter. Failure to adhere to these strictures results in a "balk" and the award of an extra base to the base runners at that time.

Cosmic Dualism

One of the probable reasons that the game of baseball appeals to so many fans is that its cosmology, its mythical structure, is also connected to a drama of cosmic dualism that is constantly played out in both individual and communal terms. A sense of dualism pervades the game: the confrontation of the pitcher with the batter, the opposition of two distinct teams, the structure of innings (during which teams alternate turns at bat and turns in the field), the clear distinction between the play of balls as fair or foul, the position of pitches as either balls or strikes, the status of the batter or base runners as either safe or out, and the covering of the ball itself.

Classically, the cosmic, dualistic conflict pits the forces of good against the forces of evil, light against darkness, creation against chaos, or it presents the Gnostic tension between flesh and spirit. In baseball, although there may be occasions when the nature of the conflict appears to be that of good versus evil, the basic confrontation is between the forces of creation and those of destruction, the classic battle between life and death—safe or out, winner or loser. The dramatic presentation of the cosmic dualism is found in the individual battle between the pitcher and the batter. As suggested earlier, the pitcher is the agent of creation, the one who, keeping his foot in contact with the rubber (the *omphalos*), hurls the white ball (the undefiled world) toward home plate (the southernmost point in the cosmos, the place of warmth and rest) in an effort to prevent the batter (the destructive force) from knocking the ball over the fence (beyond the reaches of the universe), circling the bases (circumnavigating the globe), and scoring a run. The battle between pitcher and batter, in fact, also reenacts the most ancient armed conflict, the wielding of sticks and the hurling of stones. It is appropriate that the battle between the cosmic forces begins at the cosmic mountain (the pitcher's mound), which is the point of intersection of the three cosmic spheres, and climaxes at *home* plate, the territory over which control is sought.

The alignment of the pitcher with the forces of creation is reinforced by the metaphorical designation of the warm-up area for pitchers as the bullpen, for the bull has long been associated with fertility and creation. The association of the pitcher with a bull, however, does not mean that the pitcher is singularly masculine. Indeed, the act of throwing the ball connotes the masculine act of ejaculation. But the pitcher also wears a glove, which is reminiscent of the womb and with which he hopes to catch or retrieve the ball in an effort to prevent the batter from getting on base and scoring a run. This bisexuality of the pitcher corresponds to some priestly rites often connected with the rituals and myths at the *omphalos*.

In contrast to the pitcher, who stands in touch with transcendent forces, the batter digs in at *home* plate, wielding the refined limb of a tree (usually either ash or hickory) that is the fruit of the earth. The batter is concerned about his present world, not creating a new world. He is earthy. He represents an earthly chaos that challenges the creative powers of the pitcher. The batter's charge is to knock the ball out of this world—to prevent the new world (the ball hurled as a potential out) from affecting this world—so that he can run around the bases safely and score a run. The pitcher attempts to create a perfect game, allowing no batter to reach a base, while the batter attempts to destroy this quest for perfection and to establish in its place a sense of completion, a full circling of the bases. In this way, Gardella notes, "Baseball demonstrates the difference between perfection and completion more clearly than any phenomenon of everyday life."[21]

On a larger, communal scale, the dualism of baseball pits the home team, which is always dressed in a white uniform, against the visiting team, which always wears road gray. The contrast in colors of the uniforms indicates the fans' estimation of the alignment of the two teams as representatives of the forces of good and evil, light and darkness, purity and contamination, in the cosmic conflict. The fans normally consider

---

[21] Gardella, "Baseball Samadhi," 15.

the home team as "good" and the visiting team as "bad." Yet there is no innate reason why either team should be thought of as being "good" or "bad," as being representatives of cosmos or chaos, life or death, creation or destruction, since each team alternates in the roles of pitching/fielding and batting, of attempting to establish order and to disrupt it. This duality of roles that the teams assume is a social extension of the mythical bisexuality of the pitcher himself, who (until the advent of the designated hitter in the American League) also gets to take a turn at bat—to become one of the destructive forces while identifying with that activity of his team. The fact that each team assumes both creative and destructive roles further supports the idea that baseball's structuring myth is like that of the *omphalos.*

At the end of the game, however, one team must prevail. Unlike football and hockey in which tie games are possible, baseball requires a winner and a loser. The winning team is the one that exercises greater control over baseball's cosmos by exerting power over the ball and its pure vision of perfection by pitching effectively, hitting authoritatively, and circling the bases often.

Conclusion

There is a story about Reinhold Niebuhr, the American-born theologian, taking fellow theologian Paul Tillich, who was a recent immigrant from Germany, to a baseball game. After several innings Tillich was still having trouble getting the knack of the game. As play progressed, an impressive "twin killing" was turned by the home team. Fans throughout the stands roared with approval and applause. Puzzled by such an overwhelming response to a play that had not seen the ball hit over the fence or even far enough to score a base runner, Tillich sought an explanation from Niebuhr. Failing to communicate the significance of the event in understandable baseball terms, Niebuhr finally said, "It's a *kairos*, Paulus, it's a *kairos*."[22] With that explanation, Tillich understood. (For Tillich, *kairos* was the category of time and history about turning points, occasions of depth rather than events continuing the normal chronometric measure of time.) Although the story in its present form might be embellished or even apocryphal (in which case it would be a representative part of baseball's lore), it adequately encapsulates the way in which a heroic event in baseball is sometimes seen as an event wherein some force larger than life is present, an event wherein the course of events is transformed by the nature of the event itself.

In American culture, baseball has exhibited such power to compel allegiance, to generate meaning, and to elicit and foster hope. Baseball has certainly manifested a number of characteristics of religion. Yet it is the mythos of baseball—its order through design, ritual, and conflict, the complex combination of which resembles the ancient *omphalos* myth—that underlies its compelling power, that undergirds its creation of meaning, and that nourishes its arousal of hope. And for the fans and players, as Donald Hall has so eloquently and aptly put it, "The diamonds and rituals of baseball create an elegant, trivial, enchanted grid on which our suffering, shapeless, sinful day leans for the momentary grace of order."[23]

So we return to the rain delay conversation between two teenage boys in the bleachers at Wrigley Field. "Why," one asked, "is the pitcher's mound higher than any other part of the field?" The historian of religion wanted to turn and say,

---

[22] This anecdote was related on several occasions by my mentor Langdon Gilkey, who had been a student of both Niebuhr and Tillich.

[23] Donald Hall, *Fathers Playing Catch with Sons: Essays on Sport (Mostly Baseball)* (New York: Dell Publishing Company, 1986) 51.

"Because it's a cosmic mountain. It adds order to our lives." But respecting the youthful love of baseball and its mysterious lure, the religious scholars remembered the remark without imposing academic analysis at a time when they shared some sort of liturgical experience of communion with the other faithful Cub fans enduring yet one more delay before defeat.

Writing about Americans' fascination with sports, Catherine Albanese, a historian of American religion, has noted that "by setting up boundaries and defining the space of the game, sports have helped Americans fit a grid to their own experience in order to define it and give it structure."[24] In baseball, the myth of the center provides the structure around which the game is oriented, and its utilization of creation mythology links it to the dualism that pervades the game. The implied and exemplified myth of the center generates and sustains the religious import—"the momentary grace of order"—of baseball for millions of Americans who have often not analyzed their attraction and devotion to the game.

---

[24] Catherine Albanese, *America: Religion and Religions* (Belmont CA: Wadsworth Publishing Company, 1981) 322. In the context of her imaginative and illuminative chapter on cultural religion, Albanese also suggests that the contestative character of baseball establishes the sport as a model for promoting a cultural code of "loyalty, fair play, and being a good sport in losing" (322).

4

Conjuring Curses and Supplicating Spirits: Baseball's Culture of Superstitions

Curses! In October 2003, long after the Cubs customarily began their annual hibernation, they held on to the Central Division lead and growled bravely past Atlanta to go fishing for Marlins to culminate the National League playoffs. Simultaneously, fulfillment of the fantasies of Red Sox faithful, some in the fifth generation since their ancestors' hopes had been realized, seemed possible. Pedro would pitch a seventh game, certainly propelling the Sox to the real series. A replay of 1918 hovered as baseball's two cosmic curses seemed to converge: Boston's suffering since the departure of the Bambino and the Cubs looking for a scapegoat for their failures since 1945. In the 1918 World Series the Red Sox had beaten the Cubs, ushering in the end of the war to end all wars. The new millennium's prospect of the Cubs and Sox—the Red ones—meeting in the World Series generated similar cosmic conflicts. For the persevering fans of Chicago and Boston, the end of the world must have seemed at hand, and the perfect kingdom must have been thought near.

The Cubs, of course, have not appeared in a World Series since the hurling of the curse of the Billy Goat by the high priest of Cubs' fans in 1945. Then, Billy Sianis, owner of the Billy Goat Tavern, an official watering hole for bleacher bums and sports writers, was forbidden from bringing his pet billy goat named Murphy into Wrigley Field by a seat usher or, or according to other accounts, by P. K. Wrigley himself. The ticket that Sianis sought to use for Murphy was box 65, tier 12, seat 5. Murphy was denied entry because the animal's smell could not be masked even by Doublemint. Kicking mad, it is said, Sianis cursed: "No Billy goat in the Friendly Confines?! Then there will never be a World Series played at Wrigley Field again." And so it has been for the past six decades.

For the Red Sox, the curse of the Bambino had proven equally tantalizing since it had prevented their winning a series every year since their early September victory over the hapless Cubs in 1918. Red Sox owner Harry Frazee's sale of Ruth to Jacob Ruppert and the Yankees in 1920 has been called "baseball's Original Sin"[1] since Frazee himself had yielded to the temptation of the Big Apple. He wanted to transfer the paradise of Fenway to success on Broadway for a musical that just said "No," to Nanette, twice.[2]

Yet the wisdom of Yankees prophet Yogi once again prevailed during baseball's high holy days in 2003. The games in October were not over until they were over. The games were not over even when fat ladies started to cackle on the corner of Clarke and Addison one night, followed shortly thereafter by a soprano chorus going coloraturo on the prematurely painted World Series logo on the grounds at Fenway. No, the late innings' curse for the Cubs prevailed again, with Bartman robbin' Moises Alou of a fair catch of a foul ball, followed in the Big Apple by Pedro mimicking the late-inning limp of

---

[1] John D. Spalding, "Undoing Baseball's Original Sin," http://www.beliefnet.com/story/134_13405_1.html, accessed 14 October 2003.

[2] Frazee had used the profits from the sale of Ruth to finance the production of the musical "No, No, Nanette."

Buckner. Moises would lead the exodus of Cubs' faithful, but this time he would not get a chance to part the Red Sox.

The curse of the Bambino lived even in this new millennium—from Bucky to Buckner to Boone! Just to make the taste of the Eden's apple that much more delicious for Yankees fans, let me note that like Buckner, Pedro was left in an inning too long, and like Bucky, Boone was a left-sided, right-handed infielder who had hit for modest power during the regular season. Yet both Bucky and Boone lofted late inning blasts that propelled the Sox to purgatory.

For decades, Red Sox devotees had sought to determine the precise origin of the curse of the Bambino. What is certain is that in the half dozen years before the Babe's departure from Beantown, the Red Sox had won the World Series on average every other year. And Babe carried that success with him to New York, helping the Yankees to climb Jacob's ladder to the top of the American League.

The signs for curse removal in 2003 looked more certain than a cellar finish by the Tigers. The twenty-fifth anniversary of the pontificate of Pope John Paul II, a remarkable cleric who had reversed modern Petrine succession by becoming the first non-Italian pope in half a millennium, was celebrated on October 16 of that year. If ever a day could enjoy a miracle of some sort—perhaps a papal dispensation or the exorcism of a curse—then surely having a faithful Dominican Catholic on the mound for the Red Sox would secure a victory for an Irish Catholic city's team over baseball's Goliath, the terrorists otherwise known as the Bronx Bombers.

Sometimes, however, even popes prove fallible, and the prayers of millions of Red Sox fans proved futile, about which Grady knew far too *Little*. Surpassing his seven days of creating new hopes for Red Sox, their Dominican Saver faded faster than applause for Frazee's production of *No, No, Nanette,* and the Curse of the Babe was resurrected in a new millennium.

On Tuesday, 17 October, the headline of the *Boston Globe* confessed, "Heartbreak Again," and the Sports section confirmed the divine and demonic elements in defeat to be "Extraordinary." The *Boston Metro* put it more bluntly, turning to musical theater for its inspiration, like Frazee had done almost a century earlier. Its banner caption for a full page picture was simple: "Damn Yankees." And prominently advertised on the sports pages of the *Boston Globe* was a forthcoming musical production whose title captured the city's sentiment; the promise of the return from Broadway of the stage-hit *Les Misérables* only intensified the memory Frazee's flop.

In the house that Ruth built, the Fenway faithful found that evil lurked more destructive than in Eden. Following seven creative innings, San Pedro succumbed to the Little temptress, and although attempting to shun the Big Apple, he finally ate it in the eighth.

Although a Dominican, the Bosox St. Peter [Martinez] failed as a papal pretender. He delivered no sermon on the mound. Instead, his priestly power reverted past Melchizzidek to the order of Aaron himself, who dashed the hopes of all who, like Naomi, had vowed devotion to follow, as scripture puts it, "whithersoever Ruth goest."

The eleventh inning of the seventh game proved no lucky combination for the Sox. A white-knuckler of a game knuckled blithely to Boone, who directed the first pitch from Wakefield beyond the outfield—so far, in fact, that it exiled the Red Sox to the Wilderness Road.

A few days earlier in the Second City half a continent away, Moises also failed to sacrifice the goat of curses and lead his Cubs to the elusive, promised World. Alou had leapt, not high enough, to wrest the ball away from Bartman, who had acted more like his namesake—the Simpson imp—than a dutiful Cubs' devotee. The World Series: This paradox of paradise, the Promised Land beyond the Jordan (especially for the faithful in Chicago), again evaded Moises and was left to Aaron. Such is the fulfillment of curses, whether making a golden calf the scapegoat or removing the Bambino from Madonna.

The Character of Curses and Their Function in Baseball

Curses live, not because they are empirically powerful, but because they are believed by influential individuals who inspire communities to accept their attitudes and actions. Curses derive their power from a spiritual sensibility that is often denigrated by opponents as relying on superstition. Yet the religious underpinnings of cursing recur throughout religious traditions across centuries, continents, and cultures. In religious terms, curses are "closely related to blessing" in the sense that the same people usually are empowered to do both and that the forms of curses and blessings are similar. In other words, religious leaders are the ones empowered to do both since some religious traditions consider curses uttered by unauthorized pretenders as being "magical or sacrilegious." Specifically, gods, priests, shamans, and other spiritual leaders who have gained prominence through advanced age or public suffering exercise legitimate power to invoke "misfortune, including death or destruction, upon people or things."[3]

The religious power of curses also draws upon their character as speech acts: When delivered by a properly recognized authority, curses *perform* the act that they prescribe. In ancient Semitic languages, for instance, curses were thought

---

[3] Lester K. Little, "Cursing," *The Encyclopedia of Religion*, 16 vols., ed. Mircea Eliade (New York: Macmillan, 1987) 4:182.

to contain and convey the power of the act that they signified. Utterance itself enacted. Thus, the person at whom a curse was hurled would actually, physically duck, so that the curse would fly over his or her head.

Another distinct characteristic of curses is their function. They can serve to harass enemies or combatants, to enforce law or tradition, to demand doctrinal or moral conformity, and to protect sacred sites and relics. In dealing with enemies, one technique of curses is to paralyze opponents by causing dissent or to destroy them by separating them from their source of energy and power. Curses are also used to teach a lesson about the need for moral action, as Moses did in demanding the freedom of his kinsmen and as Jesus did in cursing the tree that provided no shade. Although curses often declaim destruction, they frequently function as "instruments of negotiation," as suggested by Moses' success.[4] (But in baseball the duration of the Cubs' and Red Sox' failure makes one wonder what they must have been negotiating or, at the very least, who their agents might be!) As another distinct set of curses, protective ones often seek sanction for sites associated with the deceased, to respect their place of death, or to secure the memorial of their burial.

In baseball, curses tend to conform to the first and last of these categories—either dealing with opponents, as the curse of the Bambino is intended to execute, or protecting sacred sites, as the curses against the Cubs and Angels were thought to be directed. Because Anaheim Stadium was thought to have been built on a Native American burial ground, former owner Gene Autry and other team executives believed that the failure

---

[4] Ibid.

of the Angels to win was based on a protective curse initiated by Native Americans.[5]

Another indication of the religious power of curses is the manner of their possible annulment. The rituals for removal also engage spiritual leaders who, it is thought, have the power to deliver curses. In this regard a number of ceremonial attempts to abrogate or merely dull the power of curses have been undertaken by faithful devotees to the major league teams. Take first the Angels, since they were the first of the three teams to win the World Series. Gene Autry, that singing cowboy, hired a tribal shaman several years ago to perform a ritual to remove the curse. But during the cowboy's lifetime, it didn't make a squeeze play's difference. The Angels never made it to the series while the Autrys owned the team. Following Autry's death, Mrs. Autry even considered interring his ashes beneath home plate, thereby respecting the Native American use of the site. But such a destiny, it was finally felt, would not cause the Angels to sing Gene's signature song, "Happy Trails to You." Instead, the reversal of the Angels' destiny took the miracle of Mickey Mouse to turn the Big A's burial ground into fantasyland, to make the Angels' dreams come true, and to "ever let [them] hold [their] banner high."

In somewhat different ways, the Red Sox' diaconate made multiple attempts to reverse the curse of the Bambino. The Sox "tried everything from sage-burning ceremonies to an exorcism at Fenway Park performed by...Father Guido Sarducci of *Saturday Night Live.*"[6] Little did the Red Sox realize that they probably needed a tragic Catholic priest from the *Sopranos* more than the comic antics of Fr. Guido. More amazing still than these two attempts to exonerate the Red Sox,

---

[5] Chris Dufresne, "The Hex Files," *Los Angeles Times*, 27 May 1999, D10.

[6] Spalding, "Undoing Baseball's Original Sin."

however, are ones involving the heights of Mt. Everest and the depths of Willis Pond in Sudbury, Massachusetts. One Red Sox penitent reports that "he traveled to Nepal to ask a lama, renowned for his powers, to lift the curse. The lama told him to climb Mount Everest and to place at the summit a Red Sox cap, which the lama had blessed. He was then to return to base camp and burn a Yankees cap as an offering."[7] The Red Sox devotee accomplished the fantastic feat, only to see the Red Sox end the season by blowing their first place lead.

Or consider the efforts of Red Sox novitiates in February 2002. Because the precise origin of the curse of the Bambino is not known, scholars of the pseudopigraphal Gospel According to Fenway surmised that the curse might have begun before the Ruthian sale. An apocryphal story holds, for instance, that following the series against the Cubs in 1918, the last successful series for the Sox before the sale of Ruth, Ruth had rented a cottage adjacent to Willis Pond, and then baptized his piano by pushing it in after a night of partying. Anticipating the diamond anniversary of this Ruthian immersion, a five person scuba team braved the icy pond waters in February to retrieve the instrument so that the Red Sox could play a winning tune again. Alas, the water was so murky that they only discovered a sunken lawn chair. Not fully discouraged, they returned later with sonar equipment to sound the depths, again, but like the Sox' typical October play, to no avail.

In Chicago throughout the past half-century, various attempts have been made to expunge the curse of the Billy Goat. Yet like those related to the desire to reverse Ruth's curse, the Cubs' attempts have also failed. By mid-century, P. K. had wriggled his way into correspondence with Sianis, beseeching him to define the necessary penance and lift the

---

[7] Ibid.

curse. But the tavern owner replied simply: Forget it. Besides, Sianis said, Murphy had already died of a broken heart.

Almost two decades after Wrigley's rebuff, St. Leo (Durocher) led the Cubs to a nine-game August lead in 1969. Finally, Sianis consented to lift the curse—only to discover that the Mets, not the Cubs, were destined to drink that year from the miraculous trough at Lourdes. And the next year, the goat of cursers, Sianis himself, died *sans* Cubbie lamentations. Within three years, however, the curse officially returned when Billy's nephew Sam attempted to take Socrates, the tavern's new mascot, to Wrigley Field for a mid-summer game while the Cubs led the division by seven lucky games. But apparently fearing that hemlock might displace ivy, the Cubs methodically denied Socrates, and Sam revived the curse of the Billy Goat. Since then, however, Socrates was invited to graze outfield near the walls of ivy on opening day in 1982 and to open the League Championship Series against the Padres in 1984. His sowing of wild oats that afternoon was effective as the Cubs pounded five homeruns and won by an unlucky score of thirteen to zero. But failing to fly to San Diego, Socrates went platonic, as did the Cubs, who lost their mission with the Padres.[8]

Circumventing appeals to the Sianis family to reverse the curse, other efforts have been made for the Cubs to make it to the series. For one, the Cubs themselves have made on-field efforts to improve their play and overcome their full fall futility. About the time that Billy Sianis died, they acquired an all-star first baseman only to find that instead of overcoming the curse of the goat, he was becoming a hobbled Billy (Buckner) in such a way to make himself a goat for the Red

---

[8] Dave Dravecky and Mike Yorkey, *Called Up: Stories of Life and Faith from the Great Game of Baseball* (Grand Rapids: Zondervan, 2004) 93.

Sox. In a more comprehensive effort in the spring of 2004, the Illinois legislature passed an official resolution that the "Cubs' Curse shall be no more." And earlier in the winter of 2004, Cubs fans, like the February divers in Massachusetts, turned from the symbolic elements within the curse itself to more practical, ritual means of annulling the curse's power. At Harry Caray's sports bar in Chicago, the Bartman ball was subjected to cursing by the supplicant Cubs. In December, Grant DePorter, managing partner of the restaurant, purchased the ball at Internet auction for the tidy sum of $113,824.16. For two months the ball was displayed inside a case protected by thirteen surveillance cameras, two anti-theft alarms, and security guards on duty around the clock. During the ball's exhibition, almost 30,000 fans cursed it, suggesting ways for it to fulfill its destiny—destruction: Among their demands were to "roast it, incinerate it, crush it, drown it, drop it into a bucket of acid, split it in two with an ax, put it in front of a firing squad, launch it into outer space, shove it into a shredder, scatter its remains at sea, even freeze it in liquid nitrogen and shatter it into a million pieces."[9] DePorter himself remarked, "This ball is baseball's anti-trophy. I had a pit in my stomach, for sure" he confessed, "because it was so expensive. But what would happen if we didn't destroy it and some Marlins' fan got a hold of it? What if someone used it to psych out the Cubs next year? No, it's got to go."[10]

And it did. On Thursday evening, 26 February 2004, at a street party in Chicago, much of the nation, joined by bar patrons in fifty countries throughout the world, watched a live telecast on MSNBC as the Bartman ball was exploded by Michael Lantieri. A life-long Cubs' fan, Lantieri had been the

---

[9] P. J. Huffstutter, "Cursed Ball about to Get Whacked," *Los Angeles Times*, 25 February 2004, A20.
[10] Ibid.

mechanical effects supervisor for the *Jurassic Park* film, and with the assistance of Rawlings Sporting Goods, he had practiced destruction on similar baseballs by various means. One person who did not attend the party was Steve Bartman himself, since he had suffered death threats like those directed to the ball itself.

The Culture of Curses and Superstition

Curses in baseball derive their power not from the utterance itself or from the prestige or notoriety of the performer, but from an underlying culture of superstition. From a statistical perspective, superstitions emerge out of mistaken identity—the mistake of attributing causation to correlation. The coincidence of two events does not mean that they are causally related. Rather, coincidence is often random and statistically insignificant.[11] In baseball, players frequently attribute their success to a coincidence between, for instance, a food or drink ingested before a successful game or a pattern of preparation before a game. In so doing, they lay the groundwork for a ritual act based in superstition.

Beyond baseball, superstitions are often identified as folk beliefs that contradict reason and appeal to magic while the established beliefs of a culture are accepted as true religion.[12] The affirmation of a real presence of Christ in the Eucharist, for instance, might contradict reason as much as the acceptance of telepathic forms of faith healing celebrated by shamans. But the dominant Christian culture identifies the dogma of real presence as orthodox belief and a matter of faith, while it

---

[11] Michael Mandelbaum, *The Meaning of Sports: Why Americans Watch Baseball, Football, and Basketball and What They See When They Do* (New York: Public Affairs, 2004) 51.

[12] Mary R. O'Neil, "Superstition," *The Encyclopedia of Religion*; ed. Mircea Eliade (New York: Macmillan, 1987) 14:163.

decries as mere superstition structurally similar beliefs associated with shamanistic acts. In other words, "superstition" is a pejorative label attached to beliefs that are not accepted within the dominant religious tradition.

Related to baseball, several years ago a major feature in *Sports Illustrated* focused on the culture of superstition in sports, and it suggested that "superstition envelops [baseball] like a shroud." Among baseball's fervently held superstitions, for instance, are the beliefs that "it's bad luck for a pitcher to strike out the first batter" or for a pitcher to catch a ball thrown by the second baseman between plays. Other rules apply in areas beyond the reach of umpires: "Don't cross bats. Don't wash your uniform or change your sanitary socks during a winning streak. Step over the baseline, not on it."[13]

Some superstitions, of course, are "endemic to baseball" while others have been adapted from various childhood games and religious practices throughout the history. For example, says Jack McCallum, "Stepping over the foul line is no doubt an offshoot of the old childhood superstition that says, Step on a crack, break your mother's back. That superstition, incidentally, can be traced to the belief that a crack represented the opening of a grave, and to step on that crack meant that you might be walking on the grave of someone in your family."[14] Even the childhood crack-hopping game is derived from religious attitudes about death. Somewhat similarly, the ritual of not washing articles of clothes during a winning streak is connected to the idea that both banes and blessings might be washed away by the cleansing power of water. Several years ago, on-field opponents and even fans of the Salt Lake City Trappers were olfactorily relieved when the Trappers, who had

---

[13] Jack McCallum, "Green Cars, Black Cats, and Lady Luck: Superstition in Sports," *Sports Illustrated* 68/6, 8 February 1988, 89.

[14] Ibid., 89.

practiced the no-wash rule, lost a game after a professional record twenty-nine wins in a row.

Because most athletes who practice superstitious rituals have previously proven the excellence of their athletic skills they do not rely on their superstitious actions to improve their performance. Instead, they believe and behave in certain ways to assure their best performance. Basically, they treat their superstitions as "a crutch, a secret weapon, a way to get a little edge."[15] In this regard, former Yankees pitcher Lefty O'Doul commented on his practice of stepping over the baseline: "It's not that if I stepped on the foul line I would really lose the game, but why take a chance."[16] Even saintly Christy Mathewson wrote in his 1912 book *Pitching in a Pinch* that a jinx or curse can "make a bad pitcher out of a good one and a blind batter out of a three hundred hitter."[17] After going hitless in a game some years ago, White Sox outfielder Minnie Minoso figured that his bad luck resulted from his uniform. So still in cleats, he showered with it on. After he got three hits the next day, eight of his teammates joined him fully clothed in the shower.

Minoso's actions typify the behavior of baseball players, as suggested by former Detroit Tigers prospect turned anthropologist George Gmelch, who has studied the behavior of baseball players. In general, Gmelch notes, baseball "is an arena in which players behave remarkably like Malinowski's Trobriand fishermen.... Since their livelihood depends on how well they perform, many use magic to try to control the chance

---

[15] Ibid., 88.

[16] Quoted in Dravecky and Yorkey, *Called Up*, 19.

[17] Quoted in McCallum, "Green Cars, Black Cats, and Lady Luck," 89.

that is built into baseball."[18] Routinely, players like Minoso develop rituals when they enjoy unusual success. "When a player does well, he seldom attributes his success to skill alone," Gmelch observes. In fact, after a particularly good performance, a player is likely to do what he did differently that day that brought about such success. The player then decides to repeat what he did in preparation for the successful day's performance in an attempt to renew the good luck of his excellent play. "And so he attributes his success, in part," Gmelch concludes, "to an object, a food he ate, not having shaved, a new shirt he bought that day, or just about any behavior out of the ordinary. By repeating that behavior, he seeks to gain control over his performance."[19]

Yet as much as athletes might indulge their superstitions, they avoid calling their actions and attitudes superstitious. Some think of them as habits, even the detailed, timed pre-game ritual of Wade Boggs, who cycled repeatedly through a dozen recipes so that he could eat chicken before each game. He also practiced a five-hour routine that determined actions at certain times and places, including the time that he would leave his home for night games, the length of time that he would sit in front of his locker, and his running of wind sprints at 7:17. In addition, he made sure that as he finished taking grounders in infield practice, he would leave the field by stepping on third, second, and first, in that order, followed by taking two steps in the coach's box and loping in four strides to the dugout. Not superstition, he said, merely habit.

---

[18] George Gmelch, "Baseball Magic," http://www.dushkin.com/olc/genarticle.mhtml?article=27128, accessed August 2005. (Revised version of George Gmelch, "Superstition and Ritual in American Baseball," *Elysian Fields Quarterly* 11/3 [Summer 1992]: 25–36.)

[19] Ibid.

The elaborate rituals executed by Boggs reflect the habits of many players who seek to control their success by attributing their good fortune to something extraordinary, something unrelated to their skills in playing baseball. Among those who undertook an extensive series of actions but who did not enjoy Boggs's success is Dennis Grossini, a former Detroit pitching prospect who managed his time and diet with precision akin to that of Boggs. The reason for doing so many little things, Grossini suggests, is that because when "you can't really tell what's most important,…it all becomes important." Consequently, he confesses, "I'd be afraid to change anything. As long as I'm winning, I do everything the same."[20]

Despite their measured behavior, players and managers often reject the notion that their actions are grounded in superstition. For one, former Mets' manager Bobby Valentine categorically and paradoxically dismissed the notion that baseball plays are subject to superstition. Following Shawn Estes's loss of a no-hitter after the Shea Stadium scoreboard flashed the notice of his quest, Valentine was asked whether Estes had been jinxed by the Jumbo-Tron's insensitivity to the norm of not mentioning a no-hitter in progress. "I don't believe in superstitions," Valentine remarked. "They're bad luck."[21]

Rejecting superstitions because of his faith in God rather than faith in luck, former pitcher Dave Dravecky is an evangelical Christian perhaps best known for his making a comeback from cancer, then breaking his arm, ending his career, and requiring pitching-arm amputation. Although he took no part in superstitious behavior, as he puts it, he had a routine of stepping off the mound, rubbing the ball with both

---

[20] Quoted in ibid.
[21] Quoted in Dravecky and Yorkey, *Called Up*, 23.

hands, kicking the pitching rubber, and peering home to get the sign from his catcher. His purpose in going through the same motions, pitch after pitch, he said, had nothing to do with superstition. Instead, his series of actions was a ritual, he said. For rituals, the orthodox affirm, give players "a sense of control and stability in an unstable environment" while superstitions appeal to luck.[22] The distinction between superstitious behavior and ritual, however, is akin to that between superstition and "true belief." Orthodox believers pejoratively apply the label of superstition to empowering rituals practiced by those whom they call agnostics, atheists, and apostates. But in baseball's superstitious culture, the bad luck of a batting slump or losing streak is not credited to the lack of personal self-control or the failure to execute a play; instead, it is identified with the inability to perform rituals properly.

Conclusion

In baseball, the culture of curses thrives because of the larger system of superstitions from which it draws its energy and support. Belief in curses identifies a cosmic cause for failure, thus absolving players for their ineptitude and fans for their lack of faith or dutiful support. Belief in curses also cuts the sainted players some slack. Although Johnny Blanchard, a third-string catcher for a Yankee dynasty, earned almost a fist-full of championship rings, neither Ted Williams nor Carl Yastrzemski ever won a World Series ring, while neither Ernie Banks nor Ron Santo ever even came to bat in a post-season game. The curse means that receiving just rewards is not the issue because it was not Ted Williams's or Ernie Banks's fault that their teams never prevailed. Rather, it was a force of the demonic, of a consequence, of a curse.

---

[22] Dravecky and Yorkey, *Called Up*, 22.

In the spirit of the Billy Goat and the Bambino, curses have been conjured against the Cubs and the Red Sox, and with supplication faithful devotees of both teams have sought the spirits' annulment of the hexes. Of course, the Curse of the Bambino was annulled or avoided in 2004 when the Red Sox made history, stealing a base in the ninth inning against the Yankees' super-closer Mariano Rivera and then scoring tying and winning runs against him in game four of the American League Championship Series. That miracle was followed by the improbable sweep of the Yankees in the following three games, giving Boston the honor of becoming the first major league team to overcome a three-game deficit in a seven-game playoff series. The remarkable comeback of the Red Sox continued in their spectacular four-game sweep of the Cardinals, who had accumulated the most wins of any major league team during the season. With an irony befitting their incredible recovery against their arch-nemesis from New York, the Red Sox attained their high point by turning to their Lowe starter, Derek. It was Derek Lowe who won game seven against the Yankees, and it was Lowe, again, who topped the Cardinals with a shutout performance on that fateful evening of 27 October 2004.

In the last half century, the Red Sox had twice ascended to game seven: once against the Reds, when Carlton Fisk's hopeful arm waving had seemingly kept his long drive fair and had made a miracle possible by winning Game Six, and the other against Mookie's Mets in 1986 when, reversing the source of miracles, Wilson's apparent game-ending grounder—again in game six—eluded Buckner's bend. Although the Yankees had already been eclipsed in both seasons, in neither series could Boston attain the grail of ultimate victory. Throughout the years the efforts of fans and players to annul the Curse of the Bambino had proved futile. But with a cosmic convergence previously unimagined in these incantatory attempts by the Red Sox faithful, Boston became World Champions for the first time since the end of World War I. On 27 October 2004, at 11:40 p.m., the Red Sox recorded the final out against the Cardinals. A little more than an hour earlier, a total lunar eclipse had occurred. And with the "supervision and supervention" of the moon's power, the superstitious might say, the Curse of the Bambino was emasculated.

In Chicago, however, cosmic forces did not intervene in 2004. In the minds of devoted Cubs' fans, the Curse of the Billy Goat was compounded by another curse, the "Cover Curse" of *Sports Illustrated*. For the annual baseball preview featured Cubs' pitcher Kerry Wood on its cover and ran the lead story: "Hell Freezes Over. The Cubs Will Win the Series This Year." Perhaps the gurus at *Sports Illustrated* misapprehended their vision of the champion. If the cosmic reversal of hell freezing over did not occur for the Cubs, then at least the Red Sox eclipsed the bewitching lunar power of the Bambino.

5

Safe at Home:
Baseball as American Civil Religion

"Baseball is about going home and how hard it is to get there and how driven is our need. It tells us how good home is. Its wisdom says you can go home again but you cannot stay. The journey must always start once more, until there is an end to all the journeying."[1]

Although in recent years scholars from various disciplines and pundits in multiple media outlets have popularized the idea that baseball is a form of religion in America, one of the earliest affirmations of baseball as an American religion was offered by Morris Cohen almost a century ago. Writing about baseball as a "national religion" in *The Dial* in late July in the summer following end of World War I, Cohen wonders about future scholars looking back on early twentieth-century American culture. When the scholar "comes to speak of America's contribution to religion," he queries, "will he not mention baseball?" Cohen bases this amusement on his recognition that "by all the canons of our modern books on

---

[1] A. Bartlett Giamatti, *Hartford Courant*, 18 October 1978, quoted in Frank Deford, "A Gentleman and a Scholar," *Sports Illustrated* 70/17, 17 April 1989, 98.

comparative religion, baseball is a religion, and the only one that is not sectarian but national."[2]

Cohen identifies baseball as a religion because he understands that religion provides redemption from the mundane and trivial concerns of individual experience by connecting the faithful in a kind of "mystic unity" with a larger realm of life in which all persons participate. He goes on to add that baseball functions as a religion not merely because it provides an absorbing fascination with the play of the game on the field, but also because it provides a kind of "mystic unity" with one's team, connecting a community in ways that allow it to compete against another community. However, in terms of the personal transformation that baseball accomplishes, Cohen revels in the fact that "every one of the extraordinarily rich multiplicity of movements of the baseball games acquires its significance because of its bearing on that outcome." And, he concludes, "Instead of purifying only fear and pity, baseball exercises and purifies all of our emotions, cultivating hope and courage when we are behind, resignation when we are beaten, fairness for the other team when we are ahead, charity for the umpire, and above all the zest for combat and conquest."[3]

It is obvious that the radical optimism of the Progressive Era underlies Cohen's doxology about the wonders of baseball, for he features the virtues of respect and restraint for losing opponents (a practice that declined, if not evaporated, following the Great Depression and World War II), and he celebrates the expression of compassion to umpires. This latter expression of pleasure with umpires is a phenomenon now

---

[2] Morris R. Cohen, "Baseball as a National Religion," *The Dial* 57 (26 July 1919): 57, reprinted in Louis Schneider, ed., *Religion, Culture, and Society: A Reader in the Sociology of Religion* (New York: John Wiley and Sons, Inc., 1964) 37.

[3] Cohen, "Baseball as a National Religion," 37.

missing in years following the routine argumentative antics of managers Earl Weaver, Billy Martin, and Lou Pinella; the protest actions of Roberto Alomar, who spit at umpire John Hirschbeck, and George Brett, who chest bumped umpire Tim McClelland for disallowing a home run and calling him out for excessive pine on his bat; and the frequent complaints of Roger Clemens and Barry Bonds about called balls and strikes.

A decade after the appearance of Cohen's essay in *The Dial*, perceptions of the religious significance of baseball had permeated American culture and its civic leadership to such an extent that Herbert Hoover asserted that "Next to religion, baseball has furnished a greater impact on American life than any other institution."

The assertion of Hoover and the argument by Cohen certainly apply well to the stature of baseball in American society during the Progressive Era. It was during that time, in fact, that baseball "reached the height of its identity as America's national pastime."[4] Focusing on the economic and social roots of the moniker applied to baseball, G. Edward White insists that, although baseball does not reflect an intrinsic American character, it "became the national pastime because those at the upper echelons of the sport as an enterprise consciously, and unconsciously, transformed it from a working class, 'rough,' urban sport to a game that simultaneously embodied America's urbanizing commercializing future and the memory of a rural, pastoral past."[5]

---

[4] Christopher H. Evans, "Baseball as Civil Religion: The Genesis of an American Creation Story," in *The Faith of Fifty Million*, ed. Christopher H. Evans and William R. Herzog II (Louisville: Westminster John Knox Press, 2002) 37.

[5] G. Edward White, *Creating the National Pastime: Baseball Transforms Itself, 1903–1953* (Princeton: Princeton University Press, 1996) 319.

As early as the beginning of the Civil War, however, baseball had begun to be identified as the congealing factor for Americans when Henry Chadwick referred to the sport as the "national game." According to some accounts, almost two decades earlier, Walt Whitman, who aspired to create a new, fully American voice and vision, wrote in a mid-summer 1846 issue of the *Brooklyn Eagle* that he had observed "several parties of youngsters playing 'base,' a certain game of ball." It is certainly possible that Whitman saw the groups of kids playing the distinct American version of "rounders" that was to become baseball since the first recorded games of baseball were played in New York a year earlier. The attribution of Whitman's observation also indicates that some time later in 1846 he reflected specifically on what the new game might mean. "I see great things in base ball. It's our game.... The American game," he asserted. "It will take our people out of doors, fill them with oxygen, give them a large physical stoicism. Tends to relieve us from being a nervous, dyspeptic set. Repair these losses, and be a blessing to us."[6]

Although Whitman developed an intense love of baseball during the next forty years, it is not certain that he actually wrote these celebrative remarks at this early date.[7] But Chadwick's reference to baseball as the "national game" during the Civil War indicates that baseball had taken on a social meaning beyond the camaraderie that teammates might enjoy.

---

[6] Quoted in Baseball Historian.com, http://www.baseball historian.com/html/american_heroes.cfm?page+52. Commercial site sponsored by Balazs Enterprises and dedicated to the posting of historic baseball references. Site accessed on 4 December 2005.

[7] Charles S. Adams, professor of English at Whittier College, has followed debate about this controversy. He presented his findings in a lecture on "Whitman and Baseball," Whittier College, 1 December 2005.

At that time baseball was thought to be the national game primarily because it seemed to manifest America's desire for efficiency. Now in an era of play clocks for football and shot clocks for basketball, that consideration seems off base since baseball is often regarded as the slowest of the current major professional team sports. Yet during the latter half of the nineteenth century, baseball was being contrasted to cricket and town ball, both of whose play and duration seemed to sprawl.

The roots of baseball as an American civil religion lie in its nineteenth-century acceptance as the national pastime when it came "to symbolize national virtues of freedom, justice, and equality."[8] But this trinity of civic virtues applied to a privileged sector, not in the sense of being restricted to a lordly class; but the reality of racial prejudice and economic oppression certainly stained this set of values. In contrast to this sentimental celebration of baseball in the nineteenth century, historian Stephen Reiss describes the situation and society's attitude at that time even more bluntly: "The national pastime encouraged people to think that the United States was a democratic country where all white men were entitled to equal social justice, equal political rights, and equal opportunities for advancement."[9]

In some accord with Reiss's assessment, W. P. Kinsella's Native American sage and baseball guru in *The Iowa Baseball Confederacy* portrays the ideal of baseball in glorified terms

---

[8] Christopher H. Evans and William R. Herzog II, "Introduction: More than a Game: The Faith of Fifty Million," in *The Faith of Fifty Million* (Louisville: Westminster John Knox Press, 2002) 2.

[9] Stephen A. Riess, *Touching Base: Professional Baseball and American Culture in the Progressive Era* (Westport CT: Greenwood Press, 1980) 230.

while pointing still to its racism, whether overt in the practice of segregated professional play during that era or latent in the structure of the game itself. In the novel, one of Kinsella's works of magical realism that employ baseball as an empirical game that defies chronometric time, Drifting Away remarks on the very issue of baseball and its inherent racism. As a Native American sage and baseball guru, Drifting Away comments, "Baseball is the one single thing the white man has done right. Think of the circles instead of the lines—the ball, the bat, the outfield running to the horizon, the batter running around the bases. Baseball is as close to the circle of perfection as white men are allowed to approach."[10]

As President Hoover's remark about baseball's importance being second to that of religion suggests, the game reached its height of public acclamation as the national pastime during the Progressive Era, a period preceding the sins of the Black Sox scandal, yet one during which baseball's institutionalized racism flourished. One of the distinctions of the Progressive Era was its variety of social-reform initiatives. In this hopeful period of social change, historian Christopher Evans notes, "Baseball became a symbol of postmillennial liberal Protestant zeal that contributed to the personal and social uplifting of all Americans." For many of the secular and religious Americans, then, baseball served as "a spiritual tonic that offered solace and relief to a tired and 'overworked' nation."[11]

Although baseball evinced a compelling allure during the Progressive Era, we must consider whether it continues to exercise such a formative force at the turn of the new millennium. Noting that somehow baseball has always seemed to be "more than a game," Evans avers that baseball became a

---

[10] W. P. Kinsella, *The Iowa Baseball Confederacy* (Boston: Houghton Mifflin Company, 1968) 177–78.

[11] Evans, "Baseball as Civil Religion," 37, 39.

transcendent symbol of hope. Even today, he concludes, "The national pastime continues to appeal to many who hope that the lure of the Elysian Fields will turn our hearts away from the world's despair, in order that we may glimpse a vision of a world better than our current one."[12] Despite its continuing popularity—evidenced by professional baseball's record attendance in the new millennium—the rise of interest in youth soccer, the fascination with collegiate football and the BCS formula for determining the national championship contestants, the wagering associated with the NFL, the internationalization of professional basketball, and the infatuation with NASCAR have challenged baseball's preeminence among American sports. Yet Evans concludes that the components of baseball make it a civil religion—that it offers a vision of new world that improves upon our present lot.

Does the symbolic power of baseball that clarifies vision and generates hope actually reflect a religious dimension of the game? Former Commissioner A. Bartlett Giamatti wonders about and addresses this fundamental question: "If there is a truly religious quality to sport, then, it lies first in the intensity of devotion brought by the true believer, or fan. And it consists, second, and much more so, in the widely shared, binding nature—the creed-like quality of American sport."[13] Although Giamatti did not specify what kind of religion baseball might be, his language of "devotion," "true believer," and "creed-like quality" certainly indicates that he understood that baseball is a religion. Giamatti's intuition that baseball is a religion is supported by sociologist James Mathisen, who avers that "when a people gather and reaffirm their beliefs and

---

[12] Evans and Herzog, *The Faith of Fifty Million*, 7.

[13] A. Barlett Giamatti, *Take Time for Paradise: Americans and Their Games* (New York: Summit Books, 1989) 23–24.

traditions, their ritual acts and shared creed are intrinsically religious."[14]

Civil Religion

Writing in mid-twentieth century, theologian Will Herberg pondered the religious character of "the American way of life" and its relation to religion in his pioneering work, simply titled *Protestant, Catholic, Jew*. Following Durkheim, he recognized that to a significant degree all functioning societies share "a *common* religion." And Herberg determined that "the American Way of Life" is "the 'common faith' of American society."[15] At least since the Revolutionary period, Herberg contends, this "common faith" or "civil religion" (a term that he did not yet explicitly employ) has characterized American experience, and throughout the intervening centuries this common faith has exercised a reciprocal and pervasive influence on the traditional faiths of the American people.

As the concept of civil religion became accepted following the publication of Robert Bellah's charter essay in *Daedelus*, the concept was associated overwhelmingly with the political dimensions of American life. In collaboration with other scholars of religion and American studies two decades after the publication of his seminal work, Herberg adopted the terminology of "civil religion" while reiterating his point about the pervasive and perduring interaction of "the common faith" and the American character. For "the operative religion of a society," he maintains, "emerges out of, and reflects, the

---

[14] James A. Mathisen, "Civil Religion," in Donald W. Musser and Joseph L. Price, ed., *Handbook of Christian Theology*, New and Enlarged Edition, (Nashville: Abingdon Press, 2003) 99.

[15] Will Herberg, *Protestant, Catholic, Jew* (Chicago: University of Chicago Press, 1955) 74, 81.

history of that society as well as the structural forms that give it its shape and its character."[16]

As the concept has been refined and elaborated in subsequent years, it has been expanded and applied to other dimensions of American life. Developing the idea that American civil religion shapes the national identity by bestowing or deriving sacred significance from a variety of secular spaces, traditions, texts, rituals, and institutions, various scholars have now applied the notion of civil religion to various social organizations and cultural trends. One of the foremost proponents of this expansion, Catherine Albanese has aligned sports with the common faith of many Americans, specifically examining the function of an American sports calendar as a kind of liturgical calendar.[17]

Although Albanese succinctly identifies the distinguishing facets of religion as beliefs, ethics, ritual, and community, Ninian Smart has proposed a more comprehensive set of attributes that distinguish religion and that embrace the cultural, social, and political forms that can be considered as civil religion. He argues that a network of six categories—experience, myth, ritual, doctrine, ethics, and social—can be used to analyze whether or not an organization or movement constitutes a religion.[18] The various elements of religions—the aspects of worldviewing described by Smart—are not discreet, disconnected categories. Instead, they are interwoven, interlocked, overlapping strands that draw upon and reinforce each other.

---

[16] Will Herberg, "American Civil Religion: What It Is and Whence It Comes," in *American Civil Religion*, ed. Russell Richey and Donald G. Jones (New York: Harper & Row, 1974) 76–77.

[17] Catherine Albanese, *America: Religion and Religions* (Belmont CA: Wadsworth, 1981).

[18] Ninian Smart, *Worldviews: Crosscultural Explorations of Human Beliefs*, 3rd ed. (Upper Saddle River NJ: Prentice Hall, 2000).

Now using these divisions, we can determine whether and how baseball can be the "national religion" that Cohen proffered almost a century ago.

Baseball Experience

According to historian of religion David Chidester, baseball affords the opportunity for many of its fans to enjoy "extraordinary moments of ecstasy and enthusiasm, of revelation and inspiration."[19] These emotions, impressions, and expressions comprise the core of religious experience. Because they are truly extraordinary in character, these moments of ecstasy, enthusiasm, revelation, and inspiration have the potential to transform ordinary work and the doldrums of daily routines. In this regard, baseball is like other sports that exercise the power to induce a peak experience because performance and competition in sport offer an immediate possibility of encounter with alterity—by achieving a personal best performance, by executing a play perfectly, or by attaining victory. "Sport offers occasional entry into an extra dimension of human experience," David Vanderwerken and Spencer Wertz contend. "The fleeting transcendent moment is of sport alone and cannot be approximated in everyday life…[because] sport is better than life."[20]

For players, baseball provides opportunities for experiencing flow[21] or for enjoying a peak experience[22] when

---

[19] David Chidester, "The Church of Baseball, the Fetish of Coca-Cola, and the Potlatch of Rock 'n' Roll," in *Religion and Popular Culture in America* ed. Bruce David Forbes and Jeffrey H. Mahan (Berkeley: University of California Press, 2000).

[20] David Vanderwerken and Spencer K. Wertz, *Sport Inside Out: Readings in Literature and Philosophy* (Fort Worth: Texas Christian University Press, 1985) 3.

[21] For elaboration on the concept of flow as a religious experience, see Mihalyi Csikszentmihalyi, *Flow: The Psychology of*

the execution of a play is perfect, as in turning a seemingly impossible 6-4-3 double play, freezing the batter with a sharp-breaking curve on the outside corner, making a home-run saving catch, executing a double-steal, pulling the hidden ball trick, laying down a suicide squeeze bunt, or hitting a walk-off home run. In baseball, even an "ordinary," frequently practiced play can provide an experience of personal and communal success: for example, hitting a routine ground ball to the right side of the infield with a runner on second base and none out; charging a slow roller, scooping it up bare-handed, and throwing to first in a single motion to beat the runner by half a step; going from first to third on a Texas-League single to right field; or blocking the plate while awaiting the throw, making the catch, and applying the tag. In all of these ways, the timely performance of ordinary plays or the spectacular execution of an unexpected play—like Derek Jeter's running, backhanded flip of the overthrow from right field to Jorge Posada who made a sweeping tag of Jeremy Giambi at home plate in the 2000 American League playoffs—generate extraordinary moments that intensify hope, increase a sense of community with teammates, and provide momentary success that can be celebrated as an intimation of immortality.

Not only does baseball provide a spiritual experience and the possibilities of religious connection for players, author Thomas Boswell reflects how his mother, a fan, enjoyed a

---

Optimal Experience (New York: Harper and Row, 1990); and Susan A. Jackson and Mihalyi Csikzentmihalyi, *Flow in Sports: The Keys to Optimal Experiences and Performances* (Champaigne IL: Human Kinetics, 1999).

[22] For elaboration on the concept of peak experience as a religious experience, see Abraham Maslow, *Religions, Values, and Peak-Experiences* (New York: Viking Press, 1960) especially appendix A.

religious experience from her *watching* of the games: "Although my mother wasn't a baseball fan in the fanatic sense, she loved to go to baseball games. She said it made her feel like she was in church…. For her church was ritual epiphany, a place to go where she knew the composition of feeling she'd have when she got there and could depend on its reappearing. Basically, that's how she felt about baseball, too."[23]

Boswell's mother is not alone in her derivation of spiritual meaning by watching the game and rooting for her team. In fact, she is only one among a stadium full of fans who, while describing their experience somewhat differently, indicate baseball's religious import for their own lives. My own story, related in the final chapter of this book along with those of several other authors, is among them. *Safe at Home*, the memoir of Marc Jolley that is featured as one of the works in the Mercer series Sports and Religion, provides a sustained account of a way in which baseball blends with experience and faith to shape one's life.[24] And more than a hundred other former players, authors, and public figures join with other fans by writing briefer reflections on the significance of baseball for their own experience in *What Baseball Means to Me*.[25] Our common experience about the significance of baseball in our lives and for our viewing of the world is summed up in one of Branch Rickey's oft quoted lines: "Man may penetrate the outer reaches of the universe, he may solve the very secret to

---

[23] Thomas Boswell, "The Church of Baseball," in *Baseball: An Illustrated History*, ed. Geoffrey C. Ward and Ken Burns (New York: Knopf, 1994) 189.

[24] Marc A. Jolley, *Safe at Home: A Memoir of God, Baseball, and Family* (Macon GA: Mercer University Press, 2005).

[25] Curt Smith, ed., *What Baseball Means to Me: A Celebration of Our National Pastime* (New York: Warner Books, 2002).

eternity itself, but for me, the ultimate human experience is to witness the perfect execution of the hit-and-run."[26]

Baseball Myth

Helping to shape personal experience, a myth is a story about beginnings or about significant transformations—interruptions, disruptions, or corruptions that changed how things had been into how things really are or how they might be. Basically, myths are charter stories that indicate why the shape of a tradition or organization is a particular way. Myths exert a kind of timeless character, always impinging on the way things are, yet somehow evading chronological calculation or verification. Even as myths operate in a timeless realm, they also function in a way that transcends spatial limitations, although spatial specifications, like temporal ones, might be included in the stories themselves. According to Mary Gerhart, who has reflected extensively on the religious significance and nature of myth, "By suspending ordinary time and space, myths establish an extraordinary origin and destiny for human beings."[27] Thus, while myths identify the cosmic origin and destiny of human beings, they empower hearers to exercise the fullness of their strength and they inspire them to pursue perfection.[28]

In America's political civil religion, a myth that exhibits this power to reveal something of the American charter is a

---

[26] Quoted in David H. Nathan, ed., *The McFarland Baseball Quotations Dictionary* (Jefferson NC: McFarland and Company, 2000) 232.

[27] Mary Gerhart, "Myth," in *New and Enlarged Handbook of Christian Theology*, ed. Donald W. Musser and Joseph L. Price (Nashville: Abingdon Press, 2003) 339.

[28] Joseph Campbell with Bill Moyers, *The Power of Myth* (New York: Doubleday, 1988) 132.

story about George Washington. As the Father of the Nation (a designation that indicates origin, power, and fertility), Washington was so honest as a child that, as the story goes, he confessed to his father that he had cut down "the" cherry tree. Add to this story the one about his power—that he was so strong that he could hurl a silver dollar across the Potomac—and one gets an image of a powerful, honest person who, without being perfect, is an exemplary human being fit for leadership of a nation that would become a world power. Correspondingly, in baseball, the prodigy of its heroes is signified by a story about the early abilities of Nolan Ryan, who, according to his high school coach, had thrown a softball from the goal line through the uprights of the opposite end zone more than 100 yards away.[29] In terms of hitting prowess, the mythic powers of Babe Ruth were so great that, as the story goes, he could take two strikes, then step out of the batter's box and deliberately point to the spot where he would homer in the 1932 World Series at Wrigley Field.

Even verifiable stories take on mythic significance when they occur in extraordinary moments or circumstances. In a speed test in Chicago in 1940, Bob Feller out-pitched a speeding motorcycle although Feller was dressed in street clothes. Captured on film, the motorcycle was traveling at eighty-six miles per hour when Feller released the ball, which surpassed the speeding machine by thirteen feet in the distance between the pitching rubber and home plate. Using mathematical calculations then, promoters determined that he had thrown the ball at 104 miles per hour. Yet he exceeded that speed on a delivery in another test undertaken at the Aberdeen Ordnance Plant in Washington, DC. There, before the timing

---

[29] Jonathan Fraser Light, *The Cultural Encyclopedia of Baseball* (Jefferson NC: McFarland and Company, 1997) 321.

provided by today's generous radar guns, his pitch was timed at 107.9 miles per hour, thus making it the fastest pitch ever recorded.[30] The mythic significance of other recorded baseball feats include the remarkable courage displayed by Lou Gehrig who, dying, stood before the honoring standing-room only crowd at Yankee Stadium and declared, in halting voice and with tear-streaked cheeks, that he considered himself to be "the luckiest man on the face of the earth."

Certainly, the mythic lure of baseball includes these tales of Ruth and Ryan, of Feller and Gehrig, but the mythic power of baseball extends beyond these stories related to its heroes—or saints.[31] Baseball myths, in fact, begin by identifying the origin of the game itself, lending it immediate national significance and authority. Writing about this charter myth of the origin of baseball—its creation similar to constructed accounts of divine design—Stephen Jay Gould suggests that "the civil religion of baseball connected the origins of baseball to a sense of pastoral purity."[32]

The wonder of myth, however, is not relegated exclusively to its celebration of traditional heroes and their accomplishments. Instead, as a narrative construct, myth is also able to stimulate dreams and cultivate hope. Connecting myth and baseball in this way, former Commissioner A. Bartlett Giamatti proved an articulate sage. Inscribed on a plaque in the library in baseball's tribute to myth, the Hall of Fame, his words reverberate the multivalent power of myth: "Baseball is one of

---

[30] Bob Feller with Burton Rocks, *Bob Feller's Little Black Book of Baseball Wisdom* (Chicago: Contemporary Books, 2001) 26–27.

[31] For a comprehensive work that views baseball as a myth that makes sense of human experience, see the sophisticated confession and literary analysis in Deeanne Westbrook, *Ground Rules: Baseball & Myth* (Urbana: University of Illinois Press, 1996).

[32] Evans, *The Faith of Fifty Million*, 28.

the few enduring institutions in America that has been
continuous and adaptable and in touch with its origins. As a
result baseball is not simply an essential part of this country; it
is a living memory of what American culture at its best wishes
to be."[33]

One of the formative myths for America, as well as for
baseball, relates to freedom—democracy's full embrace of
freedom and a person's compelling desire to attain or preserve
it. At the juncture of freedom and democracy, Giamatti
concludes that baseball and myth become part of the same
American story. "Baseball," he writes, "is part of America's
plot, part of America's mysterious, underlying design—the plot
in which we all conspire and collude, the plot of the story of
our national life. Our national plot," he concludes, "is to be
free enough to consent to an order that will enhance and
compound—as it constrains—our freedom. That is our
grounding, our national story, the tale America tells the
world."[34]

Baseball Doctrines

Although Giamatti identifies a binding, "creedlike quality" in
American sport, the doctrinal dimension of baseball is more
specific than the nebulous, implied statement of faith that
creates the cult of baseball devotees.[35] According to Smart, the
doctrinal dimension of religion—or its facet featuring
beliefs—fulfills several functions, the foremost being that of
establishing order among the mythic elements of the religion.
As part of its organizational response to myths, the doctrinal
dimension of religion also is intended to "safeguard the

---

[33] Cited in Evans, "Baseball as Civil Religion," 31–32.
[34] Giamatti, *Take Time for Paradise*, 83.
[35] Ibid., 23–24.

reference of myths…to that which transcends the cosmos."[36] In other words, formal beliefs connect the mythic stories, their heroes, and their truths to a cosmic realm that suggests the universal applicability of the beliefs—that the transcendent nature of the reference is universal, rather than merely local or regional. The doctrinal dimension of religion, however, not only looks to the primordial days of mythic actions; it also focuses on the present day by helping to establish the continuing relevance of religion's truth-claims as expressed in current concepts and images. For instance, the metaphysics of "process thought," especially as formulated by Alfred North Whitehead at the beginning of the twentieth century, have been used to explain enduring Christian doctrines to the present age in ways that avoid the often dated dichotomies of "form and substance" that typified earlier explanations of distinct Christian tenets, such as those dealing with incarnation, the Trinity, and resurrection.

In a similar manner one might think of baseball's rules as ensconcing baseball's beliefs because rules determine the game's order; but the beliefs associated with baseball have more to do with myths of the game than with the values that regulate its plays or become manifest in their execution. The rules of baseball, as we will see in one of the subsequent sections of this chapter, are more closely related to baseball ethics than with baseball doctrines or beliefs because baseball rules establish the measures for fair play in the game. Although baseball superstitions (the subject of the preceding chapter) are folk beliefs, the doctrinal dimension of baseball is most easily identified with baseball wisdom, or general truths about the game; for superstitions are most frequently idiosyncratic (arising from a single player's experience or a team's

---

[36] Smart, *Worldviews*, 88.

performance) rather than universal. Most often, the truths of baseball are articulated in a pithy manner, occasionally as malapropisms, by players and pundits. Prominent among those who have formulized baseball truths in this mangled manner are Casey Stengel and Yogi Berra. But the wisdom of baseball is more frequently associated with the philosophies of Hall of Famers and thinking strategists, like Bob Feller or Branch Rickey, who is sometimes referred to as "baseball's last wise Man."

As noted at the beginning of this section, the doctrinal dimension of religion primarily deals with organizing myths, especially ones perceived as conflicting with each other. Because baseball myths often compete against each other, such as pitting the speed of Feller's fastball against the awesome power of Ruth, the purpose of baseball doctrines is to regulate their relation: Which indeed would be more dominant? Pitching or Hitting? In terms of pitching, various experts have offered their wisdom about its dominance. According to Sandy Koufax, for instance, "Pitching is the art of instilling fear" in the batter. Or fireballing Bob Gibson, noted for owning the inside corner, personalized the doctrine, believing that, as he put it, "one of the most valuable weapons in a pitcher's command is the brushback pitch." Or more wirily, Warren Spahn suggested that "the best pitch looks like a strike, but isn't." [37]

Whether utilizing speed, plate position, or pitch deceit, the truth about pitching success focuses on the pitcher's necessity to learn control, as Babe Ruth, himself both a record-setting pitcher and the Sultan of Swat, asserted: "The first thing any pitcher has got to develop—the biggest single item in his whole stock and trade—is control." But control is more

---

[37] Quoted in Criswell Freeman, comp. and ed., *The Wisdom of Old Time Baseball: Common Sense and Uncommon Genius from 101 Baseball Greats* (Nashville: Walnut Grove Press, 1996) 110–13.

than merely being able to hit the inside corner of the plate with a blazing fastball, like the intimidating Gibson, or never walking a batter. Instead, Juan Marichal asserted, "Control does not mean throwing strikes every time. It means throwing where a particular hitter will not hit it." Similarly, Koufax considered that "the wildest pitch is not necessarily the one that goes back to the screen. It can also be the one that goes right down the middle." [38]

Balancing pitchers' wisdom about needing to exercise control and deceive the batter, hitters' wisdom focuses on establishing plate discipline and developing confidence. According to all-time hit leader Pete Rose, "A hitter's impatience is the pitcher's biggest advantage." Similarly, Hall of Fame outfielder Johnny Mize mused that since "the pitcher has to throw a strike sooner or later,…why not hit the pitch you want to hit rather than the one that he wants you to hit?" Or more succinctly, Ruth offered the advice, "Don't swing at 'almost strikes.'"[39] Ruth's sage suggestion certainly applies to most hitters, but not to all, since Hall of Fame catcher Yogi Berra, former Pirate catcher Manny Sanguillen, and recent American League MVP Vladimir Guerrero often hit bad pitches quite well. Berra once hit a ball into the stands on a curve ball that bounced in front of the plate, and Sanguillen walked so rarely that former Pittsburgh general manager Joe Brown once remarked that "when Manny takes a pitch, it's either a wild pitch or paralysis set in."[40]

Whether a batter exercises a disciplined eye at the plate and refrains from swinging at bad pitches, or whether he

---

[38] Quoted in Freeman, ed., *The Wisdom of Old Time Baseball*, 110–13.

[39] Ibid. 100–101.

[40] Quoted in Nathan, *McFarland Baseball Quotations Dictionary*, 40.

swings as freely as Guerrero and Alfonso Soriano, hitting itself can be understood as a science, as former batting champion George Brett believed; yet even he recognized that hitting needs to be approached less by scientific analysis than as an art that is practiced. In other words, as Yogi Berra expressed it, "You can't think and hit at the same time," or as Branch Rickey summed it up with a kind of biblical intonation, "A full mind is an empty bat." Similarly, Stan Musial elaborated on Ty Cobb's dictum that "batting is more mental than physical,"[41] specifying that "the secret of hitting is physical relaxation, mental concentration—and don't hit the fly ball to center."[42]

Common to both pitchers' wisdom and that of hitters is their grounding of success in self-confidence. Former Dodger and Yankee pitcher Tommy John, who made the initial comeback from experimental elbow surgery that now bears his name, put the matter most succinctly: "My philosophy has always been simple. Believe in yourself." And sportswriter Grantland Rice identified the hallmark of any champion as self-confidence. But "in order to have confidence," Monte Irvin noted, "you have to perform well. Then confidence builds on itself." Not surprisingly, a determined spirit also goes hand in hand with self-confidence, as noted by former Dodgers' manager Tommy Lasorda. "The difference between the impossible and the possible," he believed, "lies in a person's determination."[43]

In turn, a player's determination—his pursuit of success—is manifest most often in hard work, hustle, and a willingness to take a calculated risk. Hard work, of course, produces sweat, which, according to Branch Rickey, "is the greatest solvent

---

[41] Quoted in Freeman, *The Wisdom of Old Time Baseball*, 102.

[42] Quoted in Nathan, *McFarland Baseball Quotations Dictionary*, 41.

[43] Quoted in Freeman, *The Wisdom of Old Time Baseball*, 44–45.

there is for most players' problems." There is "no cure," he continued, "no soluble way to get rid of a bad technique as quick as 'sweat.'"[44] Yet the hard work required for developing skills and achieving success is rooted in the deep desire or passion to do one's best. Known as "Charley Hustle" for his intense and aggressive play, even running out bases on balls, Pete Rose observed that "you'd be surprised how many shortcomings you can overcome by hustle."[45] Or again from Rickey: "Wanting to do something—desire—is the greatest difference between a championship team and a team in the second division."[46]

The tandem qualities of desire and discipline provide the context for success and what is sometimes called "good luck." One of Rickey's most frequently cited principles is his belief that good luck does not happen by chance; instead, he contended, it is the outcome of thorough preparation. "Things worthwhile generally just don't happen," he believed. "Luck is a fact, but should not be a factor. Good luck is what is left over after intelligence and effort have combined at their best. Negligence or indifference or inattention are [sic] usually reviewed from an unlucky seat. The law of cause and effect and causality both work the same with inexorable exactitudes. Luck is the residue of design."[47] Or as Joe McCarthy, manager of seven Yankees World Series Championship teams, summed things up: "Success doesn't just happen. You've got to make it happen."[48]

---

[44] John J. Monteleone, ed., *Branch Rickey's* Little Blue Book: *Wit and Strategy from Baseball's Last Wise Man* (New York: Macmillan, 1995) 2.

[45] Quoted in Freeman, *The Wisdom of Old Time Baseball,* 54.

[46] Monteleone, *Branch Rickey's* Little Blue Book, 4.

[47] Ibid., 11.

[48] Quoted in Freeman, *The Wisdom of Old Time Baseball,* 70.

Working as general manager and manager respectively in championship organizations, Rickey and McCarthy knew how to develop and guide teams to excel. A third factor that Rickey identified in creating a climate for success is the willingness to accept risk. "A great baseball player," he believed, "is one who will take a chance."[49] Citing as an example of the effective acceptance of risk, Rickey reflected on the success of Maury Wills, the first major league player to steal more than a hundred bases in a modern-era season. "There is hardly any excuse in the majors for cowardly baserunning," Rickey mused. "Shortstop Wills of the Los Angeles club should turn red the faces of twenty men in the National League who can run as fast as he can. I knew a National League outfielder who had all the skills to steal as many bases as he wished but one season stole just four."[50] The hundred-base difference in their seasonal marks was rooted in Wills's willingness to accept risk, epitomizing Rickey's general belief that one should "never surrender opportunity to security." Former Pirate All Star pitcher Vernon Law put the matter quite vividly: "You'll never reach second base if you keep one foot on first."[51]

Expressed in the wisdom about the game, baseball beliefs have more to do with strategies for pursuing excellence rather than rules for regulating its play. In addition to the pithy truths identified in the previous paragraphs, there are a number of general baseball dicta that hold true. Among them: a batter should take a pitch on a 3-0 count unless the situation of the game—the score, the number of outs, the hitter, the on-deck batter, or the number of runners on base—submonishes that general strategy. Another: with none out and a runner on second base, the hitter should try to hit the ball to the right

---

[49] Quoted in ibid., 71.
[50] Monteleone, *Branch Rickey's* Little Blue Book, 15, 42.
[51] Quoted in Freeman, *The Wisdom of Old Time Baseball*, 24, 71.

side of the infield in order, at minimum, to advance the runner
to third. And one related to defense: in the outfield, a player
should catch a fly ball while stepping toward the base where he
wants to make his throw, thereby increasing his momentum on
the throw and increasing the likelihood of its accuracy.

The most vibrant doctrines of a religion are those that
apply not only to the exercise of the faith, but also to life itself.
In that regard, several of the truths about baseball extend to
daily living in ways that prompted Thomas Boswell to reverse
the anchor of the metaphor comparing baseball and life and to
title his engaging series of essays *How Life Imitates the World
Series*. Convinced that baseball is indeed the greatest sport ever
played, Boswell speculates about how the discussion might go
in heaven about which game was the greatest ever played.
Accepting the likelihood that it would be impossible to
distinguish the "best game ever," two games, he suggests, will
need to be mentioned at the beginning of the discussion: the
1951 playoff game between the Giants and Dodgers with
Bobby Thomson hitting the walk-off, three-run homerun; and
the Yankees' defeat of the Red Sox in the 1978 playoff game,
with Bucky Dent lofting the fly-ball over the stretching height
of the Green Monster. Both games featured late-inning
homerun heroics, and both featured each league's classic
rivalry in a season-ending, single-game elimination.[52]

In addition to Boswell's universal truth that "life imitates
the World Series," other tenets also apply equally to life as well
as to baseball. Many of those have to do with the realization of
failure and the necessity for hope. In general, Bill Veeck noted,
"There is no substitute for winning and no known cure for
losing." Despite the experience of deep joy in winning and the

---

[52] Thomas Boswell, *How Life Imitates the World Series* (New
York: Penguin Books, 1982) 15.

lack of an antidote to dull defeat, it is possible to learn something from each outcome. "You can learn a little from victory," Christy Mathewson determined. "You can learn everything from defeat." In losing, one can learn which specific mistakes caused failure, and one can learn anew the prospects afforded by hope, for in the words of Bob Gibson, "without hope there is nothing."[53]

Especially since baseball is not restricted by a clock, the possibilities of rescuing the team's victory or reclaiming personal dignity remain alive until the very end, the last out of the last inning. Merely ask old Yankee fans about their hopes even as Tommy Henrich—batting with two-outs, none on, and down by a run—swung and missed the third strike thrown by Fireman Casey in the top of the ninth inning at Ebbets Field in the 1941 World Series clash between the Dodgers and the Yankees. Or consider the evasive roll of the bouncing ball hit by Mookie Wilson to Bill Buckner with two outs, the Red Sox ahead, and the 1986 World Series Championship within the reach of Buckner's glove. Unrestricted by the movement of a clock, baseball answers instead to each game's approximation of infinity, which is always a possibility until the final out has been recorded.

That realization is the heart of one of baseball's infallible dicta, uttered by Yogi himself: "It ain't over till it's over." Even then, it is possible to redeem oneself and one's team, if not the defeat itself. Buck O'Neill reflected on this opportunity for getting another chance, more than a hundred times a season. "In baseball there's always tomorrow," he said. "Maybe you got me today, but tomorrow, I'm coming back." Or in the words of Manny Trujillo, former second baseman for the Chicago Cubs

---

[53] Quoted in Freeman, *The Wisdom of Old Time Baseball*, 136, 139, 33.

who enjoyed repeated opportunities to deal with defeat, "The best thing about baseball is that you can do something about yesterday tomorrow."[54] As facile as these assertions about having new life in the game "tomorrow" might initially seem, they resemble great tenets of faith in established religious traditions, wherein the faithful gather hope for life or existence beyond the seemingly final defeat of death. "The anguish and depression that seize one's psyche in defeat," Michael Novak maintains, "are far deeper than a mere comparative failure— deeper than recognition of the opponent's superiority." Indeed, he concludes, "defeat hurts like death."[55] What this experience of defeat as death means is that in a very real sense each sporting opponent is death itself. Yet following defeat, there is, as O'Neil and Trujillo indicated, another game or another season during which one might pursue the abundant life of victory, for again according to Novak, "To win a contest is to feel as though the gods are on one's side,...as if the powers of being course through one's veins and radiate from one's actions."[56]

As noted at the beginning of this section, a primary challenge for the development of doctrines and their acceptance as beliefs is to work through and systematize competing elements in myth. The brief examination of truths about pitching and hitting address in part the dilemma about which mythic power might prevail, Feller's fastball or Ruth's prodigious swing. Yet for all of the truth identified in the pitching doctrines articulated by Koufax, Spahn, and Marichal or the hitting wisdom revealed in the tenets of Ruth, Rose, and Musial, none

---

[54] Quoted in ibid., 66, 67.

[55] Michael Novak, *The Joy of Sports: End Zones, Bases, Baskets, Balls, and the Consecration of the American Spirit* (New York: Basic Books, 1976) 47.

[56] Ibid., 47–48.

of their musings resolves the issue about whether pitching or hitting dominates the other. But Casey Stengel, with his inimitable way of summing things up, fathomed the dilemma by perceiving the paradoxical solution that "good pitching will always stop good hitting, and vice versa."[57]

Baseball Rituals

"In ritual," Edward J. Reilly suggests, "baseball approximates something of the religious experience."[58] Certainly, rituals are prominent in baseball, and rituals are often rooted in religious behavior. In baseball, ritual dramatically integrates other dimensions of religion identified by Smart, especially myths, experience, social, and beliefs. For one thing, rituals are related to myths in the sense that a "ritual is the enactment of myth."[59] Among other ways, rituals are connected to experience in the sense that outings or trips to games function as minor pilgrimages, and the experience of being at a ballgame, of participating in the rituals of cheering for one's team, generates a bond among fans. Rituals also are related to beliefs in the ways that the ritual practitioners frequently assume that their control over outcomes will be determined by the precision of their execution of the ritual performance.

In simplest terms, a ritual is a repeatable action whose meaning exceeds its performative function. In general, rituals illuminate personal experience and social memory that are formative for personal identity and communal alliances. A more expansive definition is provided by Roland Delattre, who avers that ritual consists of "those carefully rehearsed symbolic motions and gestures through which we regularly go, in which

[57] Quoted in ibid., 142.
[58] Edward J. Reilly, *Baseball: An Encyclopedia of Popular Culture* (Lincoln: University of Nebraska Press, 2005) 253.
[59] Campbell with Moyers, *The Power of Myth*, 32.

we articulate the felt shape and rhythm of our own humanity and of reality as we experience it, and by means of which we negotiate the terms or conditions for our presence among and our participating in the plurality of realities through which our humanity makes its passage."[60] The symbolic character of rituals indicates that the actions convey meaning beyond their functional outcomes, and this excess of meaning implies transcendence, thus identifying the intrinsic character of ritual with religious behavior. By dramatizing mythic and cosmic events, rituals address people's "need for belief that is lasting, experience that is constant, existence that leads the individual into communion with others in the temporal sphere and toward a reality beyond the here and now."[61] This description of the purpose, function, and character of rituals plumbs the religious core of ritual itself (because of its links to an "Other" realm of meaning), and it also effectively summarizes its connection to Smart's other categories of worldview analysis.

The symbolic aspect of rituals also suggests that in some sense their meaning is social or communal, rather than merely personal or eccentric.[62] As such, rituals bear significance within a particular culture, even when a single person might be responsible for executing the actions, as with a monk making a sacrifice. At such an event, the reenactment of the ritual is understood by others present, as well as by absent persons who embrace the tradition.

While the range of religious rituals stretches from corporate ceremonies of worship to individual practices of prayer, all ritual actions metaphorically express a social or

---

[60] Roland Delattre, "Ritual Resourcefulness and Cultural Pluralism," *Soundings* 61/3 (Fall 1978): 282.

[61] Reilly, *Baseball*, 253.

[62] Paul Tillich, *Dynamics of Faith* (New York: Harper and Brothers, 1957) 41–54.

communal understanding of power and possibility. Acts of worship and prayer achieve more than merely gathering people to hear a lecture, to sing together, to experience the aerobics of genuflection, or to share a communal meal. As acts of worship, for examples, the performance of baptism and the celebration of the Eucharist accomplish more than the application of water to a person and the distribution of bread and wine for nutritive purposes. These ritual acts connect the participants to a larger realm of meaning, one most often associated with formative events in the tradition. And because rituals are repeatable acts whose meaning is well-known by the participants, they often lend the participants a sense of comfort.

The complexity of rituals extends beyond the specific and often sweeping meaning of the performative actions them- selves. As Ronald Grimes identifies in his comprehensive guide to ritual analysis, the study of rituals distinguishes the actors who officiate and participate in the ritual actions themselves, the material objects employed in the acts, the sounds or ritual language employed in the rites, the spaces where the action is perceived or projected to be efficacious, and the sense of time within the action itself.[63] As with the interlocking components of worldviewing, so too the various aspects of ritual are interwoven in ways that they cannot exist as discreet elements; their identity and significance can be understood as they are classified, but their character and meaning are determined by their interaction with the other constitutive ritual components. For instance, to continue with the example of the Eucharist, the priest or minister (as a ritual actor) consecrates (using ritual actions and language) the bread and wine (ritual objects) at an altar or table (defining the ritual space), thus reenacting the

---

[63] See Ronald L. Grimes, *Beginnings in Ritual Studies* (Lanham MD: University Press of America, 1982) 19–33.

sacrifice of Christ or commemorating the fellowship experienced with his disciples at the Last Supper (fusing a past event with the present action in ritual time). The duration of the act of consecrating, distributing, and consuming the elements can be measured in few minutes, but the ritual time of the celebration is time immemorial, time that takes participants back to the charter event, to the Last Supper. Yet the ceremony is not merely a reference to a bygone event. Instead, it is the dramatization of a myth, re-creating, as Smart puts it, "an event which myth describes, making it real now."[64] Ritual time, then, is a kind of timelessness that involves the fusion of the past with the present in dramatic fashion. And while the past and present are linked within the ritual act, so too are participants bound together as a comprehending community.

In sports the ritual time of contests is often distinguished by periods (like hockey), quarters (like football), or halves (like basketball), but in so doing each of the sports establishes the length of its distinct period by a game clock. But no clock times an inning of baseball for the purpose of setting a limit on its length. In fact, the battle between a pitcher and batter might last for minutes, with a batter fouling off pitch after pitch in an effort to keep his at-bat alive. And a pitcher might prolong an at-bat by tossing time and again to first base to hold a threatening base-stealer close to the bag. Reflecting on possible reasons why baseball establishes such a grip on its fans, William Freedman suggests this expansiveness of time, the refusal of baseball to be regulated by a clock: "There is time between pitches, time between tosses to first, time between batters, time between innings, time for everything to register

---

[64] Smart, *Worldviews*, 124.

and sink in."[65] In this way baseball appeals to the imagination, and it provides the temporal space for conversation between pitches, plays, and innings. In other words, while the game is being played, fans can share with family, friends, or nearby fans their lore and love of the game itself.

In baseball, time is rarely measured by chronometric means, although when the Athletics still played in Kansas City, their owner Charlie Finley tried to impose the twenty second rule on opposing pitchers, particularly Pedro Ramos. Surprising players and fans and raising the ire of the commissioner's office, Finley installed a scoreboard clock that counted down the seconds between the pitcher's receiving the ball and delivering it to the batter. Despite the accepted absence of a clock in governing a game, the length of games is measured in terms of hours and minutes, with records established for the shortest and longest regular season and post season games. The shortest game in history lasted less than an hour, with the Giants beating the Phillies 6-1 in fifty-one minutes (28 September 1919) and the longest always subject to extra-innings and civic curfews. But baseball time is calculated in terms of innings, games, and seasons much more so than minutes, hours, and days. It is possible that a baseball game, like cricket until its league professionalization toward the end of the twentieth century, could extend for days, theoretically even infinitely. As long as an out would need to be recorded, the team's at-bat could continue. In part, the possibility for an infinite tie (extending eons beyond the longest one on record—a twenty-six-inning 1-1 tie between the Brooklyn Dodgers and the Boston Braves in 1920) directed W. P. Kinsella's fictional contest at Onamata, Iowa, where the Cubs

---

[65] William Freedman, *More Than a Pastime: An Oral History of Baseball Fans* (Jefferson NC: McFarland and Company, 1998) 11.

managed to play a two thousand-inning exhibition game against the all-star team from the Iowa Baseball Confederacy.[66]

In multiple ways and venues, authors and scholars have aligned the ritual dimensions of baseball with its mystical lure, often specifically identifying baseball rituals as being religious. Foremost among the ritual points of identity has been the description of the ritual space of ballparks as green cathedrals, with Edward Reilly even noting that a "domed roof or open air [stadium] parallels the vaulted roof of a medieval cathedral built to approximate the eternal vault of the heavens."[67] Similarly, increasingly during his study of the 273 ballparks called "home" by major league and Negro league teams, Philip Lowry became convinced that the longer and more intensely he studied ballparks and stadiums, the more he began to recognize their resemblance to houses and places of worship.[68] The reverential character of a ballpark has also been identified by W. P. Kinsella, who attributes such a spiritual perception to his fictive hero Ray Kinsella who, in turn, muses about the sacred sensation that a ballpark evokes. Considering a moonlit visit to old Metropolitan Stadium in Bloomington, Minnesota, Kinsella asks his traveling companions if either of them has spent time in an empty ballpark. "There's something both eerie and holy about it," he asserts. "A ballpark at night is more like a church than a church."[69]

---

[66] W. P. Kinsella, *The Iowa Baseball Confederacy* (Boston: Houghton Mifflin, 1986).

[67] Reilly, *Baseball*, 253.

[68] Philip Lowry, *Green Cathedrals: The Ultimate Celebration of All 273 Major League and Negro League Ballparks Past and Present*, rev. ed. (Reading PA: Addison-Wesley Publishing Company, 1992) 1–2.

[69] W. P. Kinsella, *Shoeless Joe* (New York: Ballantine Books, 1983) 135.

The inspirational character of baseball is also celebrated and displayed in an artistic and poetic collection titled *Diamonds Are Forever*.[70] A number of its literary and pictorial pieces intimate the eternal, especially as that sense arises out of the sacred character of the space. In that regard, it is important to note that a church was built on the former site of old Shibe Park in Philadelphia, and Wrigley Field is located on the site of a former Lutheran seminary. While these sites maintain a sense of reverence in transition from church to ballpark and vice-versa, the modern placement of ballparks near the intersection of freeways (like Anaheim and Atlanta), along prominent waterfronts (in Baltimore, San Francisco, Cincinnati, and Pittsburgh), or in dramatic hilltop settings (such as Dodger Stadium in Los Angeles) also demonstrates their civic prominence in ways that churches and temples often have sought to be distinguished.

In addition to the spiritual character of ballparks evoked by their architecture and location, a baseball field itself also suggests an intrinsic, mythical orientation of the game. As noted in the earlier chapter on "The Pitcher's Mound as Cosmic Mountain," the sacred character of the baseball field is, in part, distinguished by the rituals of consecration that occur at a season's beginning—the ceremonies of opening day—and before each game, with the ceremonial tossing of the first pitch, the managers' exchange of line-up cards, the umpire's explanation of ground rules, and the singing or playing of the national anthem, which adds civic sanction to the game.

Another ritual dimension of baseball that signifies its religious character is its language: Not only does baseball appropriate specific religious terms, such as sacrifice and

---

[70] Peter H. Gordon, ed., *Diamonds Are Forever: Artists and Writers on Baseball* (San Francisco: Chronicle Books, 1987).

perfect game, it also develops distinct linguistic meanings for other terms, thus creating a ritual language of its own. Terms like homerun, strike out, single, cellar, closer, dying quail, gopher ball, hot corner, suicide squeeze, infield fly, bleachers, double-play, clean-up batter, rhubarb, grand slam, Texas-Leaguer, RBI, Triple Crown, saves, and ERA (which itself is a kind of Trinitarian mystery)—to name only a few baseball phrases—create a linguistic system that is distinct to the sport; and many of the terms have made their way into established dictionaries and provide roots for metaphors about the cosmic significance of baseball—like Thomas Boswell's engaging title *Why Time Begins on Opening Day*. Dictionaries devoted to baseball lingo are popular;[71] but there are also other linguistic expressions that are part of the rituals of the game. For one, the catcher uses fingers pointed down and to the side to indicate the kind of pitch and its location that he wants the pitcher to throw. The umpire uses a fist upraised, usually apparently gesturing up and away from his shoulder, to indicate that a batter or runner is out; or with a double-handed, mid-body outward slice of his arms, the umpire might signal the runner safe. Trying to mislead the non-cognoscenti, a third base coach delivers a series of signs to the batter about whether to swing a pitch, whether the runner will be taking off on a steal, or whether the batter might need to lay down a bunt. One of the distinctions of a sophisticated ritual is that it employs a language of its own, thus privileging the insiders from the outsiders, the faithful from the pretenders. In addition to these gestured signals for plays, fans also enjoy participating in the ritual expressions of booing the umpire, cheering a timely-turned double-play, starting or joining a

---

[71] For example, see Patrick Ercolano, *Fungoes, Floaters, and Fork Balls: A Colorful Baseball Dictionary* (Englewood Cliffs NJ: Prentice-Hall, 1987).

"wave," standing to applaud a well-pitched game, and curtain-calling a hitter from the dugout to recognize a dramatic home run. Wherever these ritual actions are performed, a special baseball language is also at work.

The ritual language of baseball, of course, is understood by its ritual actors—not only players, coaches, and managers, but also umpires and fans. In a comprehensive sense, the ritual language of baseball extends beyond the distinct names for plays or elements of the game and beyond the use of specific signals to call for pitches or a hit-and-run play. In non-functional ways players also engage in actions designed to improve performance—or at least to invoke good luck. Enthusiastic Dodger Mickey Hatcher in the late 1980s and early 1990s popularized the use of rally caps to prompt late-inning comebacks by his teammates. By turning their caps inside out and sometimes putting them on backwards, teammates utilized a symbolic language in their actions, hoping to reverse the course of inept play in previous innings. Fans also often engage in actions that might influence players and, thereby, change the direction of the game: In Minnesota, the use of "homer hankies" became common during home playoff games for the Twins in 1987, and at Anaheim in 2002 the odd wagging of rally monkeys by devout Angels' fans seemingly aided their quest for the World Series Championship. Or at various points in Atlanta's post-season competition, fans have imitated a sing-song warrior cry and raised and lowered their arms in demonstrating a tomahawk chop to urge the Braves to rally or to taunt opposing pitchers, for example, but always to show their own allegiance to and identification with the Braves.

One of the most easily identifiable ritual actions associated with baseball is the journey of pilgrimage, which is often made with family members as one makes an initial trip to a ballpark or as seasoned fans trek to a special game. Such was the case

with my first trip to a major league game. With my father and
mother, I went to St. Louis in 1960 to see Ernie Broglio pitch
against Bob Friend, and the following year I went to Chicago
to see two games between the White Sox and the Yankees. In
other chapters of this book I relate in greater detail the
pilgrimage elements of the formative journeys, from the
planning and anticipation to their challenges and completion.

A more constant focus for pilgrimage for baseball devotees
is the Baseball Hall of Fame in Cooperstown, New York.
Among those who have written about their journey to the Hall
of Fame in terms of its being a pilgrimage are journalist Tom
Stanton and historian Christopher Evans, a United Methodist
minister. For Stanton, the trip to Cooperstown fulfilled a deep
desire—virtually an obligation—that he had held for almost
three decades. In mid-life, he was able to complete "the
journey of a lifetime" with his aged father and somewhat
disaffected brother. For years, Stanton had considered the Hall
of Fame to exercise "the same mythical quality as the North
Pole," orienting all in baseball's hemisphere toward its
magnetic pull and seeming about as far away as the Arctic
Circle itself.[72] Resonating with Stanton, Evans also describes
his experience of the life-long lure to the Hall of Fame. "In its
own way, Cooperstown invokes for the baseball fan a feeling of
transcendence, a sense that one has entered into a timeless
realm of heroic deeds and eternal bonds between parents and
children," he meditates. "For a few precious hours, my visit to
Cooperstown transported me into a realm where the stresses of
my own life seemed insignificant."[73]

It is not surprising that the Hall of Fame evoked such a
numinous response. Enshrined there are tributes to the mythic

---

[72] Tom Stanton, *The Road to Cooperstown: A Father, Two Sons, and the Journey of a Lifetime* (New York: St. Martin's Press, 2003) 19.

[73] Evans, "Baseball as Civil Religion," 35.

heroes and their incredible achievements in the game. And in terms of the space itself, the architecture of the Hall of Plaques was designed in the shape of a chapel, with light pouring in from above, casting an ethereal brightness that one associates with both reverence and revelation, an experience that might typify a faithful person's orientation or perception.

The connection of ritual to beliefs or the doctrinal dimension of religion as identified by Smart can be seen most clearly in the phenomenon known as superstition, like that of Hatcher and his teammates believing that their reversing the orientation of their hats would help the Dodgers' hitters to reverse the outcome of their previous ineffectual swings. In the preceding chapter I have identified a number of the superstitious behaviors of players and fans that are based on the belief that their adequate performance would improve their play and empower a particular outcome. Wade Boggs's precise and elaborate series of timed actions in preparation for a game, for example, extended the arena of his beliefs, requiring that he begin his routines before arriving at the ballpark (by eating certain foods) and then regulating his actions in pre-game practice (by bunting a specific number of times and by running at an exact time). The purpose of performing these seemingly unrelated acts is to provide the actor with the confidence that he is exercising control over the situation—in Boggs's case, that he would get multiple hits during the game.

The turning of rally caps by the Dodgers' players and the display of marionette monkeys by Angels' fans also evince another aspect of ritual—the use of ritual objects. There are certainly material objects used in the play of baseball, some absolutely essential (like ball, bat, and base) and others having been introduced at various points to improve play (such as a glove, catcher's mask and protector, uniforms and caps, pine tar rag, fungo bat, and resin bag, as well as field objects like the backstop, dugout, and foul poles). Most of these objects do not seem to bear much special meaning since they are functional within the game, making it indeed possible. Special significance can be acquired, however, when a particular jersey, bat, or ball, for instance, is involved in a historic game or play, such as the million-dollar value placed on Mark McGuire's seventieth home run ball. The Baseball Hall of Fame, of course, is filled with the balls, uniforms, gloves, and bases used in no-hit performances or final games at a particular ballpark.

Although these ritual objects facilitate the play of the game itself, they attain their excess of meaning from their association with specific players, plays, and games. Fans, however, are not excluded from the use of ritual objects. Among the most prized possessions of devout baseball fans are foul balls or home run balls that they have caught in the scrum for their recovery. On my own shelves, I prize a number of balls from various stadiums: batting practice balls that I have caught at Dodger Stadium, Oakland's ballpark, and Tropicana Field at Tampa Bay, but even more importantly a foul ball hit by Ed Kirkpatrick at a game at Wrigley Field, and a home run ball smashed by Ben Ogilvie at Comiskey Park. What makes these balls so special is not merely the fact that they were hit by major league players but also the way that I caught them, juggling the home run ball before snapping it from falling back onto the warning track and spearing Kirkpatrick's foul with one extended hand. And what adds to the significance of this latter trophy is that I caught it in the company of good friends, several of whom (especially Michael Kinnamon) were far better athletes than me. But a minor league ball is among my most prized because it is the first one that I caught when, with my father, I went to a game between the Richmond Virginians and the Syracuse Chiefs and stood in the aisle behind home plate to watch one more pitch before ducking into the concession

stand. Former Dodger catcher Norm Sherry fouled a pitch
back onto the screen, where it rolled up to edge of the press
box, turned to the lip of the screen, and fell into my believing
black glove in that early spring game of 1964. But the
significance of baseball's ritual objects is not tied exclusively to
professional feats. For the most prized baseball among the
autographed balls and game catches that I have been graced
enough to grab is the ball given to me by my older son on
Father's Day 1994. It is identified by a scrawled date and
description as his first high school hit, a double that he crushed
to right center field.

For fans, other ritual objects also manifest significant
attachment and bear important meaning. Scorecards and ticket
stubs from games when historic performances were witnessed
or from memorable familial or friendly outings to the ballpark
can help one, in tangible ways, to recall or reconstruct the
intense emotions of the event. Paper megaphones, which were
functionally used by concessionaires to hold the servings of
popcorn that they sold, and free homer hankies, which were
distributed by a local newspaper as an advertising gimmick,
also can become revered souvenirs, relics for helping to
remember and relive meaningful occasions.[74] Other objects
associated with the game or its players also can become ritual
objects: replica jerseys, which were never worn by a player in a
game, allow fans to mask their daily identity and to identify
with the heroism or uniqueness of the player whose number
the jersey bears. Similarly, baseball cards have grown in
collectible popularity in part because they can evoke the
childhood olfactory memories of pink strips of bubble gum and
more innocent days when baseball heroes roamed outfields and

---

[74] Victor and Edith Turner, *Christian Pilgrimage* (New York:
Columbia University Press, 1978) 196–97.

fearsome pitchers blazed fastballs whose speed approached that
of light itself. Ordinary baseballs or pictures signed by players
in uniform become somehow empowered with an autograph of
a demigod. Often young fans and life-long devotees treat a
baseball hero's autograph like a priestly blessing, connecting it
with the promise and accomplishments of the player himself.
Or miniature replicas of ballparks can serve as reminders of
journeys to games or of a fan's desire to make such a trip to see
the site where heroes had actually touched the earth, especially
on the sacred diamond that remained off-limits to fans. Each of
these objects, whether utilized by players in order to pursue a
victory or whether enjoyed by fans treating them as relics of
heroic accomplishments or connections, serves a ritual function
of enabling the play of the game or of resurrecting memories
of one's hopes and dreams associated with baseball.

The most prominent reliquary of the material elements of
baseball is, of course, the Baseball Hall of Fame in
Cooperstown, New York. There, not only are the ritual objects
of historic games on display, but the veneration of baseball
heroes is institutionalized. With a purpose of appealing to this
cult of the saints, *Sports Illustrated* was launched in the 1950s
with Robert Creamer as one of its senior editors. Throughout
his career that spanned four decades, Creamer paid particular
attention to fans' fascination with heroes as he ghost wrote
Mickey Mantle's *The Quality of Courage* and authored definitive
biographies of Babe Ruth and Casey Stengel. Although each of
his books is targeted for adult audiences, Creamer well
understood a young fan's reverence for his baseball heroes.
"The small boy does not know that the best third baseman in
baseball is human: that he fights with his wife, worries about
bills and occasionally swears at the bat boy," Creamer once
wrote in *Sports Illustrated*. "All the small boy knows is that the
third baseman is a hero, and a hero always does the right thing.

It would be sinful to disillusion him, to tell him that Babe Ruth was a glutton, that Enos Slaughter has had five wives."[75]

The issue that Creamer identifies about the human foibles of sports heroes is one that sportscaster Bob Costas reflected on at the time of the memorial service for Mickey Mantle. Costas's fondness for Mantle is evident in a comment that he had made when asked why he carries two of Mantle's baseball cards in his wallet: "I believe everyone should carry some type of religious artifact on his person at all times," Costas remarked.[76] The Yankees' switch-hitting centerfielder with the smile of an affectionate toddler was known to have consumed too much alcohol and to have philandered during his playing days. Yet Mantle, Costas perceived, "came to accept and appreciate the difference between a role model and a hero. The first he was not," Costas concluded, while "the second he will always be."[77] Adults who can make the distinction, then, between "role model" and "hero" are liberated from the denial or disillusionment that threaten Creamer's typical child, exemplified by the anonymous (and mythic) boy who cried out to Shoeless Joe Jackson, "Say it ain't so, Joe."

On the field players and umpires are surely the actors most directly involved in performing the actions of the game. Functionally, managers and coaches, by attempting to design plays and align positions, influence the outcome of each play, even if only by leaving the pitcher in the game to face another batter or by setting the batting order itself. Players' involvement with the success or failure of particular plays is more readily perceptible than that of their managers—like Bobby Thomson's dramatic three-run, walk-off, pennant-

---

[75] Quoted in Light, *The Cultural Encyclopedia of Baseball*, 320.

[76] Quoted in Nathan, *The McFarland Baseball Quotations Dictionary*, 196.

[77] Quoted in Freeman, *The Wisdom of Old Time Baseball*, 84.

winning homer against Ralph Branca and the Dodgers in the 1951 National League playoff game or like Mickey Owen's dropping the third swinging strike against Tommy Henrich with his Dodgers team ahead and two outs in the ninth inning of game four in the 1941 World Series, thus prolonging the game and ultimately sending his team home sad in yet another World Series defeat to the Yankees.

Even as players and managers provide the focal action in the play of the game itself, fans also serve as ritual actors when they cheer, stand, participate in a wave, or sing "Take Me Out the Ballgame" during the seventh inning stretch. As a congregation of the faithful, fans also seek to influence the outcome of a play or game by their rally cries (like Braves' fans plaintive intoning of a war cry) and antics (like Angels' fans clapping thunder sticks to distract the Giants and empower the Angels' hitters during the 2002 World Series). In addition to these ways of participating as a group, it is also possible for fans to participate in the game in individual ways, such as keeping score or merely watching the game while wearing the jersey of one of the two teams. A few fans, however, have become notorious participants in the actual play of the game, like young Jeffrey Maier interfering with Tony Tarasco's ability to catch Derek Jeter's warning-track fly ball in Game One of the 1996 American League Championship Series, resulting in a homerun for Jeter rather than an out recorded by the Orioles; or oblivious Steve Bartman catching a foul ball descending toward Moises Alou's in-reaching glove in Game Six of the National League Championship Series in 2003.

By promoting social interaction through group cheers, by dramatizing mythic feats of the game, by canonizing heroes of the game, and by providing dynamic means for establishing their identity, baseball rituals enable fans to express their love of the game and their devotion to their favorite players and teams. In short, as Ray Kinsella averred to "Jerry" Salinger in *Shoeless Joe*, "Baseball is a ceremony, a ritual, as surely as sacrificing a goat beneath a full moon is a ritual. The only difference is that most of us realize that it *is* a game."[78]

Baseball Ethics

By themselves, the ethics of a worldview, a tradition, an institution, or a game do not necessarily have to do with a formulaic identification of good and evil actions, with helpful and hurtful attitudes, or with concepts of social justice that apply in normal daily interactions. Instead, the ethics of a tradition or a game are located in the rules of the game, in the correctness of the participants' adherence to those rules, and in the values expressed in the play of the game itself. "In sports," as philosopher Randolph Feezell puts it, "cheating is often understood in relation to the status of rules." And cheating, he proposes, involves breaking a rule in order to gain "an unfair advantage."[79] Yet since some rules are routinely broken as part of a team's strategy to win the game and since opponents also expect to engage in similar actions, when available, mere rule breaking might not constitute cheating since neither team might gain a competitive advantage when both expect to engage in actions not within the rules of the game. The balance of competition, that perspective suggests, then reverts to umpires and officials to establish and enforce what constitutes fair play.

In baseball, "right and wrong" actions—the backbone of ethics—come into play in participants' responsibility to the rules and spirit of the game. A spikes-high slide into second

---

[78] Kinsella, *Shoeless Joe*, 72.

[79] Randolph Feezell, "Baseball, Cheating, and Tradition," in *Baseball and Philosophy: Thinking Outside the Batter's Box*, ed. Eric Bronson (La Salle IL: Open Court, 2004) 112.

base to upset the turning of a double-play or an injurious collision with a catcher blocking home plate might be seen by naïve onlookers as hurtful or evil. But for competitive players and devout fans, baseball's rules allow for such actions within the game, and consequently, they are not against the ethics of the game. By contrast, such intense, competitive acts tend to exemplify the competitive nature of the game itself.

Unlike a Christian ethic that enjoins believers to pursue justice and to live compassionately, baseball establishes rules of competition that embrace aggressive play, accept stealing as part of the game, and utilize practices of deception. Devout Methodist Branch Rickey recognized the distinct ethic of baseball; yet because of its confinement to the field of play, he did not consider the permissive rules of baseball to be in conflict with the Christian ethic of compassion. At times, in fact, he blended images from his Christian faith and its ethic to describe the baseball tactics and their goals: "In pitching we want to produce delusions, practice deceptions, make a man misjudge," he believed. "We fool him—that's the whole purpose of the game. The ethics of the game of baseball would be violated if man did not practice to become proficient in deception. In other words, you can't go to heaven if you don't try to fool the batter."[80]

Certainly, Rickey's endorsement of baseball's ethic that encompasses deception contravenes ethics based primarily on the Ten Commandments or a set of moral maxims. Yet even more unacceptable to such traditional expectations about the foundations of ethics might be baseball's establishment of rules governing when and how stealing might be fair. Not only does baseball institutionalize how bases can be stolen, its rules also allow for players and coaches to steal a catcher's sign for pitch

---

[80] Monteleone, *Branch Rickey's* Little Blue Book, 25.

selection or a pitch-out, or an opposing coach's sign for a hit-and-run play. Yet baseball's acceptance of stealing a catcher's signs is confined to the players and coaches on the field itself. As a case in point, several years ago former Giants' pitcher Al Worthington was sitting in the bullpen when he noticed that employees of his team were seated in the bleachers nearby. He watched them use binoculars to spy on the catcher and to relay his signals to the dugout. After the game Worthington confronted his manager about the tactic and threatened to leave the team if the practice were not halted immediately. Rather than suffer public scrutiny that might follow Worthington's threatened departure, the manager stopped the practice right away.[81]

In a similar way to baseball's approval of sign-stealing among the players and coaches on the field, the game also embraces the use of deceptive plays in a number of different ways. Routinely, pitchers disguise their change-up delivery with the same arm motion and point of release that they use for their fastball, and the catcher wags a series of finger combinations to confuse coaches and base-runners about the pitch selection and location that he is calling. At times when runners are on the corners, a pitcher will fake a throw to third base before wheeling to fire a pick-off throw to first, attempting to catch a sluggish runner there; and occasionally an infielder will pretend to return the ball to the pitcher before trying to pull the hidden ball trick to tag a runner out. More dangerous for players on the field is the deception called for by a batter who appears to be in a bunt situation. To deceive the defense, the batter might square around to prepare to lay down a sacrifice, but when the third baseman begins to charge hard

---

[81] Mark J. Hamilton, "There's No Lying in Baseball (Wink, Wink)," in *Baseball and Philosophy: Thinking Outside the Batter's Box*, ed. Eric Bronson (La Salle IL: Open Court, 2004) 134–35.

toward the plate or infielders start to wheel in motion, the batter might pull the bat back and swing away, hoping to slap the ball through the infield. The risk, of course, is that the batter might hit the ball so hard at the third baseman that the fielder would not have a chance to get his glove up and protect himself from possible injury.

One of the most inventive plays of deception was planned by Ty Cobb when he managed the Tigers while continuing to play left field. With Babe Ruth coming to the plate in the late innings with runners on base and the game on the line, Cobb signaled from his position that the pitcher should intentionally walk Ruth. The catcher complied and, standing upright, held the target up and away from the Babe. After checking the runners at their respective bases while Ruth waited with his bat resting on his shoulder, the pitcher came set and blazed a fastball over the plate for a strike, with the catcher reaching back to catch the apparently errant pitch. Enraged, Cobb charged in from the outfield, scolded the pitcher, slammed the ball back into the catcher's glove, and motioned wildly for the pitcher to walk Ruth. Again, the catcher stood, called for the ball outside, and reached back across the plate to catch another fastball delivered over the plate by the pitcher. As Cobb again stormed the infield, he called for a relief pitcher, and he yelled at the departing pitcher as he took the ball from him. As the relief pitcher took his warm up tosses, Cobb talked with him and gestured animatedly about walking Ruth. Returning to the outfield and getting set, the scenario of the previous pitches was repeated, with the pitcher throwing a fastball for a called third strike while Ruth, in disbelief, struck out without swinging. Following the game, Cobb indicated that he had planned the play months earlier and had waited to use it at an opportune time.

Other plays based on deception, however, break rules and therefore constitute "cheating." An example of a play in that category is the "double squeeze" play that was used successfully by a high school coach who taught his team to use it in a specific situation. In a high school game with two umpires—one calling balls and strikes behind the plate and the other roving the bases—and with runners on second and third with less than two outs, the coach might call for a squeeze play. Because of the umpires' focus on plays at first base and the home plate, the runner on second base would cut well inside third base, shortening his route to home by three full strides. Such a play is intended primarily to deceive umpires, not the opposing players, and its goal is certainly to gain a competitive advantage by getting credit for scoring a run without touching third.[82]

Yet one prominent perspective among players and fans is that "it's not cheating if you don't get caught." According to one of the hosts on an ESPN radio show, Tony Gwynn believes that more than half of major league players cheat. Attempting to use Gwynn's assertion to egg on Cal Ripken, who was the show's guest star, Rob Dibble then added, "Everybody cheats in baseball." But rather than affirming Dibble, denying the question, or offering an estimate of the extent of the practice of cheating among major league players, Ripken merely posed the fundamental question, "What is cheating?"[83] Is cheating merely the breaking of rules, or does cheating include attempts to deceive umpires?

In this regard, a common practice that does not break baseball's rules but tries to deceive the umpire involves a catcher's skill in framing a pitch, as Ivan "Pudge" Rodriguez

---

[82] Hamilton, "There's No Lying in Baseball (Wink, Wink)," 127.

[83] Ibid., 110–11.

was so adept at doing. More subtle than the act of catching the ball in the glove while moving or sliding it toward the plate, the skill of framing calls for catchers to freeze their pose with their glove—but perhaps not the ball itself—covering the corner of the plate. The intent, of course, is to get the umpire to call a close pitch a strike, even a pitch that the catcher knows to be a ball. The question then becomes does a catcher who consistently frames pitches "just off the plate" seek to gain a competitive advantage by deceiving the umpire? Although no rules are broken by such a practice, it might be considered cheating.

Related to the issues of baseball's distinct rules and ethics is the unwritten book of etiquette that accompanies good sportsmanship among players. For instance, when Barry Bonds or Manny Ramirez hits a tremendous home run, it is considered a breach of baseball's etiquette for either to stand at home and gawk at the ball's flight. Similarly, it is considered inappropriate, although not unethical, for a pitcher like Randy Johnson to taunt a batter, perhaps throwing a fastball behind a batter—like John Kruk—to unnerve the batter and gain a distinct competitive advantage. Following a dramatic home run it is certainly possible to display good sportsmanship and intense competitiveness while "not showing up" a pitcher, as Ted Williams consistently did by running the bases at normal speed with his head down. Among other things, Williams did not want to raise the pitcher's ire and generate a disadvantage for himself in his next at bat.

Among former players who perceived that the ethics and etiquette within baseball are distinct from extrinsic moral codes and religious ethics is former Negro league star Buck O'Neil. When interviewed for the Ken Burns series on the history of baseball, O'Neil was asked simply, "What has a lifetime of baseball taught you?" Without a hitch in the swing of his reply, he asserted, "It's a religion for me…[because] if you go by the rules, it is right. It taught me and it teaches everyone else to live by the rules, to abide by the rules."[84] Yet even though O'Neil recognized the limitation of baseball's rules to the game itself, he transferred the principle of playing by the rules to daily life, not restricting its application to sport.

Although the ethics of the game are established by its rules, the integrity of baseball in American culture is challenged, in the minds of many critics, by the personal behavior of players off the field, especially when their actions (including alcohol and steroid abuse, gambling, and violent behavior) influence the level of their performance on the field. Pitchers Grover Cleveland Alexander, Don Newcomb, and Ryne Duren basically drank themselves out of their livelihood before Newcomb and Duren became administrators in alcohol prevention and rehabilitation programs for major league teams. With a similar problem, Phil Douglas, who amassed almost 100 career victories as a pitcher for the Chicago Cubs and the New York Giants during the early twentieth century, got so drunk that he wrote a letter to a friend on another team, offering to sit out games or to affect their outcome in such a way that his friend's team might win the pennant. For this action, Commissioner Landis banned him permanently from baseball. The most recent prominent exile from baseball is Pete Rose because of his habits of gambling on baseball games, even though he has maintained that he never wagered on a game in which he could influence the outcome. The steroid scandal associated with Balco has also dimmed the season performances and career accomplishments of Jose Canseco and Rafael Palmiero. And fighting, often associated with

---

[84] Buck O'Neil, "Why would you Feel Sorry for Me?" in Geoffrey C. Ward and Ken Burns ed., *Baseball: An Illustrated History* (Alfred A. Knopf, 1994) 231.

drunkenness, has been a continual problem that has affected teams and their play, even when the fights occurred beyond the diamond and the locker room. One of the more dramatic fights reported involved a celebration of Billy Martin's birthday at the Cocacabana Club in New York in the late 1950s. Not only was Hank Bauer accused of slugging a patron rather than a baseball, several younger Yankees (including Mickey Mantle, Whitey Ford, and Yogi Berra) were also involved. As a result, Martin was traded shortly thereafter to Kansas City, thus altering the shape of the entire team.

More typically, players get into trouble or display disruptive behavior because of the excessive free time that they often experience when their team is on a road trip. In Branch Rickey's opinion, "the most dangerous moral hazard in the field of professional sport is leisure," because many players consider themselves employed or at work only four hours a day.

> "Nothing to do" is the most damnable thing that can come to a youth. I am sure that I have lost two major-league pennants because of rainy days. Every temptation that can come to a boy in the immoral field—women, wine, and gambling—presents itself so easily to idle youngsters. Idleness even more than monotony wrecks the morals of boys and girls more than anything I know. Through the ages, it has been the greatest enemy of adolescents. When one has nothing to do, he is so apt to do the so-called pleasurable thing, the thing closest at hand requiring no thought or industry—and usually indulges in the course of least resistance.[85]

Rickey's worries about the hazards of leisure are echoed by Satchel Paige in his more specific warning that one should "go very light on the vices, such as carrying on in

---

[85] Monteleone, *Branch Rickey's* Little Blue Book, 112.

society—[because] the social ramble ain't restful."[86] Even more precisely, the *Spalding Guide* at the turn of the twentieth century suggested that "the two greatest obstacles to success of the majority of professional ball players are wine and women."[87]

The ethics of baseball are not only codified by the rules of the game and interlaced with players' off-field behavior. The ethical dimension of the game is also manifest in values embedded in its rituals and underlying its social relationships. Among these values are equality, freedom, and a rugged sense of individualism.

The equality in baseball is set up in a number of ways. Among other things a player does not have to be tall in order to play (as Freddy Patek demonstrated) or lithe (as Smokey Burgess displayed) or fast (as Gus Triandos showed). As Tommy Lasorda put it, "It's still the best game in town because you don't have to be big to play, and everybody plays."[88] In this sense, then, as A. G. Spalding early perceived the balance of the game, the genius of baseball is that it is "a democratic game."[89] Indeed, that is the democratic key—everybody plays. Every player takes a position in the field, every player has a chance to have the ball hit or thrown to them, and every player gets a turn at bat. The equality or balance of baseball is also manifest in the alternation between offense and defense. Each team gets three outs and then gives the other team three

---

[86] Leroy (Satchel) Paige, as told to David Lipman, *Maybe I'll Pitch Forever: A Great Baseball Player Tells the Hilarious Story behind the Legend* (New York: Doubleday and Company, 1962) 277.

[87] Quoted in Light, *The Cultural Encyclopedia of Baseball*, 9.

[88] Quoted in Freeman, *The Wisdom of Old-Time Baseball*, 20.

[89] A. G.   Spalding, *America's National Game: Historical Facts Concerning the Beginning, Evolution, Development and Popularity of Base Ball* (Lincoln and London: University of Nebraska Press, 1992) 14.

outs. A clock does not regulate play or prevent a team from getting its full turn at bat.

Off the field, too, baseball has promoted equality. Although professional baseball remained segregated until Branch Rickey's signing of Jackie Robinson, followed almost immediately by Bill Veeck's inking Larry Doby to a contract in the American League, it led American institutions to integrate voluntarily half a decade before verdicts began to desegregate public transportation and public education. In other words, before the late 1940s, segregation was not primarily a problem of professional baseball, but of American society; it was baseball, led by Branch Rickey who not only signed Robinson in order to win but in order to begin to set things right, that helped to initiate racial integration for American institutions, especially since games were played in the open to be viewed by the public.

A second value that pervades the play of baseball is freedom. According to Giamatti, "Baseball simulates and stimulates the condition of freedom"; but Giamatti focuses on the responses of fans rather than the play of the game itself and its rituals, asserting that "baseball, in all its dimensions best mirrors the *condition of freedom* for Americans that Americans ever guard and aspire to." For baseball, he concludes, "is part of America's plot, part of America's mysterious, underlying design—the plot in which we all conspire and collude…to be free enough to consent to an order that will enhance and compound—as it constrains—our freedom." [90] Although Giamatti does not specify ways in which the game itself exemplifies the value of freedom, it is possible to identify several dimensions of free play that a player might select. For one, a batter is free to swing at a pitch in the dirt or to take a

---

[90] Giamatti, *Take Time for Paradise*, 83.

blazing fastball over the heart of the plate for a called third strike. A base-runner is free to break on a pitch, even without receiving a steal sign from the third-base coach or knowing that a hit-and-run play is on. An infielder is free to position himself in anticipation of the direction that the batter might hit the ball. An outfielder is free to throw the ball behind the base-runner, hoping that he will have strayed too far from the base and can be tagged out before safely returning. And a pitcher, of course, is free to shake off signs from the catcher until signals for the pitch that he wants to throw are given.

To a certain extent, language common to the game also picks up on this theme of freedom. When players are pursuing a high fly ball, for instance, they are often said to be "roaming the outfield," and batters typically are allowed to "swing away." Ironically, however, although the game and language about it might reflect the value of freedom, baseball's reserve clause prevented players from exercising their own freedom until the mid-1970s. For more than a century after the establishment of professional baseball, players—unlike other workers in America—were bound to a team and not able to negotiate freely with other teams.

A third American value that is a part of baseball is its rugged individualism, which is rooted in the freedom afforded by the game. The hallmark of individual competition in baseball is the concentrated contest between pitcher and batter that begins every play. Even while action occurs within the context of a team's play, the expression of rugged individualism is manifest in the number of categories for which an individual player's statistics are computed and for which awards are made for highest achievement. While teams vie for one single World Series championship trophy each season, players can garner multiple awards for individual accomplishment: for examples, the Cy Young Award, Fireman of the Year, Home Run and RBI crowns, batting champion, and more.

In the end as in the beginning, the intention of baseball's ethics, Giamati professed, "is to delineate a world whose rules have no meaning anywhere else, but where every act is significant. Baseball has the largest library of law and lore and custom and ritual, and therefore, in a nation that fundamentally believes it is a nation under the law, well, baseball is America's most privileged version of the level playing field."[91]

Baseball Community: Its Social Dimension

Even as the ethics of baseball feature a distinct balance or equality between teams, each getting its own turn to score without the risk of having its outs fumbled away or intercepted by the opponent, so too a sense of equality characterizes the social dimension of the game, which is the final dimension of worldviewing identified by Smart.

The social equality of baseball is not restricted to the power that the game exercises over its fans, unifying folks from diverse economic and ethnic backgrounds to form a congregation of the faithful. Essentially, baseball serves as a cross-heritage melting pot. From Ruth to Robinson to Rodriguez, from Kluszewski to Clemente to Clemens, from Mantle to Marichal to Matsui, baseball bridges cultural and linguistic divides, it establishes temporal continuities among successive generations of players and fans, and in so doing, it provides the foundation for establishing a real community, a group of devout baseball nuts, the truly faithful. Early in the twentieth century, *Baseball Magazine* identified this equality within baseball as being intrinsically tied to the American character.

---

[91] Giamatti, quoted in Deford, "A Gentleman and a Scholar," 98.

The assurance provided in the Declaration of Independence—that all persons are created equal—surely applies to baseball, for at a game, the magazine noted, "Banker and bricklayer, lawyer and common laborer" sit side by side, cheer with each other, talk equally with passion and knowledge about the game, and share stories of their heroes.[92]

Doris Kearns Goodwin observes that "a sense of camaraderie grew among Dodger fans that made the experience of going to Ebbets Field unforgettable."[93] The fellowship that fans experience at the ballpark is frequently grounded in their devotion to the home team, but it grows most immediately out of their participation in ballpark rituals. In particular, at Ebbets Field, as umpires would make an unfavorable call, a rag tag band would strike up a taunting round of "Three Blind Mice." When an opposing pitcher might be taken out of the game for a relief pitcher, the musicians might play the old favorite "Somebody Else Is Taking My Place." At such moments, the angry response by the opposing players intensified the bond that the Dodger faithful enjoyed. At the ballpark, Goodwin recalls that she "felt part of the invisible community of Dodger fans, linked by shared emotions and experience to thousands of strangers who, for a few hours, were not strangers at all."[94] Or in the words of Ray Kinsella, fans are not "just ordinary people"; instead, they are "a congregation."[95]

On the occasion when Goodwin attended the game with hundreds of others from her neighborhood in the annual "Rockville Centre Night" at Ebbets Field, she experienced a sense of community that was pure, both in terms of the shared

---

[92] Quoted in Ward and Burns, *Baseball: An Illustrated History*, 86.

[93] Doris Kearns Goodwin, *Wait Till Next Year* (New York: Simon and Schuster, 1998) 49.

[94] Ibid., 133.

[95] Kinsella, *Shoeless Joe*, 72.

bond with Dodger devotion and in terms of the familiarity and fondness for her daily playmates and neighbors. "It was as if my block, my school, my church had been snatched up and transported to a gigantic ocean liner for a trip to some fantastic land," she reflects. "I recognized all the people, of course, but they were not the same. The familiar setting of our lives, the context that we shared, had changed and, in changing, had imparted a different dimension to my existence. The invisible barriers dividing the natural compartments of my life had been dissolved, leaving me a resident of a larger world."[96]

The communal bonding fostered by baseball is common not only in relation to major league stars and their seasons, but also it characterizes players' and families' relationships throughout baseball, extending even to local youth leagues. "Baseball connects Americans with each other, not just through bleacher friendships and neighbor loyalties, but, most importantly, through generations," the poet Donald Hall muses as he considers why baseball enables fathers and adolescent sons to play catch. "When you are small, you may not discuss politics or union laws or profit margins with your father's friends, but you may discuss baseball. It is all you have in common because your father's friends do not wish to discuss the assistant principal or Alice Bisbee Morgan."[97] In a more specifically spiritual way psychiatrist James Lomax also remarks on the bonding potential of learning baseball from his father, who was both his first catcher and first coach. "In the 1950s," he recalls, "my dad taught me—mostly by what he (and we) did rather than what he said—that baseball, like religion throughout the centuries, was about intimate connections and attachments.

---

[96] Goodwin, *Wait Till Next Year*, 133–34.

[97] Donald Hall, *Fathers Playing Catch with Sons: Essays on Sport [Mostly Baseball]* (San Francisco: North Point Press, 1985) 49–50.

Almost every day after he would come home from work, we would play catch in out back yard." [98]

Not only does baseball provide an occasion for fathers to play catch with sons, whether with the fictive Kinsellas in *Field of Dreams* or typical families in both urban and rural America, it also provides an opportunity for family members to reconnect and to fulfill childhood dreams, as Tom Stanton experienced with his middle-aged brother and elderly father. Baseball attracts multiple generations because it bridges memory with play, blending experience with innocence: "They are the memories of a time," Giamatti muses, "when all that would be better was before us, as a hope, and the hope was fastened to a game."[99]

As one of Smart's dimensions of worldviewing, the social bonding of baseball occurs across familial generations, class differences, and ethnic distinctions. For individuals, as we have seen throughout this chapter, baseball reaches into the depths of self and provides a sense of personal identity. In a corresponding communal way, as Christopher Evans has suggested, baseball also "deals with matters of the soul."[100]

Baseball as American Civil Religion

Several years before he was elected commissioner of Major League Baseball, A. Bartlett Giamatti addressed the incoming class in 1984 at Yale University, where he was serving as president. Recognizing that they were a cross-section of the country—representing multiple regions, religions, ethnicities, and economic classes—he sought to articulate common elements in their experience before becoming Yalies. "Because

---

[98] James D. Lomax, "Opening Day," *American Journal of Psychiatry* 161/2 (February 2004): 224.

[99] Giamatti, *Take Time for Paradise*, 82.

[100] Evans, *The Faith of Fifty Million*, 10.

no single formal religion can embrace a people who hold so many faiths, including no particular formal faith at all," he said, "sports and politics are the civil surrogates for an America ever in quest for a covenant."[101] He perceived well the common faith among Americans: their allegiance to nation as an exemplar of freedoms and democracy, and their fascination with sports, even before their first attendance at a Harvard-Yale fall classic. After becoming commissioner, he worked on a monograph on baseball and American culture that was published posthumously as *Take Time for Paradise*. In it, he professed his belief that "sport is an instrument for vision, and it ever seeks to make the common—what we all see, if we look—uncommon. Not forever, not impossibly perfect, but uncommon enough to remain a bright spot in the memory, thus creating a reservoir of transformation to which we can return when we are free to do so."[102] Here in mythic and functional terms, he describes sport as a religion since it provides vision and transformation of the common to the uncommon, since it facilitates an escape from the tedium of reality into a celebration of alterity and possibility, and since it renders intimations of immortality, even if only in ritual or in record.

Throughout his excurses on utopia, Giamatti avers that leisure is more indicative of people's values than their work. Since they work to survive and since they play in freedom, he reasons, images of paradise have shaped much of Americans' mindsets, and they provide "a dream of ourselves as better than

---

[101] A. Bartlett Giamatti, (address to incoming freshmen, Yale University, New Haven CT, 1984); quoted in Frank Deford, "A Gentleman and a Scholar," *Sports Illustrated* 70/17, 17 April 1989, 94.

[102] Giamatti, *Take Time for Paradise*, 15.

we are."[103] So too baseball prompts us to consider that there is a time and place more nearly perfect than our present day.

Not only does baseball provide opportunities for envisioning a new way of being in the world and of viewing the world, it also takes into account the deep history of where we have been. In this regard, baseball "opens a portal to our past, both real and imagined, comforting us with intimations of immortality and primordial bliss," John Thorn propounds. "But it also holds up a mirror, showing us as we are. And sometimes baseball serves as a beacon, revealing a path through the wilderness."[104] Even when baseball's lore features the mythic feats of bygone heroes, it surveys paths to a new world, paths to "the Kingdom of Baseball," as Christopher Evans puts it, revealing "the game as a communal symbol of hope."[105] Baseball, then, is not merely "the game of our past, our nation's and our own," Thorn professes, "it is the game of our future, in which our sons and daughters take their places alongside us, and replace us. It reflects who we have been, who we are, and who we might, with the grace of God, become."[106]

This language of "the Kingdom of Baseball" resounds with the hope of the Social Gospel era, which coincided with baseball's early glory days. As leading theological proponents for the Social Gospel movement, Shailer Mathews and Washington Gladden believed that baseball aligned itself with the imperative to address the social ills of the day. Because baseball requires teamwork while demanding individual discipline and displaying a player's determination, baseball, they believed, could demonstrate the transformative power of

---

[103] Giamatti, *Take Time for Paradise*, 43.

[104] John Thorn, "Why Baseball?" in Ward and Burns, *Baseball*, 58.

[105] Evans, *The Faith of Fifty Million*, 48.

[106] Thorn, "Why Baseball?" 61.

the Kingdom of God. Yet the history of baseball in its institutionalized form of professional play has betrayed this mission to usher in the Kingdom or, at least, to provide a proleptic sample of the perfection signified by the Kingdom. Like the church which is the institutionalized form of Christianity itself, baseball has succumbed in various epochs of its history to racism, sexism, greed, exploitation of players, and triumphalism. Despite this failure of baseball to achieve various social ideals, it is nevertheless religious because it "offers a unique form of play, a chance to participate in a meaning and order beyond ourselves which satisfies mind, body, and soul," James Wall concludes. For "the kingdom of baseball, after all, is a gift as well as a task."[107]

As we have seen in the analysis of baseball using the six dimensions of worldviewing identified by Smart, baseball itself can be understood as a religion. But why, we must finally ask, is it distinctly American? One of the ways is that its myths appeal to the American mindset, which is often oriented to pastoral and utopian visions. Another is the identification of America's government as a democratic ideal with the game. Not only does this distinct alignment between baseball and democracy influence thinking about the relationship between politics and the game (as, for instance, in considering the establishment of the reserve clause and the granting of baseball's exemption from antitrust regulations), it also prompts the practice of ballpark rituals that express communal patriotism.

The sanctifying civic ritual that routinely consecrates baseball for American culture is the performance of the national anthem before games. Like powerful symbols that arise from a cultural need for condensing a social expression,

---

[107] James Wall, "The Kingdom of Baseball," *The Christian Century* 119/12 (5 June 2002): 36.

the performance of the national anthem emerged as a response to solidify the patriotism of baseball's players and fans. The first verifiable record of the national anthem having been played at a game was during the 1918 World Series between the Boston Red Sox and the Chicago Cubs. Performed as one piece among the patriotic songs played during the seventh inning stretch, "The Star Spangled Banner" was enthusiastically received by the crowd in Chicago. Although it had not yet officially been designated as the national anthem, "The Star Spangled Banner" would attain that recognition more than a decade later when Herbert Hoover would sign legislation designating it as the official anthem. During the period between the world wars, "The Star Spangled Banner" continued to be played on special occasions such as World Series games, opening day festivities, and fourth of July celebrations, but it was not routinely performed before regular season games until World War II, when, again, the need for public patriotic rituals generated the occasion for its play.[108]

A half century earlier, A. G. Spalding observed the tandem relation between warfare and baseball. "Ever since its establishment in the hearts of the people as the foremost of field sports, Base Ball has 'followed the flag,'" he noted. "It followed the flag to the front in the sixties [the Civil War], and received then an impetus which has carried it to half a century of wondrous growth and prosperity...and wherever a ship floating the Stars and Stripes finds anchorage today, somewhere on a nearby shore the American National Game is in progress."[109]

Although there is an alliance between baseball and the flag, as Spalding suggested, there is a sense in which baseball,

---

[108] Light, *The Cultural Encyclopedia of Baseball*, 474.
[109] A. G. Spalding, *America's National Game*, 14.

like religious traditions and communities, is separate and independent, for the antitrust exemption that was granted to baseball by the Supreme Court in 1922 effectively established—to borrow language from another court opinion—"a wall of separation" between the sport and the government. That image, of course, does not annul the frequent convergence of baseball and the government, with the president occasionally throwing out the first pitch of the season. Even that practice, however, does not dull the comparison between baseball's antitrust exemption and religions' formal separation from the state, for the president routinely has his photograph taken when attending church or when seeking the counsel of religious leaders. Even as the non-establishment clause in the Bill of Rights has assured the religious freedom of individuals and communities of faith, so too does the antitrust exemption for baseball secure its independence from federal supervision.

Conclusion

For millions of Americans, baseball has exercised a centering power that has shaped their worldview. Repeatedly, pundits have sought to explain baseball's "strangely powerful grip on the American psyche"[110] by considering its ability to provide escape, to exercise superiority, to pursue perfection, or to approach the sublime in its remarkable choreography. Reflecting on his own experience, Tom Stanton noted that "those who have never felt the sweet pull of baseball's gravity struggle to understand its hold on us [devout fans]."[111] The identification of baseball's power as the sweet pull of its gravity also suggests the rewarding and pleasant character of its strength. Somewhat similarly, former major league pitcher Jim Bouton said, "You spend a good part of your life gripping a

---

[110] Freedman, *More than a Pastime*, 10.
[111] Stanton, *The Road to Cooperstown*, 7.

baseball and in the end it turns out that it was the other way around all the time."[112] That reversal describes the character of faith as defined by theologian Paul Tillich, who specified that faith is the matter of being grasped by an ultimate concern. While one thinks that one might be groping for and clutching significant concerns, one discovers that the ultimate concern is so powerful, so overwhelming that it grasps one's very being, empowering one to reach out for other significant concerns and causes. One does not adopt a new faith or give up one's faith; instead, one's faith is a matter of deep direction that cannot be easily or abruptly uprooted or rerouted. In simple terms, one's faith shapes one's worldview. In the same way, being the faithful fan of a team, fervently *wanting* one's team to win, "is an attitude that is not under direct voluntary control." Personalizing matters in this regard, philosopher Thomas Senor suggests that a passionate fan consider the team that he or she typically roots against and then change, by sheer act of will, to become a fan of that team. The passions of fan allegiance, he concludes, are rooted so deeply in one's experience and psyche that a decisive volitional act will not change one's fervor, one's faith. "You can decide now to *act* like a fan," he avers. "You can cheer and tell people you are pulling for them, but you can't just choose to like them starting *now*."[113]

As exemplars of other players and fans, Bouton and Stanton articulate the grasp that baseball exerts on themselves. The inexorable pull of baseball as a denomination or form of civil religion is revealed in this inversion of expectation. Rather than choosing to become a passionate fan, baseball itself re-

---

[112] Jim Bouton, *Ball Four* (New York: MacMillan, 1970) 398.

[113] Thomas D. Senor, "Should Cubs Fans Be Committed?" in *Baseball and Philosophy: Thinking Outside the Batter's Box*, ed. Eric Bronson (La Salle IL: Open Court, 2004) 48.

verses matters, fervently gripping players and fans, enabling them to persevere through defeats and players' strikes and instilling hope for prolonging the game or season. In all of these ways baseball folds them into the heart of faith. "Baseball's appeal," Stanton concludes, "isn't complicated or confusing. It's about the beauty of a game; it's about heroes and family and friends; it's about being part of something larger than yourself, about belonging; it's about tradition—receiving it and passing it; and it's about holding on to a bit of your childhood."[114]

As effective as Bouton and Stanton are in identifying the fundamental power of baseball to exercise a distinct form of faith, the summons to that faith is supplied best by an evangelistic character in W. P. Kinsella's novel *Shoeless Joe*. Deleted from the film adaptation of the story is a vivid scene following Ray's return to Iowa with both Moonlight Graham and J. D. Salinger. One of the mystic players on the field of dreams and in the Kinsella's home is Eddie Scissons, the oldest living member of the Chicago Cubs' World Series team. Like Graham, he bridges past and present, playing with the old timers as the youthful version of himself while also interacting with the Kinsellas as an aged sage. Standing atop the bleachers and "looking for all the world like an Old Testament prophet on the side of a mountain," he delivers a sermon about the word of baseball, the word as baseball. Having elicited an accepting response from the Kinsellas, he proclaims, "Can you imagine walking around with the very word of baseball enshrined inside you? Because the word of salvation is baseball. It gets inside you. Inside me. And the words I speak are spirit, *are* baseball." At that point, W. P. Kinsella narrates, Eddie "shakes his head like a fundamentalist who can quote chapter

---

[114] Stanton, *The Road to Cooperstown*, 7.

and verse for every occasion."[115] Eddie continues with his oration:

> As you begin to speak the word of baseball, as you speak it to men and women, you are going to find that these men and women are going to be changed by that life-flow, by the loving word of baseball.
>
> Whenever the word of baseball is brought upon the scene, something happens. You can't go out under your own power, your own light, your own strength, and expect to accomplish what baseball can accomplish.

When believers then embody the word of baseball, they can speak its truth and hope because, as Eddie believes, "the word of baseball is spirit and it is life." [116]

Finally, Eddie testifies to the congregation of Kinsellas and the teams of old time players: "I've read the word, I've played it, I've digested it," he insists. "[I]t's in there! When you speak, there is going to be a change in those around you. That is the living word of baseball." [117] The cure for the illnesses of the world or the answers to its anxieties will not be found in the diagnoses of physicians or the prescriptions of their medicines. Instead, the cure, the answer, the hope is to be found in the word of baseball. "Praise the name of baseball," Eddie concludes. "The word will set captives free. The word will open the eyes of the blind. The word will raise the dead. Have you the word of baseball living inside you? Has the word of baseball become part of you? Do you live it, play, digest it, forever? Let an old man tell you to make the word of baseball your life. Walk into the world and speak of baseball. Let the word flow through you like water, so that it may quicken the

---

[115] Kinsella, Shoeless Joe, 192.
[116] Ibid., 192–93.
[117] Ibid., 193.

thirst of your fellow man."[118] For Ray, it is baseball that cures him, that sets him free—not only from the worries about making ends meet on the farm but from the guilt of severing ties with his father. It is baseball—with a field of dreams in the Iowa cornfield adjacent to the family home—that finally enables Ray to play catch with his catcher father, overcoming the alienation that had set in years before and experiencing the restoration of their filial bond.

For true believers, then, the word of baseball is the gospel of an American civil religion that finds safety and wholeness—completion and salvation—where the game begins and where it ends: at home.

---

[118] Kinsella, *Shoeless Joe*, 191–93.

6
Fusing the Spirits:
The Sacramental Power of Baseball

When baseball functions as a civil religion, its true believers—the passionate fans and players who shape their worldviews and daily routines around their devotion to the game—experience a kind of sacramental rejuvenation in the game itself. This salvific affirmation emerges out of the full fusion of the sporting and the spiritual, a blending that fascinates and orients the literary world of David James Duncan. In the review of Duncan's family epic *The Brothers K* shortly after its publication at the start of the 1992 baseball season, Frank Deford highlighted the novel's fusion of the spirits of fundamentalism and the national pastime. Beginning his review with a title melded from religion and baseball—"The Sermon on the Mound"—Deford struck the truth: "So much has been spouted—often piously or pretentiously—about our National Pastime as a sacred devotion that we should not be surprised when a book finally is written that deals with baseball and religion, paired. Baseball and religion are precisely the only two of our institutions that we regularly attach the defining adjective 'organized' to. We always referred to Organized Baseball and Organized Religion, but we never say Organized Business or Organized Football or Organized Journalism."[1]

Comparisons of organized baseball with organized religion have been made often in recent years by journalists such as Jack Smith[2] and Jim Murray,[3] as well as by several religious studies scholars including Chris Evans[4] and Peter Gardella.[5] Duncan's imaginative fusion of the organized worlds of baseball and religion in *The Brothers K* continued his exploration of the sporting and the spiritual, for in his first novel, *The River Why*,[6] Duncan ponders the metaphysical dimensions and implications of fly-fishing, especially as it is pursued and promised on a river in the Northwest. In *The Brothers K* Duncan proposes and plumbs a range of comparisons between religion and baseball fanaticism by explaining aspects of "organized religion" through baseball metaphors. Yet what distinguishes *The Brothers K* from other asserted comparisons of baseball with religion is that its fusion (of the spirits of baseball and religion) transcends[7] "*Organized*

---

[1] Frank Deford, "The Sermon on the Mound," *Los Angeles Times Book Review*, 5 July 1992, L3.

[2] Jack Smith, "Divine Rites," *Los Angeles Times Magazine*, 10 April 1986, 10.

[3] Jim Murray, "Wanted: Playoff Memories," *Los Angeles Times*, 9 October 1983, C1:1.

[4] Christopher H. Evans and William R. Herzog II, eds., *The Faith of Fifty Million: Baseball, Religion, and American Culture* (Louisville: Westminster John Knox Press, 2002).

[5] Peter Gardella, "Baseball Samadhi: A Yankee Way of Knowledge," *Books and Religion* 14/3 (September 1986): 15–16.

[6] It was the first work of fiction ever published (in 1983) by the Sierra Club. *The Brothers K* was David James Duncan's second novel.

[7] That transcendence is a dimension of depth or the ground of all being is an idea that recurs throughout the work of Paul Tillich. See, for example, his *Dynamics of Faith* (New York: Harper and Row,

religious denominations" and "*Organized* baseball teams" at every level: major league, minor league, little league, or even *church* league (softball).

In two more extensive and complex ways than the comparisons that align organized baseball with organized religion, *The Brothers K* thoroughly combines baseball and religion, suffusing the playfulness of one with the spirituality of the other. First, the story considers the kind of religious transformation that baseball provides in saving the life—in restoring its health and wholeness—of Hugh "Papa Toe" Chance. Secondly, it celebrates a kind of sacramental metaphysics that underlies even informal religion and ball games played on fields without fences.

The Players and Their Prayers

One of the initial ways that Duncan begins to fuse the spirits of baseball and religion is by conceiving and portraying characters who combine religious doctrine with baseball knowledge and who also blend religious piety with baseball fervor. In fact, it is through the prayers of players that we get an intimate view of their personal *con*fusion regarding the interplay between and similarity of baseball and religion.

In *The Brothers K* Hugh "Papa Toe" Chance is the father of four older boys and two younger twin girls. He is an unlucky former flame-throwing pitcher who, seemingly by fate rather than by chance (which, according to his surname, is his family heritage), has had his professional pitching hopes crushed by a mill accident that mangled the thumb on his pitching hand. But through a kind of mystical beneficence—a surgical gift

---

1957) for an introductory exploration of the idea, or his three-volume *Systematic Theology* (Chicago: The University of Chicago Press, 1967) (three volumes in one edition) for a more extensive examination of the idea.

from a yuppie physician whose contact with Hugh was re-initiated by a chance encounter—he undergoes a successful grafting operation that attaches his big toe—hence his new nickname—to his left hand, thus enabling him to grip and throw a variety of junk pitches. All of which motivates him in sentimental ways finally to make a comeback as "the stupid situation" reliever and pitching coach for a team called the Portland Tugs.

Even Laura "Mama" Chance, Hugh's wife, is portrayed as worrying about her religious love of baseball at times when she knows that she must follow her Adventist faith and its endorsement of a literalistic reading of the Bible, which offers little identifiable praise for baseball. As a teenager, Laura had turned to Seventh Day Adventists to assist her in escaping an abusive relationship with her father; yet her initial attraction to Hugh was occasioned by her own excitement for the game of baseball and appreciation of Hugh's talent in the sport. After she tells one of the wonderful stories about Hugh's baseball feats, she will "sometimes put on her Pious Face, sigh, and say, 'Sometimes I'm afraid I know baseball better than I know my own Bible.'" In fact, the last time that Kincaid, her youngest son and narrator of the novel, recalls her having said that, Everett, the oldest, agnostic son, had retorted that "God didn't even *own* a Bible, so the chances were He knew baseball better too."[8] Although she laughed, she squirmed and never again compared her memory for baseball with her knowledge of Scripture. Despite her enthusiastic support of the play and display of baseball for her husband and children, she could not tolerate the idea of playing ball on the Sabbath, much less

---

[8] David James Duncan, *The Brothers K* (New York: Doubleday, 1992), 31

could she accept the kind of the clubhouse rowdiness and crudeness that often accompany the game.

In addition to baseball-playing Papa Chance and baseball-loving Laura Chance, their sons also display various ways in which the spirits of the sport and religion intertwine. The eldest son Everett has apparently been an agnostic since birth. His expression of doubt, in fact, precipitates the Chance family's disruption. One evening he is given the unusual chance to offer the grace before the meal because his father, who normally had offered the blessing, had taken to performing late afternoon workouts following his toe-to-thumb transplant. Rather than following the family custom of listening to Papa offer grace before dinner, the family heard him thwacking fastballs against the side of a newly constructed pitching shed out back. On that pivotal evening Everett began his prayer: "Dear God if there is One"—an agnostic confession and invocation that prompted his mother to shriek and start to argue.[9]

Combining his questioning attitude with his devotion to baseball, Everett considers a kind of baseball Christology by identifying Jesus as one of Leo Durocher's poster boys, a super nice guy who finished *dead* last. As biblical proof Everett cites a text familiar to Adventists and recognizes the speaker, "the Lord God," as Jesus. Everett aligns the apocalyptic epigram in Revelation—"I am the Alpha and the Omega. The First—and the Last"—with Durocher's dictum: "Nice Guys finish last." While Everett expresses this agnosticism about the power of the divine, he does believe that baseball itself affords miracles, the possibility of moving from last to first, and he facilitates the occasion for his father's baseball salvation by contacting his

---

[9] Ibid., 168.

father's former coaches and the surgeon who eventually transplants the big toe.

Peter, the second son, also adopts a religious attitude toward baseball, although his perspective is derived from Asian religious traditions rather than Christianity. According to the youthful Kincaid, Peter reads many religious books, including the "Bog of Vod Geeta"—which is an accurate rendering of how Kincaid perceived his brother's immersion into and absorption by the Indian text. Possibly with greater baseball talent than even his father, Peter leads his high school team in hitting by adopting a Buddhist "no think" attitude toward pitches. In this attuned state of reflexiveness, Peter carries the team to the league championship and state tournament. But in a Buddhist sermon that he delivers at the sports banquet following his senior year, Peter shuns the MVP award, stunning the audience, and with a Buddhist sense of disdain for trophies, he renounces his playing of baseball ever thereafter. Although Peter went on to publish a scholarly analysis of Maharashtran poet-saints, he understood heresy or apostasy best in terms baseball, not religious dogmatics. Before the imposition of lights onto the roof at Wrigley Field, he remarked, "Nightfall is to the Cubs exactly what Charles Darwin is to the Christians."[10]

Irwin, the only son who followed past puberty the fundamentalist faith-hold of Seventh Day Adventism, is a lovable state champion javelin thrower who is the heartthrob of the Adventist teens, the Chance family, and the novel itself. Despite his fundamentalist inclinations, even Irwin has moments of blending piety and the national pastime. As a young boy, Irwin had owned a clear-glass statue piggy bank of Lou Gehrig. The money in the bank was special not only

---

[10] Ibid., 34.

because it was being saved for something special—whatever that might be—but also because of *how* it was being saved: in a little saint statue of one of the gods of baseball, the Iron Horse, Lou Gehrig. Kincaid recalls: "One time at church this missionary guy came and showed us films of himself baptizing big long rows of brown people called Laotians in an even browner river out in the Mission Fields [as opposed to the outfield] of wherever Laotians live, and Irwin got so inspired he took a hammer, smashed Lou Gehrig's head in, and gave it to the missionary. The money, that is."[11] With this simple sacrifice of the statue of a baseball hero for a religious cause, Irwin, potentially the most gifted hitter in the family, anticipates the greatest challenge to his faith—not the lure and love of baseball, but the war in Vietnam and its attempted depersonalization of the Viet Cong.

The final member of the Chance family is Kincaid, the narrator who perceives and intensifies the fusing of the spirits of religion and baseball. He is the one who remembers and retells the story about Irwin and the glass Lou Gehrig bank. Kincaid is also the one who identifies the magnitude of Irwin's church record for the number of consecutive Sabbaths for which he had memorized the assigned Bible verse. The grandeur of his streak—its seemingly unsurpassable character—can be comprehended, Kincaid figures, only when compared to Joe DiMaggio's hitting streak or perhaps the consecutive game recorded by the Iron Horse, whose fragile icon, of course, had held the coins that Irwin would give to missions.

Kincaid himself not only personifies the family heritage of chance, but he also stands for baseball in an aspiring way, for he is named after the AA minor league city in Oklahoma where

[11] Ibid., 20.

he was born during the time when his father's baseball dreams had flourished and his mother had begun to attend more diligently to Adventist ways. Since Kincaid is the only Chance brother whose name begins with the letter K, the title of the book prompts readers to wonder who then might be the other "K brothers." Although Kincaid's "K" brother(s) remain unspecified, they perhaps include the narrative spirit of baseball (with "K" as the abbreviation and expression of appreciation for the strikeout, which had been his youthful father's forte) and the repeated references to the classical literary narrators Franz Kafka and the Brothers Karamazov. It is also quite possible that the title of the book is fully metaphorical, suggesting the ways in which each of the Chance brothers—other than Kincaid himself, whose name already begins with that letter—somehow strike out with their family after striking out from home. Whatever the specific reference of the title, the brothers in this book are the sons of Hugh and Laura *and* of the spirits of baseball and religion, spirits whose fusion the story bears out.

Organized Baseball and Organized Religion

Although Duncan explores more fundamental relations between religion and baseball than the comparison, contrast, or conflict between their "organized" institutions, he begins the fusion of their spirits by setting up the parallels and polarities between organized religion and organized baseball. Initially, the pairing of baseball and religion is set out in Kincaid's recollection of watching a Saturday CBS-telecast of the Yankees and Indians during mid-summer 1960. On a typical Sabbath, Kincaid attended Sabbath school and listened to Elder Babcock's sermon. Yet the conflict between the two "organized" religions of Kincaid's parents—the conflict between Seventh Day Adventism and baseball, or at least some of its attendant (and often condoned) behavior—provoked an argument whose end had come when Hugh, who would not go to church with his wife and children and drank the first beer that his children had seen in his possession, told Laura that Jesus himself did not like churches. Kincaid recalls the event in the following way: "Papa stuck the Lucky in his mouth, lit it, and sent smoke streaming like a brush-off pitch, just past the side of her face." The cigarette was not an ordinary smoke. It was a Lucky Strike, the emblem of the chance "K" (if one is keeping score), an opportune strikeout by a pitcher. Then Hugh Chance took a chance to comment on Jesus' appreciation for Sabbath regulations about worship:

"As a kid, all [Jesus] did at church was argue with the rabbis," Papa said. "And as a grown man He went to church twice, if I remember right. Once to kick out the salesmen and ticket-scalpers, and once to cure that poor bastard with rabies."

"Well you *don't* remember right!" Mama shouted. "Christ founded a *new* church! You'd know that if you ever opened a Bible! And that new church—"

"And that *new* church," Papa cut in, his face suddenly savage, "is two thousand years old now, and every bit as senile and mean-spirited as the one that killed Him!"

"How *dare* you!" Mama hissed. "How dare you say such a thing in front of these children!"

"How dare *you* throw a fit in the name of *God* over one damned beer!"

"I've seen the hell one beer can lead to!" Mama cried.

"And *I've* seen the hell your friendly preacher calls salvation!" Papa roared. "Come unto me all ye Tea Totalin' prudes, bores and Bible-thumpers, bring your wallets and purses, and if your husband watches baseball

or sips a beer with a neighbor on *my* Sabbath pay day
then damn him to hell and whip his kids off to
Spokane!"

"*Satan!*" Mama gasped.[12]

With that argument, the polarities and conflicts in *The
Brothers K* crystallize, for the various disruptions and
reconciliations that ensue have to do with the tensive strength
and resiliency of both Bible-believing religion and modern
secular life as symbolized by baseball.

The experience of Kincaid's watching the game in such a
forbidden time frame—on the Sabbath during the time of
Pastor Babcock's weekly sermon—also shifts the sense of the
religious, the wholly other.[13] For if religious experience is one
in which a person gets in touch with that which is wholly other,
then the very viewing of Dizzy Dean and Pee Wee Reese on a
Sabbath morning in July creates a kind of experience that is
indeed different than any that Kincaid had previously known.
It is remote, transmitted mysteriously from afar, genuinely and
completely "Other." And this unique experience of alterity
germinates a kind of religious vision for Kincaid. In his liminal
state of watching the telecast on Sabbath day, Kincaid wonders
about the passion of St. Francis and the apathy of Roger Maris,
who remains uncanonized in Cooperstown by the "organized"
religion of baseball.

While watching the Yankees, Kincaid experiences a
certain premonition, a kind of prophetic vision, that the

---

[12] Ibid., 18.

[13] The idea that religion has to do with that which is "wholly
other" has laid the foundation for various comparative and historical-
cultural approaches to the study of religion. Its classic formulation is
by Rudolf Otto, *The Idea of the Holy*, trans. John W. Harvey, 2nd ed.
(London: Oxford University Press, 1950).

Yankees would come back from their two-run deficit and overtake the Indians. He also realizes (or at least in a revisionist way remembers) a certain disdain for Roger Maris. Although Kincaid usually enjoys watching home runs, he experiences a kind of dullness or boredom when Maris homers and methodically sweeps the base paths in a circular arc reminiscent of his looping swing. Unlike most baseball fans, Kincaid does not derive his disdain of Maris from a general contempt for the Yankees. But his distaste for Maris provokes a spiritual crisis. Because his disgust with Maris is so profound, he anticipates guilt for being unable to complete Jesus' command to love everyone, including Maris.

Adding to Kincaid's confusion about the manner and urgency of his need to love Maris is his conflation of Franciscan spirituality with San Francisco, the home of baseball's Giants. In particular, Kincaid imagines how St. Francis, following his transforming vision, had kissed the first leper whom he saw, only then to realize that the leper was actually Jesus. This revelation of the fused identity of Jesus with the leper prompted St. Francis to dedicate his life to the poor, the sick, and even animals. For Kincaid, the significance of this story about St. Francis is not so much historical—since the saint had been Catholic, not Adventist—as it is existential. Each Christian, he believes, must confront and embrace his or her own personal leper. In Kincaid's mind, the application of this story to his own experience is that he must get past his personal feelings of repulsion toward Maris. Like St. Francis kissing the leper, Kincaid might have to kiss the crown of Maris's crew-cut beneath his baseball cap.

For Kincaid, the challenge to kiss the leper Maris initially seems feasible as he envisions the prospect that, like the leper whose identity was revealed as Jesus to St. Francis, his kissing or licking of Maris's close-cropped hair might turn Maris into Jesus. Kincaid muses:

> But then again, what if the Jesus I turned Roger Maris into just went on playing right field for the Yankees? They'd be even more unbeatable! Everett [a Yankees hater] would *murder* me. And all the Catholics would be running around with a little ballplayer on a cross around their necks, and the ballparks'd fill with holy water and priests instead of ice-cream and peanut vendors. It'd be chaos, most likely. So I don't know. Hopefully the chance to lick it will never arise.[14]

Kincaid's christological melding of Maris with Jesus emerges out of his Sunday school indoctrination about the perfection of Jesus and his recognition of the mythic feats of Maris who is chasing the divine standard of Ruth's record.

The pairing of organized baseball and organized religion certainly provides an entree for us to begin an exploration of the full fusion of baseball and religion in *The Brothers K*. At several points in the story the comparison becomes more elaborate than this single con/fusion of Maris with Jesus, however religiously convoluted that might be, especially since their comparison results from Kincaid's desire to follow Jesus' command to treat undesirable persons in a particular way. Following the "Psalm Wars," which were fought on the Chance family's battlefield of the dinner table at grace time, Papa huddles his dissident sons together and lets them know that their mother's religious devotion should not be derided in comparison to the lure of baseball, not because baseball is less important than Laura's Adventist faith but because baseball itself is impure. According to Papa, the problems of churches are basically duplicated in professional baseball. Since he has

---

[14] Duncan, *The Brothers K*, 37.

attended churches and played in the minor leagues, he knows
the similarities between them. He explains:

> I went to church as a boy, too. Episcopal churches, most
> of these were, but they weren't all that different from
> Mama's. And I've been going to ballparks ever since. So
> based on experience, I'm telling you guys: baseball and
> churches have got the same boredom factor, the same
> hypocrisy, the same Pie in a Big League Sky, the same
> bone-hard benches, the same loudmouthed yo-yos mixed in
> among the decent fans in the pews, the same power-loving
> preacher/managers delivering the same damned "Do what I
> say or you're doomed" sermons. Hell, they've even got the
> same stinking organ music.[15]

Quite simply, Papa points out that the "organized" systems of
both religion (congregations and denominations) and baseball
(teams and leagues) are human, fallible, imperfect institutions,
not divine ideals above or beyond the fray of human life.

Despite this explanation, Kincaid protests that he still
prefers the play of baseball to the rituals of religion, and he
admits that although he might be wrong, he still prefers "Take
Me Out to the Ballgame" to "Stand Up for Jesus." Yet
knowing the rituals and rules of baseball and churches so well,
Papa concludes that it's easy to prefer the novelty of the
ballpark's song to the familiarity of the church's hymn. "But
wait'll you've heard it *five thousand times*," he retorts. "You're
gonna find out it's the same damned song."[16]

Papa knows that organized baseball and organized religion
are clones of the same human impulse, that "standing up for
Jesus" and standing up for the home team in the middle of the
seventh inning are functionally equivalent gestures of devotion

---

[15] Ibid., 180.
[16] Ibid.

and anticipation, of fidelity to a community and its beliefs and an affirmation of hope.

The comparison of organized baseball with organized religion suggests a deeper connection than the identification of their similar rituals, which intimate the metaphysical and mystical core of the game. Underlying Papa Chance's comparisons of baseball and religion are a sacramental dimension and a soteriological prospect of the game that render it religious. In *The Brothers K* two distinct events display this spiritual heart of the game. One celebrates the sacramental character of baseball in a narrative about the sheer joy in playing voluntary softball (baseball's simpler sibling) at a summer camp meeting; the other focuses on Papa's finding salvation—a restoration of health and hope—in learning to throw the Kamikaze pitch (his sons' innocent name for the spitball that he developed). While these two events link the fusion of the spirits of the sport and religion, they also perhaps reveal the heart of the novel—another possible identification of who "the Brothers K" are: Kincaid himself attempting to strike out his Sabbath school teacher at the summer camp meeting, and his father learning to throw the Kamikaze pitch for strike-outs.

Baseball as Sacrament

The lure and sacramental power of "baseball" as a game rise up in Kincaid's narration of the late afternoon softball game at camp meeting during a prior summer. The lure toward the confrontation between pitcher Kincaid and his Sabbath school teacher Brother Beal is love and its adolescent intimation, infatuation. Having a crush on Brother Beal's fiancée *Sister* Nancy Durrel, who assisted Brother Beal in his Sabbath school instruction each week, the adolescent Kincaid decided to make a pitch to her, rather than to play the game, in the last inning.

In his effort to perform heroically for Sister Durrel, whose smile radiated a beauty perhaps reserved only for the innocent, Kincaid tried to outwit Brother Beal, a former player for Walla Walla Adventist College and subsequently for a semi-pro team until his refusal to play on the Sabbath got him kicked off the team.

In baseball, deceit is a part of play, not a sin as such. But illegal moves and pitches are not allowed, even within Kincaid's deceitful desires. According to the softball rules for summer camp, Kincaid knew, fast pitches were illegal, and overhand pitches were even worse. Even so, Kincaid recalls:

> I threw one anyhow. Winding up fast to increase the surprise, I blazed a perfect strike in there—and Beal's grin *did* vanish. The problem was, so did the softball. The problem was, Beal's body coiled and uncoiled in a split second, there was an eerie *boaf!*, and that flat blob of a ball just disappeared. He obliterated it. The speed of the illegal pitch only made matters worse. I turned to the sky and started looking, finally spotting an ugly little grass-stained moon, still rising in the company of a flock of swallows, high over a meadow so far beyond anything we'd ever considered "outfield" that it was like something out of the Book of Revelation had happened. The ball flew so high and far it made our diamond and players and the entire afternoon's playing seem as if a bunch of pygmies had been shooting marbles on a rug and calling that a ballgame. But it was what happened after the ball returned to earth and bounded on into a lily pond that changed my mind about Beal for good.[17]

The flight of the ball beyond the bounds of the field and into the infinite light of the sky suggests the transcendent trajectory and distance of the hit. And the ball itself so fully

---

[17] Ibid., 70.

blended with nature, resembling an earth-stained moon and being swallowed into the flock of evening birds, that it suggested an apocalyptic image from the Bible. The ethereal reach of Beal's hit also exacted sufficient punishment for Kincaid's illegal pitch, but the ebullient nature of Beal's celebration, which defied the strictures of Adventist decorum, transformed the occasion from one of defeat to one of vicarious victory, yielding a spiritual joy incipiently akin to Resurrection's reversal.

Despite the ethereal flight of the ball and Kincaid's immediate humiliation in front of Sister Durrel, he simultaneously perceived the beauty of the human and the mythic power of protest in play(fullness) in Brother Beal's reaction:

> About the time he reached second base, a few of us began to notice something odd about the Brother's baserunning.... He wasn't running the bases at all. He was *dancing* them. Our first reaction was to gawk. There stood our big pious weenie of a Sabbath School teacher on second base, eyes closed, body motatin', zonked faced impossibly unembarrassed as his hands mojoed a solo on a sax no more visible than the Holy Ghost. Then he stepped off the bag, swivel-hipped his way toward third.[18]

Somewhat similar to the Dervish's dance in quest of mystical union, the uninhibited, spontaneous display of joy by Brother Beal represents a kind of sacramental event. He exhibited the jazz of joy, a visible performance of the invisible grace of the Holy Ghost.

That exuberant, physical expression of joy in the game revealed a deeper metaphysical or mystical connection with the wonder and otherness of the divine spirit. And in his

---

[18] Duncan, *The Brothers K*, 70.

perception of this sacramental event, Kincaid himself experienced a conversion from an attitude of envy to one of admiration. Kincaid confesses:

> What finally made it impossible for me not to like the man was how right out there on the Adventist basepaths, right in front of eighty or ninety of the kind of pious spectators who spent their every Sabbath if not their entire lives trying to forget the existence of things like butts, Beal's buns were trying to light a fire by friction inside his jeans; they were gyrating like a washing machine with its load off balance; they were thrashing against his pants like two big halibut against the bottom of a boat. And the wonderful thing, the amazing thing, was how once the older audience got over the shock of it, they began to look amused at, then fascinated by, and finally downright grateful toward his writhing reminder that yes, buns did exist, and yes, every one of us owned not one but two of the things, and yes, like the God who created them in His Image, they did indeed move in mysterious ways.[19]

By dancing the base paths and celebrating with his body, Brother Beal contravened the Gnostic principle that matter is evil or unreal. Instead, Beal's actions affirmed the physicality and goodness of creation, and they suggested that with their bodies humans can extol the wonders of creation and, by extension, the magnificence of God.

Brother Beal's running or mojoing around the bases, however, could be accomplished because of how hard he clobbered the ball. The ball indeed had flown beyond the outfield, beyond the territory even considered to be beyond the outfield, and it had landed finally in a pond. Without remarking on its descent, Kincaid did comment on its location: "Meanwhile the sun was sinking, and the softball was floating

---

[19] Ibid., 70–71.

serenely among the lilies of the pond until *kerrfloosh!* Dougy Lee Babcock dove in after it. And the Elder himself—our stern umpire—had turned so crimson watching Beal's stern that his face looked like a big fat painted brush trying to add its frantic scarlet to the sunset to hurry on the Sabbath, since once Sabbath began, dancing would become a sin and he could order Beal to stop."[20] Drawing upon the image of lilies in the field found in the Gospel of Matthew, Kincaid conjured up images of the ball itself neither toiling nor spinning—of the game itself being oblivious to work and worry, even to whether or not the sun had set and Sabbath had begun.

"But it wasn't Sabbath—not yet it wasn't," Kincaid recalled, which meant that Beal's dancing and prancing for Sister Durrel could hardly be contained, even by the base path. In fact, Elder Babcock, acting as umpire, applied the rule in fundamentalist fashion and called Beal out, not for dancing, but for straying from the straight path between the bases. Then, Kincaid remembered:

> The sky got so red and the light so golden that I couldn't even look at [Sister Durrel], she was so pretty, and all over the ballfield kids were collapsing from over-laughing as, far off in the pond water, Dougy Lee Babcock surfaced with a lily pad on his head, shouting tiny, jubilant shouts and looking like a chip off the old Elder as he raised the dripping ball aloft like the newly baptized pate of some saved sinner, while Beal waltzed, a whole world away, onto home plate, and kept waltzing on it throughout the waves of wild cheering and applause.[21]

The event was sacramental and transformative. It was revelatory and inspirational. It elicited a seeming cosmic delay

---

[20] Ibid., 71.
[21] Ibid.

and display of the sunset in order to heighten the light-filled, sensuous, human, and sacramental character of the event. Indeed, the sacrament of witnessing any clobbered ball fly beyond the liminal reaches of the field and bob between the lily pads (so that even the obstinate agnostics will note its sacramental promise of baptism) supersedes the regimented restrictions of an organized approach to religion and baseball. In the frozen moment of the ball's flight and landing, the cosmos smiled, delaying the full-setting of the sun until Beal himself had gyrated, "motated," and "mojoed" the dance of divine ecstasy for having hit the ball out of this world and into the next, thus marking some way to traverse the two—even while leaving the straight and narrow base paths as defined by the Elder umpire of the organized religion. The sacramental moment came without the sanction of organized religion or organized baseball. The sacramental character of the event emerged from its folk ways, from the mythic elements attached to its *un*organized, illegal origin. It came on an illegal pitch during the liminal moment while the sun was sinking into Sabbath's rising.

The Transformative Power of Baseball

The religious significance of baseball extends beyond the kind of dogmatic and metaphoric connections that Duncan specifically identifies.[22] The religious significance of baseball is that, as surely as Seventh Day Adventism can offer a way of

---

[22] An autobiographical account that attributes a similar sort of salvific power to baseball can be found in the brief reminiscence of J. Anthony Lukas, "Surrogate Family," *Birth of a Fan*, ed. Ron Fimrite (New York: Macmillan, 1993) 150–59 in which he attributes a restorative, religious power to the Yankees of the 1950s and 1960s. A confessional analysis of his reflection is part of the final chapter of this book.

purpose, acceptance, and wholeness to the formerly child-molested Laura, so too baseball can transform the body and soul of her unlucky, Lucky Strike chain-smoking husband Hugh. His conversion from the sullen, sulking, nicotine-stained mill-hand to a drug-free father starts with an appeal from his son Kincaid, who urges him to *love* baseball like the way Kincaid's speech-impaired Sabbath school classmate Vera loves the Lord and expresses her faith. Weekly, Kincaid pointed out, she offered heartfelt prayers with malformed words that exposed her soul and human limitations, despite the laughing of her classmates at her nasal attempt to pronounce words clearly.

After the twelve-year-old Kincaid criticized his father for smoking, for having given up to the rotten string of bad luck that had brought him a limp left (pitching hand) thumb and no disability compensation or injury settlement from the paper mill where he worked, his father punched him so hard in the eye that he began to bleed in his mouth. Aghast that he had hurt his son and truly repentant for his abusive act, Papa begged Kincaid to tell him what to do to make it up to him. At first, Kincaid said nothing because he was afraid that he would start to sob or choke on blood if he opened his mouth to speak. From some unknown depth, however, the words began to form and erupt with the plea that his father fight past his disdain for the mill where he worked and to pursue what he loved—baseball. "All I want is for *you* to fight, Papa," he had concluded. "To fight to stay alive inside! No matter *what*."[23] With this moment of testimony and personal appeal, Kincaid shares the gospel—proclaiming the restorative power of baseball and imploring his father to accept the challenge to love baseball and fight for it and for himself.

---

[23] Duncan, *The Brothers K*, 99.

Having heard truth in the challenge from his son, after work the next day Hugh ran four miles, as he did every day thereafter. The unlucky pitcher who had thrown strikes now threw away his Lucky Strikes. Shortly thereafter he erected a year-round pitching shed in order to allow him to throw hard, not for the purpose of starting a comeback, but to light the first flicker in the fight to regain the meaningfulness and joy of throwing hard strikes. As Papa told his youngest son, "'Don't think of it as baseball, Kade. Call it my hobby, or some weird kind of worship maybe. Call it psalmball, or shedball, or thumball if you like. But remember it's not baseball. It's not a comeback."[24]

Certainly the wild flings that plagued the "shedball" throwing prevented the Chance boys from thinking that their father could really make a comeback. Although the recognition of salvation might be sudden, the fullness of its experience can be delayed, even in evangelical families of Adventists. The restoration of wholeness is often not an instantaneous miracle; it often takes work, discipline, rehabilitation, for full health to be restored. So, too, the process of restoring Papa's thumb and pitching control by finagling an agreement with a creative orthopedic surgeon was a long process whose specific path was not envisioned in its beginning.

Papa's conversion—his willingness to follow Vera's model of protesting one's own physical limitations and fighting to exercise life itself—was dramatic. Among other things his absence from the dinner table created a vacuum that needed to be filled: In his absence the children started to rotate the chore of saying the blessing before the evening meal. And it was on the occasion of Everett's first opportunity to say grace in Papa's absence that he questioned the existence of the God.

---

[24] Ibid., 113.

Charging him immediately with blasphemy, his mother soon thereafter tried to excommunicate him, Peter, and Kincaid from the family in order to adhere to the strictures of her Seventh Day Adventist convictions and to promote their advantages to Irwin and her twin daughters. The process of Papa's salvation, however, disrupted the family, leaving a "graceless" hole that only Adventist preconceptions could adequately fill.

Conclusion

Although *The Brothers K* is not primarily a novel about baseball,[25] but about a family whose passions include organized baseball and organized religion, it understands and expresses life in the fusion of the spirits of play and devotion that often get institutionalized in baseball and religion. *The Brothers K* captures baseball fever and religious fervor at several different levels of competition. It is fascinated with the major league level in a true fan's absorption in watching the late innings of a telecast on CBS by Dizzy Dean and Pee Wee Reese of a Yankees-Indians game in the glorious Yankee summer of 1960. It is enthralled with AAA baseball from the time of Hugh and Laura's first date to see a Pacific Coast League game to that of Papa "Toe" Chance's amazing comeback with the Portland Tugs. It celebrates the thrill of baseball hopes at the high school level, remembering Papa's youthful exploits on the

---

[25] The book is not without its baseball errors. Despite the precision and vividness of description of the 1960 Sabbath day game between the Indians and the Yankees, Duncan failed to check from which side of the plate Moose Skowron batted. He correctly recalls Skowron's power to right center field, but Skowron batted right handed, not left, as the book narrates. This little error, however, tabulates as a mid-season, mid-game miscue rather than a Buckneresque bobble of mythic proportions at the Day of Judgment.

mound and watching Peter excel at second base in the second Chance generation of all-state stars. The story even captures a sense of joy that comes from playing baseball at a semi-professional level with an armed forces team during the Korean War. But most importantly, the story grasps the salvific and sacramental power of baseball itself in the "pick-up," playground level of softball at summer religious camp and in the backyard variety of throwing strikes against a mattress on the wall of the garage.

The sense that baseball is either mystically or metaphysically significant finally causes the story to cohere, although the novel's length and diversity of story lines occasionally challenge credulity. Nonetheless, the impression that baseball is connected to human destiny is articulated in one of the opening segments of the novel and pervades the story. A letter from G. Q. Durham, then manager of the Kincaid (Oklahoma) Cornshuckers—supposedly a AA farm team of the Washington Senators in the late 1950s—to Everett Chance, then eleven years old, reflects on the convergence of baseball and religion: "You, me & your papa are 3 of the tiny percentage of souls on this miserable earth who've figured out that playing ball is the highest purpose God ever invented the human male body for. The rub is, once you've known & done it what you go through when you lose it is a death, pure and simple."[26]

Although Durham starts out by indicating that baseball is connected to some divine purpose, he ends up fusing the spirit of baseball with religion in a more significant way. Baseball is not merely the highest purpose or goal for men; it is, in fact, a

---

[26] Duncan, *The Brothers K*, 12.

kind of wholeness unto itself. It provides a kind of salvation; it becomes one's life, one's health, and one's well-being and whole being so that its loss results not in the mere deprivation or degradation or decimation of a game—but in death of self.

7
Now and There, Here and Then: Kinsella's Millenarian World of Baseball

Among his many stories about baseball, W. P. Kinsella repeatedly employs apocalyptic sensibilities of time, fusing past and future into an experience of presence that C. H. Dodd, the British biblical scholar at mid-century, called "realized eschatology." Time is no more. The past is present, embedded in events and ideas, and embodied in the lives of persons and institutions. Simultaneously, the end time is present even now, not fully, but proleptically. Without past or future separate from one's current experience, the final days are *now*: Judgment is not delayed; it is rendered and binding in the moment. Obviously, Dodd adapted an existentialist perspective on time and judgment as he developed the idea of realized eschatology.[1]

In Kinsella's baseball world of magical realism, time stands still, with past and future present now in ways that make the past and future indistinguishable in the moment. The possibility for this fusion of time is articulated by the father of Gideon Clarke, the narrator of *The Iowa Baseball Confederacy*, Kinsella's novel of 1986. "It is a fact there are cracks in time," the elder Clarke assured his son on more than a few occasions.

---

[1] C. H. Dodd, *The Parables of the Kingdom*, 3rd ed. (London: Nisbet, 1950) especially chaps. 1 and 5.

He described these breaks or openings as "weaknesses— fissures if you like—in the gauzy dreamland that separates the past from the present."[2] *The Iowa Baseball Confederacy* is conceived on this premise, for Gideon Clarke sets out to prove that which has been revealed to him and his father, that all-stars from a league known as the Iowa Baseball Confederacy played a 2,000 inning exhibition game in 1908 with the Chicago Cubs, a team featuring such greats as Mordecai "Three Finger" Brown and baseball's immortalized double-play combination: Tinker to Evers to Chance.

Although the prospect for exploring the temporal, historical, and revelatory themes in *The Iowa Baseball Confederacy* is alluring, two of Kinsella's other works blend baseball and millenarian themes in more explicit ways: "The Last Pennant before Armageddon," a story that introduces Kinsella's 1984 collection *The Thrill of the Grass*, and his novel *Shoeless Joe* (1982), on which the film *Field of Dreams* was based.

The repeated failure of the Cubs to win the National League pennant since 1945, despite the continuing faithfulness of their fans, fueled Kinsella's prophetic story, "The Last Pennant before Armageddon." In it, Kinsella associates the Cubs' drive for the pennant with more significant theological issues and images of Final Judgment than one suggested by the kerygmatic recognition that Grace was the constant feature in the Cubs' lineup during the 1990s. And in one of those seasons, Grace was joined on the opposite side of the diamond by Vance Law. Yet not even the infield anchors of Law and Grace could propel the Cubs to a millenarian kingdom.

It should not be too surprising that baseball and the kind of persistent hope associated with Cubs' fans have theological

---

[2] W. P. Kinsella, *The Iowa Baseball Confederacy* (Toronto: Collins Publishers, 1986) 7.

parallels or implications. Author Tom Boswell has noted the kind of metaphysical charter accorded to baseball as he has given two of his books titles that suggest religious significance or ultimacy of baseball itself: *Why Time Begins on Opening Day* and *How Life Imitates the World Series.* And connections between the Cubs and theological themes were frequently noted by popular cartoonist Jeff MacNelly. In one of his daily strips of *Shoe*, MacNelly has Skylar, the student nerd, carry on box-seat chatter with Shoe. Sitting in the front row of Wrigley Field stands, Skylar remarks, "Of course the Cubs will someday win the World Series! It's only *logical.*" Without batting an eye, Shoe turns to his companion, looks down his beak, and responds: "Skylar, the concept of the Cubs winning the World Series is only *theo*logical."[3]

For half a century, the faithfulness of Cubs' fans and their refusal to concede the loss of hope have provided a cultural measure for the focus on the unrealizable ideal, a utopian event, a manifestation of a Kingdom which is not of this world. Cubs' fans yearn for the final validation and reward that they suppose will be afforded by a World Series Championship; yet they constantly exemplify some degree of suffering often associated with perpetual torment. Kinsella, however, does not make his story an apologue, for he contends that the primary purpose of story telling is to entertain, not to provide some esoteric insight into the structure of reality, the nature of human relationships, or prospects for the future. Many of his stories, Kinsella notes, deal with the theme of magic, so much so that Kinsella himself has been accused of believing in magic. He could only wish, for example, that dinner dishes would spontaneously wash and rinse themselves as they do for Gideon Clarke in *The Iowa Baseball Confederacy.* But Kinsella contends

---

[3] Jeff MacNelly, *Shoe*, Los Angeles *Times* (7 March 1990) E6.

that his stories often include elements of that which is mysterious or magical, especially with respect to time, because they are elements of entertaining stories.[4]

Despite Kinsella's reticence to emphasize a metaphysical or mystical dimension in "The Last Pennant before Armageddon," there is a causal—albeit coincidental—connection between the eschatological orientation and the entertaining character of the story. The idea for the story came to Kinsella when a person called him on a radio talk show and suggested the possibility of his writing a story about deceased Cubs' fans who pleaded with God to let the Cubs finally win a pennant and the World Series.[5] The story line is simple and its cast of

---

[4] W. P. Kinsella, introduction to *The Thrill of the Grass* (New York: Penguin Books, 1984) x–xi.

At this point, I must also make two parenthetical points, both of which make further connections between theology—or religious experience—and the kind of entertaining intention that Kinsella exemplifies. First, I wonder whether or not the appeal of magic and mystery has to do with human yearnings for the Other, with human fascination *with*, if not inclination *toward*, the Other, toward the divine. Secondly, I appreciate the clarity with which Kinsella perceives the entertaining purpose of story telling. For the etymology and function of entertainment, as the noted anthropologist Victor Turner has pointed out (Victor Turner, *The Anthropology of Performance* [New York: PAJ Publications, 1988] 41), are potentially religious. The word "entertainment" comes from the French words *entre* and *tenir*, meaning "to hold between." What entertainment does, then, is quite like what religion does; it provides a means or a location for a liminal experience, one in which one moves beyond the normal edges of reality and experiences the Other without completely or permanently severing connections with the world. Through the liminal experience, then, one is enabled to return to the regular world with a fresh perspective, yet informed by the experience in the "held between" or "entertained" space.

[5] Kinsella, introduction to *Thrill of the Grass*, xi.

characters small. The wonder of the story is generated by its artful telling and the twist in the plot that shifts the reader's expectations—perhaps much like Final Judgment itself. Unlike the legend in which Faust sells his soul to the devil in order to gain the thrill of victory over a temporal and sometimes pernicious foe, Kinsella constructs his story with a twist in the temptation: The Cubs' manager, Al Tiller (nicknamed the Hun), does not meet temptation in a stealthy or selfish way, for he is an honorable man whose sole desire is "to manage his baseball team in an honourable manner."[6] He confronts temptation not in an effort to secure victory for the Cubs; he must choose between maintaining his honor and *allowing* the Cubs to meet their seeming destiny of winning a pennant for the first time in half a century.

Several other colorful characters provide the background and context for his dilemma. Chester A. Rowdy, the independent and eccentric "new" owner of the Cubs, had gained his fortune by "discovering a unique worm deep in an Alabama swamp, a worm that drew fish to it the way the back of one's neck draws mosquitoes."[7] With a *savoir faire* that defies baseball logic, Rowdy hires Tiller, a career-losing manager—in fact, with the worst won-lost record of any manager—to direct the Cubs. And when Tiller wonders aloud why he, as "the dumbest manager in baseball" (according to reports in a major sports publication), had been chosen to tend to Wrigley Field's harvest, Rowdy replies, "Nobody will expect much of you, will they? If something good happens it will be a surprise."[8] For Rowdy himself, low expectations had been a way of life since early childhood, when his father, as he puts it, "figured some

---

[6] W. P. Kinsella, "The Last Pennant before Armageddon," in *The Thrill of the Grass* (New York: Penguin Books, 1984) 4.
[7] Ibid., 5.
[8] Ibid., 6.

day I might steal something without gettin' caught; that was the highest expectation anybody had for me."[9]

The other interfacing character in the story is Tiller's unnamed first love, unnamed because his passion for her still makes the calling of her name too painful. When he had been a minor league infielder at Little Rock, he had fallen passionately in love with the mayor's daughter who, as the season's end approached, announced her need for independence and fled to college in the East. There she met a Harvard pre-law student who raced "funny little boats" and, in Tiller's opinion, had the audacity to call the activity a sport. Shortly before Christmas she married him. Crushed by the loss of his love, Tiller became engaged to one of his childhood sweethearts—a good but plain woman. Shortly before their marriage he learned of the failure of his first love's marriage, and he rendezvoused with her—experiencing once again the intense passion that had raged during the previous season. But Tiller chose to do the honorable thing: to be faithful to his fiancée with whom he then established a stable if unimaginative marriage that has lasted thirty years. Tiller also knows that a few years after his marriage his first love contracted leukemia and died.

With unlimited capital playfully tossed toward three all-star free-agent third basemen, Rowdy constructed a team that appeared to be headed for a winning season, even the pennant. All that Al Tiller must do is let the players play. In June following a loss in St. Louis, Al returned to his hotel room and listened to "Talking Baseball," a radio call-in show. Among the customary cast of unusual callers was someone who claimed to be a blind archangel and who then delivered a prophecy that the Cubs would win the pennant that season but that it would be the last pennant before Armageddon. The next time that the

---

[9] Ibid., 6–7.

Cubs played in St. Louis, Tiller returned to the hotel following the broiling game in Busch Stadium and found no real escape from the torrid August heat and viscous humidity, circumstances upon which he blamed his sleep difficulties hours later.

That night, he first dreamed the apocalyptic dream that returned for six consecutive nights, with only the seventh night providing rest. In contrast to the biblical story about God having created the world and all therein in six days followed by the Sabbath of rest, the dreams about this dark New World at the end of time occur at night, in darkness, a counterpoint to the very light of Creation. Tiller's nightmarish inversion of the pattern of Creation, with six nights of torment about destruction preceding his night of rest, also certifies the reversal of perfection that had characterized Creation. Unlike the single six-day sequence of divine activity in Creation, the pattern of six nights disrupted by the dream followed by a seventh undisturbed recurred throughout the remainder of the season. Until the night before the decisive playoff game, the dream had no significant variations other than a rotation of the petitioners who plead with God on behalf of the Cubs.

Tiller, however, was not a religious man, not a person inclined to become or be selected a prophet. Quite the contrary: he had always considered petitionary prayers to be an exercise in self-centered wish fulfillment. He recalled that when he had been a child in Oklahoma his mother had dragged him to revival services. And several years later, his girlfriend, who was then quite devout, had explained basic Christian beliefs to him. But he dismissed the dogmas as being unbelievable by anyone past puberty.

After the first night of the dream, Tiller offhandedly mentioned it to his pitching coach, who laughingly urged the manager to wish for better starting pitching in order to relieve a tired bullpen crew. That night, a pitcher who had not gone more than five innings all year, pitched a four-hit complete game. Alarmed by the coincidence, Tiller never again mentioned the dream or its haunting replays to anyone.

Scared by a mysterious force in the dream and curious about the various biblical references to Armageddon, Tiller was the first patron through the doors of the Chicago Public Library when it opened on the morning after the sixth night in the first cycle of dreaming. Scouring through lexicons and concordances, he identified every biblical reference to Armageddon and learned its significance: "*The last struggle of the forces of good and evil against each other. A clash of God's truth opposed to Satan's error. To take place on Judgment Day. The end of the world as we know it.*"[10]

The regular form of the dream started with Tiller sitting on an observation balcony similar to a surgical theater. Yet there did not seem to be walls around him or the others, merely sheets of white light that varied in degrees of transparency and translucence. On the set opposite his own position, an old white-haired, white-bearded, stern looking man sat behind a desk with a white marble top. "His clothing was right out of the Old Testament," Tiller realized, "flowing robes of ice-blue lined with material of flamingo-pink colour." In front of the desk of this old man, five ordinary people dressed in modern clothing sat in a semi-circle. "'Please God,' the man furthest away from Tiller was saying, 'we'd like you to arrange for the Chicago Cubs to win the pennant this year.'"[11] Although Tiller understood the unreality of the dream, he recognized that all of the persons around the desk were

---

[10] Ibid., 12.
[11] Ibid., 9.

deceased baseball fans, each in turn beseeching God on behalf of the Cubs.

On the sixth night of the dream in each of its cycles, God finally responds to the variety of petitioners who plead the Cubs' case: "'I appreciate your interest,' God said. 'I want to assure you that I hold the Chicago Cubs in highest esteem. I have listened to your entreaties and considered the matter carefully from all angles. I am aware of how long it has been since the Cubs have won a pennant. I think that you should know that when the Cubs next win the National League Championship, it will be the last pennant before Armageddon.'"[12]

Horrified by the solitude to which his new vision condemned him—for if he should tell the press about his revelation he felt that he would be locked up for psychiatric observation while someone else would receive the glory of directing the Cubs to a pennant-clinching playoff victory—Tiller considered trying to lose the pennant in order to save the world, especially since the current political crises in Sri Lanka had provided a staging ground for a military conflict between the super powers. His agony reached its climax the night before the decisive playoff game with the Dodgers, a sixth night in the cycle of his dreaming. Desiring above all a peaceful night's rest, Tiller instead experienced a new level of torment in the nightmare. This time, the final petitioner, a woman, was not a stranger, but his first love who, like the previous petitioners, urged God to let the Cubs win the pennant. In the dream Tiller saw again the beauty of her lips and the love in her eyes that had caused him to treasure her identity deep within his own heart.

---

[12] Ibid., 12.

In the reality of the pennant race, in the season's decisive game with the score tied 2-2 in the bottom of the ninth and with his ace Eddie Guest on the mound, Tiller watched the Dodgers' hitters make two outs before fighting off a score of strikes and getting two runners aboard by walks. Making a trip to the mound, he inquired about his pitcher's stuff, while Fireman of the Year "Bullet Boyd" waited warm in the bullpen. The catcher said that Eddie still had "everything but the curveball." Weighing love against duty, passion against honor, Tiller advises, "Don't throw the curve," before sloughing back toward the dugout, prepared to suffer. *C'est fini.* So the story ends.

Fully engaged, we are left in the lurch, left straining toward the anticipated action at home plate, an action that we must complete in accord with our understanding of passion and possibility, of honor and justice. As in cases of Final Judgment in "realized eschatology," the future is present even as memories are informing who we are and what we should do. We are called upon to make the judgment now, a judgment that certainly affects others but ultimately reveals who we are, what values we hold, what courage we exercise. Confronted by the need to make a decision, we encounter a theological twist about final judgment: We must complete the act of writing the story of the world, the baseball world; but it is our story. And by the act of our writing, or supplying the ending to the game between the Cubs and Dodgers, we determine the outcome—and judge ourselves, even in the final scene.

The story is entertaining—especially to baseball fans and, even more, to Cubs' fans. But if in entertainment we are transported to a liminal occasion in which we are able to taste—if not fully ingest—the Other, then what is it that we have here tasted? What is it that we have sampled in the entertainment that enables us to savor the world differently or to evaluate some of its experiences in new ways? I suggest that there are at least three effects that emerge from our entertainment with these stories of hope for a Cubs' pennant.

First is the matter of believing, of exercising non-rational confidence, while knowing that a kind of scientifically verifiable knowledge of the outcome is not possible. The matter of belief lies at the heart of Al Tiller's perception of his dreams as revelation or delusion. For during the final Cubs' games of the season in St. Louis, he had called the radio show "Talking Baseball," and prior to going on the air he had inquired of the host about the archangel's prophecy three months earlier. The host did not recall the caller or the conversation! Had Tiller merely dreamed about the archangel too? Were his dreams the result of anxiety and stress about guiding the Cubs so near to the pennant, yet expecting them to fall short? Were they his unconscious preparation to deal with the failure to win the pennant? Why would the unreligious Tiller be convinced of their revelatory authenticity and power? Are we, as fans who have watched the Cubs swing so near and far, from the Durocher collapse of 1969 to the Padres' prayerful uprising in 1984 (coincidentally, the year in which Kinsella published "The Last Pennant before Armageddon") to the most recent post-season hibernations in Candlestick in 1989, in Atlanta at century's end, and even at home against the Marlins in 2003—are we open to or convinced of the mysterious character of reality? Are we concerned with the issue of "How Life Imitates the Pennant Chase"?

A second effect is that images of fulfillment, even for the seemingly secular rituals of baseball, are informed by—if not adapted from—the eschatological imagery of biblical literature. Although we might be living in a post-ecclesiastical age, ours is one in which persons still cling to religious affections and actions, often transferring them in unconscious ways to secular ceremonies and events that have begun to render their lives entertaining and thus residually religious if not fully meaningful.

Finally, the theme of the evasive pennant—particularly as it has eluded the Cubs—provides images of eschatological wonder and hope, even if only through the liminal character of a dream or the more entertaining possibility of a story about a dream. In such a liminal experience of entertainment within entertainment, as this dream within a dream provides, we touch the deep crevices of human experience, memory, and possibility. Transported beyond, perhaps even through, the experience of particular pain or ecstasy and into the nether realm of entertainment, we can play out possibilities without the tyranny of consequences; for in entertainment decisions can be explored and reversed, perspectives can be engaged and modified, and the world's order or chaos can be invented and played out. Thus informed by the entertainment, we return again to the rules and rituals of our everyday world and become empowered, decisive, or perhaps even resigned to act in ways that had previously been unknown or forbidden.

In a way similar to that of "The Last Pennant before Armageddon," baseball and its nostalgia provide Kinsella with *vehicles* for expressing an eschatological worldview in *Shoeless Joe*. The dominant theme in the novel is certainly a religious one—of fulfilling dreams, of reclaiming innocence, of finding faith in a post-ecclesiastical age—an age in which the *institutions* of organized, established religions no longer exercise dominant mythic and ritualistic power in the lives of contemporary secular persons.

The film adaptation of the novel portrays the field of dreams itself as a hallowed place, yet the film script omits one brief scene in the novel that specifies and celebrates the spiritual character of a baseball field. After picking up Archie

"Moonlight" Graham after leaving Chisholm, Minnesota, Ray Kinsella and his compatriots sneak into old Metropolitan Stadium in Minneapolis. There Ray muses about the nature of a baseball park: "Have either of you spent any time in an empty ballpark?" Ray asks his friends. "There's something both eerie and holy about it.... A ballpark at night is more like a church than a church."[13]

To be sure, the careful alignment of baseball with the divine is introduced much earlier in the story. When Ray had described his affections and allegiances while he was contemplating whether to heed the call and build the field, he thought aloud: "I count the loves in my life: Annie, Karin, Iowa, Baseball. *The great god* Baseball."[14] Similarly, while sitting in Fenway Park he had opined to J. D. Salinger (replaced in the film by the character Terence Mann) about the character of the baseball crowd and the virtues of the sport: "We're not just ordinary people," he said making reference to the fans in the stands. "We're a congregation. Baseball is a ceremony, a ritual, as surely as sacrificing a goat beneath a full moon is a ritual. The only difference is that most of us realize that it *is* a game."[15]

In the cinematic adaptation of the novel, visual images reinforce the religious themes and concerns that underlie the story. In the opening scenes of the film, expansive Iowa skies mysteriously channel shafts of sunlight onto select fields of corn, and in the final nighttime scene, cars queue up in pilgrimage toward the Kinsella farm. Like the novel, the film *Field of Dreams* presents mystical and metaphysical challenges to the quotidian concerns of Hawkeye farm life in particular

---

[13] W. P. Kinsella, *Shoeless Joe* (New York: Ballantine Books, 1982) 135.

[14] Ibid., 6.

[15] Ibid., 72.

and to the American way of life in general. It questions the structure of reality itself, it generates a mythic cosmology that provides release from personal guilt and inadequacies, and it explores the significance of faithful action based on revelation rather than empirical data or scientific reasoning.

In *Shoeless Joe* farmer Ray Kinsella feels guilty for having alienated himself from his father, who had loved his son, baseball, and Shoeless Joe Jackson. As a teenager Ray had refused his father's offer to play catch. But with a 1960s predisposition to do something socially relevant like read digested Marxist theory or protest a war, burn a bank, or demonstrate against a university administration, Ray rejected his father's conciliatory playfulness and left home for enlightenment at Berkeley. Motivated in part by antisocial impulses in the literature of Salinger, Ray Kinsella follows his fiancée Annie to Iowa where he settles down and continues his personal protest against American economic and social structures by buying a small farm, working the land for the love of crops growing, and espousing liberal democratic values like freedom of speech. He also yearns for rapprochement with his father, whose presence is sensed through fascination with his father's baseball hero or patron saint, Shoeless Joe Jackson.

Walking among the dense stalks of summer corn, Ray hears a voice at first faintly, then more pronounced. "If you build it, he will come." Wondering while he is wandering through the flat fields of corn, he looks for the source of the clear call. Seeing none and finding no transmitting source, he sees a vision of the baseball diamond and modest bleachers in the middle of his corn field. That night in bed with Annie, he reluctantly remarks, "I hear a voice telling me to plow under our corn and build a baseball field with lime foul lines and lights." With the devotion of a true apostle, Annie consents to the construction of the field.

Understanding that prophets must exercise individual courage in the face of popular disdain, film critic and baseball fan James Wall aligns Ray Kinsella with the Hebrew prophets. "The beauty of this story," he avers, "emerges from the cautious manner in which Ray, joined by his trusting family, decides to follow the strange command and build a baseball field, plowing up valuable corn acreage in what to doubting neighbors looks about as sensible as Noah's decision to build an ark."[16]

Completing the field and caring for it, Ray waits and wonders and doubts whether he has indeed heard and heeded the voice of, as another film critic puts it, "the great Whisperer in the sky,"[17] or whether he has merely suffered from prairie fever and imagined the still, small (but convincing) voice. After watching, waiting, and wondering, Ray finally hears the call, like "land ho." Karin, his daughter, interrupts his mediated message through television and announces, "There is a man on your lawn."

The second coming of Shoeless Joe is not on clouds of glory nor accompanied by fanfare of trumpets. It is rather anonymous, innocuous, nocturnal. But Ray's faith is rewarded with an epiphany of his father's mythic hero who has gained iconic status for Ray himself.

The voice comes again. The prophetic message again is simple: "Ease his pain." The meaning, however, is evasive: Whose pain? Annie's dream then confirms Ray's own nocturnal vision: J. D. Salinger/Terence Mann must go to a Red Sox game with him and share the communion of eating hot dogs together. In the story, Salinger/Mann has become

[16] James M. Wall, "A Playing Field for the Boys of Eternity," *Christian Century* 106/17 (17 May 1989): 515.
[17] Pauline Kael, "The Current Cinema Fascination," *New Yorker*, 1 May 1989, 75.

reclusive; basically he feels like a prophet despised and rejected: a man of sorrows and acquainted with grief. To Salinger, Ray goes to ease his pain—to take him to a baseball game. The message has been clear. But as is the case with many prophetic utterances and perceptions, the application of the message is multiple, as Ray finds out when his own father's pain is eased, when his own father arrives at the field because it has been built, when his father starts to play catch with him because Ray, too, has gone the distance.

In the late innings at Fenway Park the scoreboard flashes a message visible only to the prophets' faithful eyes. Again the text of the message is straightforward, but its meaning is unclear. The message presents information about Archie "Moonlight" Graham, and his birthplace, Chisholm, Minnesota. His record showed that he had played in a single major league game without ever coming to bat or touching a ball in play. This third message to the prophets then is: "Go the distance." On then they go to Chisolm, Minnesota, where Ray Kinsella and Salinger traverse time and discover an aged Doc Graham, spliced into their reality through one of the cracks in time that Gideon Clarke's father had known. Expressing deep content with the course that his life had taken, Doc Graham nevertheless had wanted always to bat once against a major league pitcher and to wink just before the pitcher's delivery in order to establish his independence and playfulness.

These three baseball lovers—a childhood player and now farmer, a former fan and now reclusive novelist (or computer programmer), and a deceased doctor who had appeared in a single major league game—journey together in a mystical way back to Iowa and its field of dreams. In one way or another, the dead from various baseball generations are resurrected. Shoeless Joe indeed returns. Ray's father emerges as an unmarried, young baseball prospect. Archie Graham arrives as a young player who finds the crack in time is coincident with the foul line on the field. As he crosses the lime line from fair territory into foul ground, he ages instantly, becoming the widowed Doc Graham, who himself is still magically present since his death had occurred years before the journey of Ray and Salinger/Mann to Chisholm. In this magico-realistic fusion, in this eschatological disregard for time, Doc Graham resuscitates Ray's choking child Karin.

Surrounded by corn, the field is one of dreams, one of heaven, where the game is never over because heaven, as Ray had earlier queried, is said to be the place where dreams come true. On that field young Archie Graham did face the major league pitcher at whom he winked and from whom he then took one under the chin. There and then in the cornfield-baseball field of dreams, an eschatological fusion of time and space takes place in such a way as to render coherent the prophetic messages that had been revealed: "If you build it, he will come." "Ease his pain." "Go the distance." Pre-millennialism, in evangelically-oriented eschatology, refers to the expectation of the Second Coming of the Messiah who will rescue the redeemed and judge the rest. The pre-millennial eschatology is oriented toward preparing for the Second Coming, toward initiating the Kingdom of God through some form of believers' communities, toward persevering through the process of expectation: All of these elements lie at the heart of the revelation, expectation, and fulfillment that generate the hope and purpose of the true believers in fictive *Shoeless Joe* and cinematic *Field of Dreams*. And the true believers—the Kinsellas, J. D. Salinger/Terence Mann, Moonlight Graham, the resurrected Hall of Famers who join Shoeless Joe for games in the field of dreams, and the stream of pilgrims who drive their cars toward the incredible place—share a passion for baseball as it is played for the pleasure of the game itself.

The realized eschatology of Kinsella's baseball world focuses on a kind of existential realization that Final Judgment or final reward—be it the abyss or bliss—is already underway, not in a chronological sense but in a sense of ultimacy. The hope for the transformation and fulfillment of dreams need not wait until the end of one's life. Transformation and the movement toward fulfillment can become a part of one's life as one is threatened by the meaninglessness of modern life and as one yearns for some reconciliation with lost loves. This we see in the life of Ray Kinsella.

In the novel's play *with* baseball, not *of* baseball, we can sense a new metaphysics, one composed of dimensions within dimensions, of the reality of dreaming and remembering. "For the central wisdom of [*Field of Dreams*]…is that if we can break out of the confines of modern rationality," James Wall concludes, "it is possible to experience a power that is not limited to the space-time continuum we call reality."[18] Here we would join Salinger/Mann in his liberation from a reclusive life. And there in the Iowa cornfield of dreams we could join him, walking among the seven-foot-high corn stalks, peering expectantly and jubilantly, looking back and laughing at those who have not yet been invited into the liminal realm of that which is horizon, that which is neither here nor there, now nor then. If there is no time—if indeed eternity assumes presence—then "now and then" don't matter, and "here and there" are not. In such a world of wonder and expectation we might, with Salinger/Mann, leave the public pressure for interviews and publications, turn toward possibilities of moving

---

[18] Wall, "Playing Field," 515.

through the horizon, and laugh at last at the littleness of past performances and the largess of mystery and possibility.

8

Here I Cheer:
Conversion Narratives of Baseball
Fans

As a Canadian team prepared to defend its World Series title in the early 1990s, *Sports Illustrated* editor Ron Fimrite contacted several distinguished authors, many of whom had been awarded Pulitzer Prizes and other noteworthy literary awards, and he asked them to write about how they had become such avid baseball fans. In part, what fascinated Fimrite was the observation that the authors were so taken by the sport that baseball images or heroes often seeped into their literary works, even shaping their literary worlds. In his introduction to *Birth of a Fan*, Fimrite notes that "baseball did not merely transform these writers into terminal fans; it also heightened their awareness of a larger world, introduced them to a life beyond childhood."[1]

Somewhat similarly, baseball historian Curt Smith contacted more than 170 authors and athletes, performers and politicians, and asked them to write about what baseball means to each of them. A couple of the most telling bits appear on the same page in the reflections offered by former baseball Commissioner Bowie Kuhn and baseball writer Leonard

---

[1] Ron Fimrite, ed., *Birth of a Fan* (New York: Macmillan, 1993) vii.

Koppett. For one, Kuhn enjoys the lore that baseball brings to fans and seatmates at the ballpark or to children listening to "old timers" talk about their glory days. In particular, he recalls one game when he was seated adjacent to the noted Reformed preacher Norman Vincent Peale. Peale remarked that baseball "was like the Bible because of the stories that poured forth in such joy from its people." For another, Koppett suggests that he "can imagine a world without baseball, but can't imagine wanting to live in one."[2]

Simply and theologically put, baseball facilitates a devout fan's rite of passage from the world of childhood playground to the *ekklesia* of new relationships, an always imminent realm that overflows with hope and promise. If that description of the power of baseball in eliciting devotion and fostering community seems "off base," consider the horde of Cubs' fans who exercise the optimism of Ernie Banks, who always thought that each day was a good day to play a doubleheader.

Fimrite's description of the transformative power of baseball—of its pervasive effect and enduring influence—corresponds to the phenomenon of conversion and its articulation in personal narratives that have characterized many eras and aspects of American life, ranging from the spiritual accounts of colonial Puritans, to the emancipation narratives of African-American slaves, to the protests against patriarchal structures by feminists, and to the testimonies of evangelical devotees. In continuity with these significant American life-changing narratives, the baseball affiliation stories manifest thematic and stylistic similarity to the sub-genre of spiritual autobiography that includes spiritual diaries, conversion narratives, and personal testimonies.

---

[2] Curt Smith, ed., *What Baseball Means to Me: A Celebration of the National Pastime* (New York: Warner Books, 2002) 129.

In his examination of conversion narratives in early American Protestantism, Rodger Payne reflects on "the morphology of conversion" for Puritans, Congregationalists, and converts during the Great Awakening. During the initial period of American revivalism, the discourse of evangelicals about conversion helped to generate a democratic form of religious authority and to establish "a new vernacular literature of conversion narratives and spiritual autobiographies."[3] The significance and characteristics of conversion have been clearly identified throughout Paul's epistles, and they have been succinctly summarized by Jonathan Edwards. He noted:

> [Conversion] strongly impl[ies] and signif[ies] a change of nature: such as being born again; becoming new creatures; rising from the dead; being renewed in the spirit of the mind; dying to sin, and living to righteousness; putting off the old man, and putting on the new man; and being made partakers of the divine nature.... They that are truly converted are new men, new creatures; new, not only within, but without; they are sanctified throughout, in spirit, soul and body; old things are passed away, all things are become new.[4]

Although the experience of conversion is significant, it becomes transformative as it is remembered and articulated in such a way that the constructed narration of the event shapes one's identity and provides a foundation for hope and personal growth. As Payne concludes about the early American conver-

---

[3] Rodger Payne, *The Self and the Sacred: Conversion and Autobiography in Early American Protestantism* (Knoxville: University of Tennessee Press, 1998) 9.

[4] Jonathan Edwards, *Religious Affections*, vol. 2 of *The Works of Jonathan Edwards*, ed. John E. Smith (New Haven: Yale University Press, 1959) 340–41, 391. Quoted in Payne, *The Self and the Sacred*, 4.

sion experiences, "Only the experience of conversion empowered—and compelled—the convert to speak of conversion.
Further, the experience of conversion itself became a product
of the narrative through which it was given form, structure,
and meaning."[5]

A similar process of shaping experience through stories
also characterizes reflective baseball fans. Drawing from the
depths of childhood memories and the intensity of adult
passion for baseball, the authors in Fimrite's volume construct
their affiliation narratives in such a way that renders form,
structure, and meaning to their lives. Not surprisingly,
Fimrite's contributors repeatedly connect their early love of
baseball with a desire to learn more about the game, especially
its terms and its teams, its players and its rules. As children
they consumed the sports pages in newspapers, devouring
reports and features about the best and worst teams and their
favorite players. Then learning to dissect box scores of games,
they began to (re)create games by reconstructing innings—by
narrating at-bats, hits, runs, and put-outs. Their early
fascination with baseball accounts led them increasingly to
other sections of the newspaper, to libraries for books, and
finally to paper and pen for writing themselves. Literature was
loved and lived for the young readers. But various subjects also
took on immediate significance as the young authors-to-be
pursued their baseball interests. Again, Fimrite observes:
"Through baseball we as youngsters were introduced to such
previously arcane subjects as geography (you had better know
where the major league cities were), history (better find out
who this guy Delahany is), and, since ballparks of yesteryear
were structures of considerable individuality and charm,

---

[5] Payne, *The Self and the Sacred*, 11.

architecture."[6] Of course, the customary reticence of literary types to "do math" was overcome by their desire not only to understand, but also to be able to calculate batting averages and the seemingly Trinitarian mystery, ERA. In addition, Jonathan Yardley, one of the contributors to *The Birth of a Fan*, recalls that, as he puts it, "listening to games on the radio taught me to use my imagination in the same way that listening to the Book of Common Prayer in church taught me to write."[7]

Although we might occasionally expect these sorts of memories and reflections to come from intellectuals who love the game, we might not expect their consistent perspective and tone, both of which align these reflections with the sub-genre of autobiography known as "conversion narratives." It is here—with the idea that the birth of a fan is a sort of conversion—that I want to focus our attention. By suggesting that the birth of a fan is a conversion, I build upon the premise argued in chapter five, that fandom is a kind of faith.

First, however, I must confess my own fanaticism and faithfulness. Given the reading of others' accounts as "conversion narratives," it should not be too surprising that I describe my attraction to baseball in religious terms. On 9 October 1956, I sat in my home in Jackson, Mississippi and read the lead story in the sports section of the Jackson *Clarion-Ledger*. As a new baseball fan, I read about Don Larsen's perfect game on the previous day. As a preacher's kid, I understood reality in terms of the sermons that I heard at least three times a week from my father's pulpit and more often from my mother's kitchen perch. I sensed somehow that baseball would be big for me, and so I established allegiance

---

[6] Fimrite, *Birth of a Fan*, vii-viii.

[7] Jonathan Yardley, "Stuck for Life," in Fimrite, *Birth of a Fan*, 201.

that very moment for theological reasons. If I were to be a baseball fan, then surely I must admire and seek perfection. For the first time in World Series play, I read, perfection had been realized. Perfection had become manifest at Yankee Stadium, the "House that Ruth Built." That description itself is somehow as evocative for me as the mention of similarly mythic and distant Solomon's Temple. The day before my newspaper reading, a Yankee pitcher performed a unique feat, hurling a perfect game at the time of baseball season's final judgment—the World Series. I then confessed, I guess, that I would love the *Yankees*, something that young *Southern* Baptists are not wont to do. And so I have followed them faithfully for more than forty years—at times through seeming baseball deserts when Ross Moschitto and Roger Repoz roamed the outfield wilderness impersonating successors to the perfect "7" himself, St. Michael in pinstripes—Mickey Mantle.

I'm obsessed. I'm incurably a Yankee fan. Given my nurture within a religious household and given my own career as a theologian, it is not too surprising that I describe my own experience of faithful following of the Yankees in religious terms. To adapt Luther's succinct testimony at Worms, "Here I cheer. I cannot do otherwise."[8] I might also add that in the spirit of religious protest so crucial to Protestant traditions, my two sons have converted to heretical sects—the Cubs and the Red Sox.

---

[8] Of course, Luther's testimony was uttered with prophetic fervor as he appealed to the authority of Scripture. See Roland H. Bainton, *Here I Stand: A Life of Martin Luther* (New York: New American Library, 1950) 144. By quipping here, however, I do not mean to imply that my stance is nearly as profound as his, nor is the risk in my utterance even remotely akin to the danger that he encountered as the result of his testimony.

But what about other fans? Does their following also resemble or manifest the characteristics of faith?

Two theological reasons seem to make sense about the expressions of devotion that sports fans exhibit with regard to their favorite teams, whether my personal recollections and interpretation, or the memories and analyses recorded by authors in Fimrite's collection. The more obvious one, to which we will return, is that fans often invest their allegiance with a sense of ultimacy. Their fervor reveals their faith. According to Frank Deford, the *Sports Illustrated* writer who first suggested that if Karl Marx had lived in the twentieth century, he would have opined that sports is the opiate of the people, the very love of baseball develops out of being a fan: "No matter how much you might play baseball as a boy [or girl], no matter how much you might chuck the old horsehide around, nobody ever comes to baseball without coming through the love of a baseball club."[9]

The other theological reason has to do with the ways that sports have often provided the symbols and sites for rites of passage that—in previous generations, cultures, and traditions—had often been associated with religious rituals and myths. A couple of years after the strike-shortened season in 1994, Steven Stark, a columnist for the *Boston Globe*, affirmed that baseball is back, and he identified this phenomenon well. "Like Billy Crystal's character in *City Slickers*," he observed, "baseball fanatics often use the sport to supply the sacred family experiences [that] religion once provided. Instead of a bar mitzvah or confirmation, seeing Mickey Mantle bat or

---

[9] Frank Deford, "Coming to Baseball...but Not Necessarily Being Loved Back," in Fimrite, *Birth of a Fan*, 68.

playing catch with Dad become the seminal experiences of life."[10]

That was certainly the case for my "Baptist bar mitzvah." To celebrate my early adolescent birthday in the summer of 1961, my family planned a father-son journey to give me the chance to see the Yankees play. The pilgrimage—which provided a chance for me to bond with my father as an emerging adolescent, an adult fan in the eyes of the true faith—yielded baseball memories that now take on mythic proportions. The religious significance of the trip itself was also shaped by its pilgrimage character. To minimize cost, the trip was planned to coincide with a family vacation within a long day's drive of Chicago, which was the nearest American League city to my home town. Also like a pilgrimage, our trip had to overcome personal difficulties (my raging intestinal flu that almost prevented our departure) and social obstacles (intimidation by small gangs of urban kids near Comiskey Park). Finally, the trip required sacrifice, driving late into the night on two lane highways and staying in a cramped room downtown in an alien city. For a pre-adolescent Southern boy, the world of the YMCA hotel on Wabash, adjacent to the South side loop of the "El," seemed like Nineveh.

Of course, my father and I did attend two games and witnessed heroes of demigod status accomplish mythic feats. In a losing cause on Friday night, Mantle hit a homerun batting right-handed, and the following afternoon Maris hit one of his sixty-one round-trippers that year. The Saturday game also featured Elston Howard hitting one over the roof of the left

---

[10] Steven Stark, "White American Males Get Religion in 9 Innings." (Full bibliographic data are unavailable. Several years ago, a colleague handed me a photocopy of the article, which seems to have come from a newspaper, although searches of the *Boston Globe*, *USA Today*, and *InfoWeb* have not turned up references.)

field stands, Maris throwing out Louie Aparicio at home on an attempted sacrifice fly in the bottom of the eighth, and Bob Cerv pinch hitting a game tying homer in the top of the ninth. In ten innings, the Yankees won 9-8. Maslow would call the event a peak experience, Tillich might call it *kairos*, but I simply thought of it as heaven. Even now, the scorecard from the game, the popcorn megaphone from the concession stands, and a photograph of me waving a Yankees pennant in our box seats that afternoon enjoy relic status on a shelf in my study.

Several of the authors who provide "conversion narratives" for Fimrite's volume remark on the significance of family for their early fan activity. In particular, Pulitzer Prize winner J. Anthony Lukas identifies ways in which his fondness for the Yankees helped to connect him to a larger, stabler world. Lukas won the Pulitzer Prize for non-fiction for his humane portrayal of race relations in Boston in *Common Ground: A Turbulent Decade in the Lives of Three American Families*, his 1986 contemporary history. And Jonathan Yardley, the noted literary critic of the *Washington Post* who had previously been a writer for *Sports Illustrated*, reflects perceptively on the construction and continuity of family myth about the early, formative days of being a fan. Like the writers of conversion narratives in recognized religions, Lukas, Yardley, and Doris Kearns Goodwin identify a transformative event or period, connect it to family life, and indicate how their love of the game and their devotion to a single team oriented a new engagement with and understanding of the world.

Anthony Lukas recalls how the darker world of his mother's manic depression lurked beneath the apparent success and stability of his family life. Initially, his father appeared to be prospering as a lawyer in Manhattan while his mother supervised the elegant renovation of a farmhouse on six wooded acres in White Plains. But beneath this profile of contentment lay the darker worlds of his mother's illness and his family's dysfunction. Eventually, she committed suicide, and subsequently his father abused alcohol and suffered a bout with tuberculosis. It is with "little wonder then," he writes, "that I retreated whenever possible into that other world [of imaginary playmates], where bumblebee princes soared to the stars. I was in search of a realm which made more sense than this one, a place in which beauty and virtue and talent were rewarded not by pain and death, but by the love and approbation they deserved. It was then that I found baseball."[11] For Lukas, baseball liberated; baseball redeemed. Like converts to religious communities and traditions, Lukas had experienced the desolation of his own world, seeking deliverance from his destitute state and refuge in the new world, a promised land, a hope-filled world of joy and victory where stability prevailed and justice reigned. Such a remote, transcendent world could be perceived through listening to the radio broadcasts of games of the great Yankees. "To millions of Americans," Lukas continues, "the Yanks were arrogant...spoilsports who squeezed all innocent joy from the game. But to an anxious youth still shaken by the implosion of his ordered world, the masterful Yanks were vastly reassuring. If I couldn't control my environment, they surely dominated theirs. And by some alchemy of fandom, their triumphs were mine as well."[12] In a way akin to a new Christian's experience of hope and security in the Kingdom of God, Lukas found the victorious world of DiMaggio and Dickey, of Gordon and Keller, to be the realm of deliverance that enabled the living out of routines and combating pain in the everyday world.

---

[11] J. Anthony Lukas, "Surrogate Family," in Fimrite, *Birth of a Fan*, 152.

[12] Ibid., 153.

The Yankees made other contributions to Lukas's salvation by providing a sense of community, of personal continuity. "Not surprisingly," he concludes, "what I missed most in those years was the very notion of family, the ingathering of Lukases each night in that comfortable old house, the sense that people that I loved and who loved me were there at the close of each day, no matter how I'd fared on the history quiz or how many goals I'd blown in soccer practice. Before long the Yankees became my surrogate family."[13] Certainly, a fan's identification with a favorite team as family indicates a rebirth that is remarkably similar to a Christian convert's identification with new brothers and sisters in Christ. This surrogate family is, as Annie succinctly affirmed in *Bull Durham*, "the Church of Baseball." More than merely the sense of the sacred that one gets at a fabled stadium or baseball shrine, "the Church of Baseball" is fundamentally the community of like-minded believers.

In her memoir about growing up on Long Island in the baseball rich New York of the mid-twentieth century, Doris Kearns Goodwin also reflects on the bonding potential of baseball. When she was only six years old, she met eight-year-old Johnny, a devoted Dodger fan who knew even more about the Dodgers than she did. "It was my first introduction," she recalls, "to the invisible community of baseball, which now, for the first time, was extended beyond my street in Rockville Centre, to the town of Mineola, where Johnny lived. In years to come, I would find that the lovers of the Dodgers, and, indeed, of baseball, shared common ground, reaching across generations and different social stations dispersed across the country."[14] Additionally, there is "nothing [that] inspires

---

[13] Ibid., 154.

[14] Doris Kearns Goodwin, *Wait Till Next Year: A Memoir* (New York: Simon and Schuster, 1997) 42.

camaraderie," she notes, "like sharing a victory not only of a game, but of a season." This sense of camaraderie that grows out of the social anti-structure or "communitas"[15] is also manifest during ritual occasions at the ballpark, when, for instance, fans sing "Take Me Out to the Ballpark" during the seventh inning stretch, when they clap and stomp in unison to rattle the opposing pitcher or urge on the home team hitter, when they implore the charm of the rally monkey at Anaheim, and when they join the chorus at Comiskey Park, singing: "Nah, nah, nah, nah. Nah, nah, nah, nah. Hey, hey, Goodbye." The penchant for baseball allegiance to provide such a communal connection transcends the particularity of ballparks and games. For throughout her travels even now as an adult, Goodwin encounters Brooklyn Dodgers' fans across the country who immediately bond and share a true believer's faith with her as they revel in their memories of and devotion to "da Bums" of Brooklyn.

The establishment of affiliation with a particular team, she remembers, was passed on from father to child, like one's religion, "with the crucial moments in a team's history repeated like the liturgy of a church service."[16] The challenge to her childhood friendships, in fact, seemed to have been threatened more by Lainie Lubar's fondness for the Yankees than by the Kearnses' religious differences with the Lubars. Lainie was so devoted to the Yankees that she would argue the superiority of the diminutive and wily Billy Martin as the premier second baseman, much to the dismay and discomfort of Doris, who "idolized," as she puts it, the fleet and powerful Jackie Robinson. Following the Yankees' defeat of the Dodgers

---

[15] Victor Turner and Edith Turner, *Image and Pilgrimage in Christian Culture: Anthropological Perspectives* (New York: Columbia University Press, 1978) 250–55.

[16] Goodwin, *Wait Till Next Year*, 61.

in the 1949 World Series, she recalls, her relationship with Elaine suffered for weeks. It was then, too, that Doris first understood the agony, power, and hope of the Dodger fan's refrain, "Wait till next year," echoing the eternal religious affirmation from the Lubars' household, "Next year, in Jerusalem."

Although she likens the liturgical calendar of the Catholic Church to the cycles of a baseball season, nowhere does Goodwin identify the conflation of the sporting and spiritual more thoroughly than in her consternation about celebrating her first holy Communion. As she prepared for her first confession, she suffered guilt from the malice that she had wished on the Dodgers' arch-rivals—the Giants—and she suffered guilt from the quandary about wanting to see Roy Campanella in a speaking appearance at a local Episcopal church. Devoted wholeheartedly to the Roman Catholic Church and the authority of the pope, Doris worried about the papal proscription against setting foot in a non-Roman Catholic church. Her fears were only partly relieved, she recalls, when her father assured her that the Catholic Church's prohibition pertained to participating in a religious service rather than attending a lecture by a baseball player. However, following her rapturous experience of meeting a baseball hero and hearing him speak, in a somewhat squeaky voice that belied the power of his baseball prowess, she returned home to a bedtime anxiety that only nuns could induce. Their warnings, she writes, "tumbled through my head, convincing me that I had traded the life of my everlasting soul for the joy of one glorious night when I held Roy Campanella's strong hand in a forbidden church. Jumping out of bed, I got down on my knees and repeated every prayer I could remember, in the hope that each would wipe away part of the stain that the Episcopal church had left on my soul."[17]

Days thereafter, she confessed her shortcomings to an understanding priest who heard her admit that every night she had also wished that harm would come to Robin Roberts and Richie Ashburn, Enos Slaughter and Phil Rizzuto, and Alvin Dark and Allie Reynolds. She desired that the players would suffer temporary injuries in order to permit the Dodgers a first world championship. "But how would you feel knowing that the victory wasn't really deserved," the priest asked, "knowing that if your rivals had been healthy your team might not have won? I promise you it wouldn't feel anywhere near as good as if you won in the proper way. Now, let me tell you a secret. I love the Dodgers just as much as you do, but I believe they will win the World Series someday fairly and squarely. You don't need to wish harm on others to make it happen."[18] For her penance, the priest assigned young Doris to "say two Hail Marys, three Our Fathers, and...a special prayer for the Dodgers." About her experience, Goodwin concluded: "My First Confession, received by a baseball-loving priest, had left me closer to my church than ever before."[19]

The recollection of childhood memories about baseball heroes, of familial relations with fellow fans, and of the fascination with nuances of games provides memory itself with an anchor that orients deep pleasure. Seeing her first Dodger game at Ebbets Field in 1949, Goodwin experienced distraction from all of the commotion that took the place of the clear, directive narrative of Red Barber, whose *voice* had, always earlier, *seen* the game for her. Yet after experiencing the clamor of the crowd and the joy of watching the transcendent

---

[17] Ibid., 96.

[18] Ibid., 108.

[19] Ibid.

heroes perform on the field, Goodwin felt disoriented. In an effort to restore order, her father offered to allow her to create the narrative of the game, batter by batter, detail by detail, by translating and elaborating her own scorecard. Certainly the experience of the game had been thrilling, but the order and primary pleasure resided in the ability to narrate the events, to lend a storied structure to the play that she had witnessed. "I experienced that night what I have experienced many times since," she writes, "the absolute pleasure that comes from prolonging the winning feeling by reliving the game, first with the scorebook, then with the wrap-up on the radio, and finally, once I learned about printed box scores, with the newspaper accounts the next day. But what I remember most is sitting at Ebbets Field for the first time, with my red scorebook on my lap and my father at my side."[20]

The celebration of family relationships is certainly one of the dimensions of baseball's religious power. In the simple act of *Fathers Playing Catch with Sons*, recalling Donald Hall's poetic title, we find "a momentary grace of order" that lends joy and affection to otherwise tedious and separate lives.[21] The "momentary grace of order" that baseball offers is one that adheres to rules. As Gil Renard, the pathological Giants' fan portrayed by Robert DeNiro in *The Fan* (1986) puts it, "Baseball is better than life. It's fair." The celebration of family relationships also manifests the testimonial character of writing about baseball. So keen were the stories of baseball and its significance to her relationship with her father that Goodwin vividly recalls the transformation afforded by the first night game at Ebbets Field: "I was sitting by my father's side, five years before I was born," she asserts, "when the lights were

---

[20] Ibid., 51.

[21] Donald Hall, *Fathers Playing Catch with Sons: Essays on Sport [Mostly Baseball]* (New York: Dell Publishing Company, 1986) 51.

turned on for the first time at Ebbets Field, the crowd gasping and then cheering as the summer night was transformed into startling day." So intense was their relationship through baseball that she believed that her father's "love of baseball would be forever unfulfilled"[22] if she did not recount a missed game to him, play by play, inning by inning.

Although the mind might exaggerate or transmute actual baseball events when remembering childhood activities with one's physical family, Jonathan Yardley recognizes the mythic impact of family baseball outings. "Memory is fallible and mine more so than most. But does it matter?" he muses. "Are the specifics all that important? I think not. The indisputable and central fact is that this unlikely process [of loving baseball] started in this unlikely place." Yardley recalls his youthful enthusiasm in the summer of 1948 when his father took him by train to New York to see a doubleheader between the Yankees and the St. Louis Browns. The trip, he now figures, must have required a major paternal sacrifice because of his father's full indifference to—if not thorough abhorrence of—baseball itself. "At least I *think* it was a doubleheader," Yardley continues:

> It must have been a doubleheader because my...private mythology insists upon it—insists that my father, who so hated sports, so loved his son—that he was willing to sit through two whole baseball games in order to make him happy. What if it was just a single game? What if we stayed only five innings? What shabby raw material would I then have been given from which to fabricate what has become one of the central legends of my life?

---

[22] Goodwin, *Wait Till Next Year*, 17, 18.

I'd rather not know. I've resisted all impulses to search
out the occasion in the newspaper files of seasons past.[23]

What is at work for Yardley? Among other things he
manifests the orientation of converts who write about their
experience. "There is an urgent need among them," Peter
Dorsey asserts about autobiographers reflecting on their
conversion experiences, "to justify their orientations to the
world, not just as they were at the time of writing, but as they
had been and would be."[24] In addition to his use of conversion
rhetoric, Yardley also employs language about the father loving
his son so much that he would suffer that which is
reprehensible. The image and language here surely resonate
the language of the Johanine gospel. Furthermore, the impulse
to place faith in the legends of childhood memory and meaning
resounds with the theological effort to maintain faith in the
simple stories of a religious tradition rather than the critical
analysis of texts and the deconstruction of charter myths.

Even *if* baseball did not actually prompt such a sacrifice
from his father, Yardley has oriented his life around the firm
conviction—even if legend—that his father loved him so much
that he would endure his disdain for baseball not only by taking
young Jonathan on the train to Yankee Stadium, but by sitting
through a full day of baseball with him. As Yardley draws a
conclusion to his mythic memory, he invokes more explicit
religious language: "But my father, having helped give me this
[baseball experience], then took it away. He accepted a new
job, running a school for girls in Southside, Virginia, and
suddenly I was three hundred miles from the nearest big-

---

[23] Yardley, "Stuck for Life," in Fimrite, *Birth of a Fan*, 199.
[24] Peter A. Dorsey, *Sacred Estrangement: The Rhetoric of
Conversion in Modern American Autobiography* (University Park:
Pennsylvania State University Press, 1993) 12.

league ballpark, not to mention five hundred miles from Yankee Stadium [itself]. I had barely received true baptism as a fan, and now I was excommunicated."[25]

Whether accurately recalling actual events or fusing meaning and hope with nuggets of fact, baseball memories can exert this formative power in orienting life. In this regard Robert Creamer, another of the authors featured in Fimrite's collection, does not care about the accuracy of his recollection of his first game at the Polo Grounds, an afternoon that featured a doubleheader against the Giants and Dodgers. "I can't remember if one team swept both games or if the doubleheader was split," he concedes. "It didn't seem to matter. I wasn't rooting for either the Giants or the Dodgers. All I was doing was absorbing the wonder of major league baseball, inning after inning, sucking in details that have never left me. I think I am correct in saying that I adored—not loved, but adored, as though they were gods—every man on the altar of that field. I didn't realize how sacred they were to me until just a year or two ago."[26] For Creamer, like Yardley, the impressions heightened by reconstructed memory often assume the character of charter myths for a tradition—personal, familial, and communal—and they begin to exhibit the sense of ultimacy that distinguishes true faith. For faith, as theologian Paul Tillich consistently averred, is the state of being ultimately concerned. It is more than the affirmation of dogmas that might defy logic, experience, or scientific reasoning. It is more than "true belief," as popular philosopher Eric Hoffer was wont to say several decades ago. Faith is, instead, that condition of orienting life centrifugally toward the dominant concern that has grasped one's being so

---

[25] Yardley, "Stuck for Life," in Fimrite, *Birth of a Fan*, 199–200.

[26] Robert W. Creamer, "Pop Watts, a Newspaper, and a Day at the Polo Grounds," in Fimrite, *Birth of a Fan*, 64–65.

tightly that wriggling and struggling cannot budge one from its grasp.

It is accurate to classify the baseball fandom of Anthony Lukas and Jonathan Yardley and Doris Kearns Goodwin, as well as myself and hundreds of others who have written about their love of baseball, as expressions of faith. And it thus becomes more intriguing and enlightening to read the accounts of their affiliation with and devotion to specific teams as being conversion narratives. Their stories take on the character of testimony. They manifest the passionate apology for non-rational devotion. And it is in this vein of devotion that Yardley concludes his own confession: "If God in [all] mysterious wisdom has chosen you to be a baseball fan, you can't just walk away from it whenever you decide to get 'serious.' You're stuck for life. And me, I'm not complaining."[27]

Nor me.

Amen.

---

[27] Yardley, "Stuck for Life," in Fimrite, *Birth of a Fan*, 207.

For Further Reading:

Works Relating Baseball and Religion

Histories and Analyses

Adkin, Jr., Clare. *Brother Benjamin: A History of the Israelite House of David*. Berrien Springs MI: Andrews University Press, 1990.

Aitken, Brian. "Baseball as Sacred Doorway." *Aethlon* 8/1 (Fall 1990): 61-75.

Altherr, Thomas L. "W. P. Kinsella's Baseball Fiction, *Field of Dreams*, and the New Mythopoeism of Baseball." *The Minneapolis Review of Baseball* 10/2 (Season Opener 1991): 23-32.

Ardolino, Frank. "Missionaries, Cartwright, and Spalding: The Development of Baseball in Nineteenth-Century Hawaii." *Nine: A Journal of Baseball History and Social Policy Perspectives* 10/2 (Fall 2002): 27-45.

Batts, Callie Elizabeth. "City Jewel Boxes: The History and Preservation of Two Chicago Ballparks." Master of Arts Thesis, Cornell University, Ithaca NY, 2000.

Beach, Charles Franklyn. "Joyful vs. Joyless Religion in W. P. Kinsella's *Shoeless Joe*." *Aethlon* 16/1 (Fall 1998): 85-94.

Beardsley, Steven Michael. "Safe at Home: Baseball as a Ritual of America's Civil Religion." Bachelor of Arts Thesis,

Department of Philosophy and Religion, Bates College, Lewiston ME, 1997.

Bevis, Charlie. *Sunday Baseball: Major Leagues' Struggle to Play Baseball on the Lord's Day, 1876-1934.* Jefferson NC: McFarland and Company, 2003.

Boswell, Thomas. "The Church of Baseball. " In Geoffrey C. Ward and Ken Burns, *Baseball: An Illustrated History*, 189-193. New York: Alfred A. Knopf, 1994.

_____. *How Life Imitates the World Series.* New York: Penguin, 1982.

_____. *Why Time Begins on Opening Day.* New York: Viking, 1986.

Bronson, Eric, ed. *Baseball and Philosophy: Thinking Outside the Batter's Box.* Chicago: Open Court, 2005.

Brown, Bill. "The Meaning of Baseball in 1992 (with Notes on the Post-American)." *Public Culture* 4/1 (Fall 1991): 43-69.

Butterworth, Michael L. "Ritual in the 'Church of Baseball': Supressing the Discourse of Democracy after 9/11." *Communication and Critical/Cultural Studies* 2/2 (June 2005): 107-129.

Candelaria, Cordelia. *Seeking the Perfect Game: Baseball in American Literature.* New York: Greenwood, 1989.

Carino, Peter. "'The Ballparks are Like Cathedrals': Stadia in American Culture." *Nine: A Journal of Baseball History and Social Policy Perspectives* 1/1 (Fall 1992): 1-18.

_____. "Fields of Imagination: Ballparks as Complex Pastoral Metaphors in Kinsella's *Shoeless Joe* and *The Iowa Baseball Confederacy*." *Nine: A Journal of Baseball History and Social Policy Perspectives* 2/2 (Spring 1994): 287-299.

Caterine, Darryl V. "Curses and Catharsis in Red Sox Nation: Baseball and Ritual Violence in American Culture." *Journal of Religion and Popular Culture* (www.usask.ca/relst/jrpc) VIII (Fall 2004).

Cherner, Reid. "If You Billed It around Faith, They Will Certainly Come." *USA Today*, 22 July 2005, A1.

Chidester, David. *Authentic Fakes: Religion and American Popular Culture*. Berkeley: University of California Press, 2005.

_____. "The Church of Baseball, the Fetish of Coca-Cola, and the Potlatch of Rock 'n' Roll." In *Religion and Popular Culture in America*, ed. Bruce David Forbes nd Jeffrey H. Mahan, 219-238. Berkeley: University of California Press, 2000.

Cohen, Morris R. "Baseball as National Religion." Reprinted in *Religion, Culture, and Society: A Reader in the Sociology of Religion*. Ed. Louis Schneider, 36-38. New York: John Wiley and Sons, Inc., 1964.

Cox, Adam J. "Baseball's Passionate Collectors: A Psychosocial Perspective of the Quest for Memorabilia." *Nine: A Journal of Baseball History and Social Policy Perspectives* 3/2 (Spring 1995): 248-260.

Crepeau, Richard C. "Divine Wrath: The Goat and the Bambino." *Nine: A Journal of Baseball History and Social Policy Perspectives* 13/1 (Fall 2004): 109-113.

Dailey, Thomas F. "Believing in Baseball: The Religious Power of Our National Pastime." *Logos: A Journal of Catholic Thought and Culture* 6/2 (Spring 2003) 63-83.

DeMotte, Charles. "Baseball and Freemasonry in American Culture." In *The Cooperstown Symposium on Baseball and American Culture, 2001*. Ed. by William M. Simons, 262-275. Jefferson NC: McFarland and Company, Inc., Publishers, 2002.

Dufresne, Chris. "The Hex Files." *Los Angeles Times*, 27 May 1999, D10.

Evans, Christopher H. and William R. Herzog II, editors. *The Faith of Fifty Million: Baseball, Religion, and American Culture*. Louisville: Westminster John Knox Press, 2002.

Fogarty, Robert S. *The Righteous Remnant: The House of David*. Kent OH: The Kent State University Press, 1981.

Galli, Mark. "Pirates vs. Braves: Reforming One City at a Time." *Christianity Today* 112/42 (23 March 2006).

Gardella, Peter. "Baseball smadhi: A Yankee Way of Knowledge." *Books and Religion* 14/3 (September 1986): 15.

_____. *Domestic Religion: Work, Food, Sex and Other Commitments*. Cleveland: Pilgrim Press, 1998.

Giamatti, A. Bartlett. *Take Time for Paradise: Americans and Their Games*. New York: Summit Books, 1989.

Gitersonke, Don. *Baseball's Bearded Boys: A Historical Look at the Israelite House of David Baseball Club of Benton Harbor, Michigan*. Las Vegas: Privately published by Don Gitersonke, 1996.

Gmelch, George. "Superstition and Ritual in American Baseball." *Elysian Fields Quarterly* 11/3 (Summer 1992): 25-36.

Goi, Naohiro. *The Tao of Baseball*. New York: Simon & Schuster, 1991.

Goldstein, Warren. "Winning Isn't Everything: Baseball as a Theological Discipline." *Christian Century* 120/22 (1 November 2003): 11.

Golenbock, Peter. "What Makes the Sports Fan Tick?" An interview with Peter Golenbock. *Forum: The Magazine of the Florida Humanities Council* 21/2 (Fall 1998): 18-21.

Graf, Gary. *And God Said, "Play Ball!" Amusing and Thought-Provoking Parallels between the Bible and Baseball*. Liguori MO: Liguori/Triumph, 2005.

Hall, Donald. *Fathers Playing Catch with Sons: Essays on Sport (Mostly Baseball)*. San Francisco: North Point Press, 1985.

Hall, Frank. "Sacred Baseball?" *The Minneapolis Review of Baseball* 10/2 (Season Opener 1991): 5-16.

Harrison, Walter L. "Six-Pointed Diamond: Baseball and American Jews." *The Journal of Popular Culture* 15/3 (Winter 1991): 112-118.

Hawkins, Joel and Terry Bertolino. *The House of David Baseball Team*. Images of America Series. Chicago: Arcadia Publishing, 2000.

Hogan, William R. "Sin and Sports." In *Motivations in Play, Games, and Sports*. Ed. Ralph Slovenko and James Knight, 121-147. Springfield IL: Charles C. Thomas, Publisher, 1967.

Hye, Allen E. *The Great God Baseball: Religion in Modern Baseball Fiction*. Macon: Mercer University Press, 2004.

Hollander, Russell. "The Religion of Baseball: Psychological Perspectives." *Nine: A Journal of Baseball History and Social Policy Perspectives* 3/1 (Fall 1994): 1-13.

Jackson, Susan A. and Mihaly Csikszentmihalyi. *Flow in Sports: The Keys to Optimal Experiences and Performances*. Champaign IL: Human Kinetics, 1999.

Joffe, Linda S. "Praise Baseball. Amen. Religious Metaphors in *Shoeless Joe* and 'Field of Dreams.'" *Aethlon* 7/2 (Spring 1992): 153-163.

Johnson, Paul C. "The Fetish and McGwire's Balls." In *From Season to Season: Sports as American Religion*. Ed. Joseph L. Price, 77-98. Macon: Mercer University Press, 2001.

Kimball, Richard Ian. "'bringing Fame to Zion': Tony Lazzeri, the Salt Lake Bees, and Life in the Pacific Coast League." *Nine: A Journal of Baseball History and Social Policy Perspectives* 14/2 (Spring 2006): 40-58.

Land, Gary. "Adventism and the Church of Baseball." *Spectrum: Journal of the Association of Aventist Forums* 23/2 (August 1993): 27-30.

Levine, Peter. *Ellis Island to Ebbets Field : Sport and the American Jewish Experience*. New York: Oxford University Press, 1993.

Light, Jonathan Fraser. *The Cultural Encyclopedia of Baseball*. Jefferson NC: McFarland and Company, 1997.

Lipsyte, Robert. "Sports and Values: Losing Our Grip." *Forum: The Magazine of the Florida Humanities Council* 21/2 (Fall 1998): 4-11.

Lovinger, Jay, editor. *The Gospel According to ESPN: Saints, Saviors, and Sinners*. Intro. by Hunter S. Thompson. New York: Hyperion Books, 2002.

Lowry, Philip J. *Green Cathedrals: The Ultimate Celebration of All 273 Major League and Negro League Ballparks*. Reading MA: Addison-Wesley Publishing Company, 1992.

Mandelbaum, Michael. *The Meaning of Sports: Why Americans Watch Baseball, Football, and Basketball and What They See When They Do*. New York: Public Affairs, 2004.

McCallum, Jack. "Green Cars, Black Cats, and Lady Luck: Superstition in Sports." *Sports Illustrated* 68/6 (8 February 1988): 86-94.

McBride, Michael J. and Michelle A. Cervantes. "The Coming of Age of Jean Jacques Rousseau and Nuke Laloosh." *Nine: A Journal of Baseball History and Social Policy Perspectives* 6/1 (Fall 1997): 81-92.

Murphy, Michael and Rhea A. White. *In the Zone: Transcendent Experience in Sports*. New York; Penguin/Arkana, 1995.

Neilson, Brian J. "Baseball." In *The Theater of Sport*, ed. By Karl B. Raitz, 30-69. Baltimore: The Johns Hopkins University Press, 1991.

Newman, Roberta. "The American Church of Baseball and the National Baseball Hall of Fame." *Nine: A Journal of Baseball History and Social Policy Perspectives* 10/1 (Fall 2001): 46-63.

Novak, Michael. *The Joy of Sports: End Zones, Bases, Baskets, Balls, and the Consecration of the American Spirit.* New York: Basic Books, Inc., Publishers, 1976.

Oliver, Phil. "Baseball, Transcendence, and the Return to Life." In *The Cooperstown Symposium on Baseball and American Culture, 2001.* Ed. by William M. Simons, 291-303. Jefferson NC: McFarland and Company, Inc., Publishers, 2002.

Phalen, Rick, ed. *A Bittersweet Journey: America's Fascination with Baseball.* Tampa: McGregor, 2000.

Porter, Kathleen Sullivan. "Women as 'Goddess' Archetypes in Baseball Fiction." *Aethlon: The Journal of Sport Literature* 15/1 (Fall 1997): 67-82.

Prakash, Abhijay. "Comprehending the Narrative Power of the 'Curse of the Bambino.'" *Nine: A Journal of Baseball History and Social Policy Perspectives* 13/1 (Fall 2004): 118-132.

Rader, Benjamin G. "Compensatory Sport Heroes: Ruth, Grange, and Dempsey." *Journal of Popular Culture* 16/4 (Spring 1983): 11-22.

Reilly, Rick. "What Would Jesus Do?" *Sports Illustrated* 91/3 (19 July 1999): 92.

Reising, R. W. "Visions of Sport: The Gospel According to Yogi." *Journal of Popular Culture* 16/4 (Spring 1983): 68-74.

Rielly, Edward J. *Baseball: An Encyclopedia of Popular Culture.* Lincoln: University of Nebraska Press, 2005.

Riess, Steven A. *Touching Base: Professional Baseball and American Culture in the Progressive Era.* Revised Edition. Urbana: University of Illinois Press, 1999.

Robinson, Jr., Richard. "Spirituality and Baseball." In *The Cooperstown Symposium on Baseball and American Culture, 1999,* 23-30. Ed. by Peter M. Rutkoff. Jefferson NC: McFarland and Company, Inc., Publishers, 2000.

Rosengren, John. "Let Us Play." *U. S. Catholic* 69/1 (January 2004): 12-16.

Saposnik, Irving S. "Homage to Clyde Kluttz or the Education of a Jewish Baseball Fan." *Journal of American Culture* 4/3 (Fall 1981): 58-65.

Scholes, Jeffrey. "Professional Baseball and Fan Disillusionment: A Religious Ritual Analysis." *Journal of Religion and Popular Culture* (www.usask.ca/relst/jrpc) VII (Summer 2004).

Shaughnessy, Dan. *The Curse of the Bambino.* New York: Penguin Books, 2000.

Shurgot, Michael W. "The Baseball Cap as Talisman." *The Minneapolis Review of Baseball* 10/2 (Season Opener 1991): 35-37.

Smith, Jr., Leverett T. *The American Dream and the National Game.* Bowling Green OH: Popular Press, 1975.

Snyder, Eldon and Elmer Spreitzer. "The Religious Dimension of Sport." In *Social Aspects of Sport.* Third ed., Snyder and Spreitzer, 262-278. Englewood Cliffs NJ: Prentice-Hall, 1989.

Solomon, Eric. "Jews, Baseball, and the American Novel." *Aethlon: The Journal of Sport Literature* 14/1 (Fall 1996): 47-69.

Spalding, John. D. "Undoing Baseball's Original Sin." http://www.beliefnet.com/story/134_13405_1.html.

Stafford, Tim. "Baseball and the Atonement: Living Vicariously through Jesus and the Oakland A's." *Christianity Today* 32/6 (8 April 1988): 22-24.

Swift, E. M. "The Pox on the Sox: Who Needs Success? The Red Sox' Biblical Misfortunes Are a Unifying Force." *Sports Illustrated* 100/16 (19 April 2004): 34.

Tworkov, Helen. "The Baseball Diamond Sutra." *Tricycle: The Buddhist Review* 2/3 (Summer 1993): 4.

Vanderwerken, David L. and Spencer K. Wertz. *Sport Inside Out: Reading in Literature and Philosophy.* Fort Worth: Texas Christian University Press, 1985.

Vlasich, James A. *A Legend for the Legendary: The Origin of the Baseball Hall of Fame.* Bowling Green OH: Bowling Green State University Popular Press, 1990.

Voigt, David Q. "American Sporting Rituals." In *Rituals and Ceremonies in Popular Culture.* Ed. Ray B. Browne, 125-140. Bowling Green OH: Bowling Green University Popular Press, 1980.

Warnock, Jim. "The Mormon Game: The Religious Uses of Baseball in Early Utah." *Nine: A Journal of Baseball History and Social Policy Perspectives* 6/1 (Fall 1997): 1-14.

_____. "Playing Centerfield in the Lord's Ball Club: Billy Sunday's 1914 Denver Campaign." *Nine: A Journal of Baseball History and Social Policy Perspectives* 4/1 (Fall 1995): 62-83.

Weber, Bruce. "A 'Cathedral' to Some, the Stadium to Others." *New York Times,* 31 October 2001, C12.

Westbrook, Deeanne. *Ground Rules: Baseball and Myth.* Urbana: University of Illinois Press, 1996.

Will, George. *Bunts: Curt Flood, Camden Yards, Pete Rose, and Other Reflecions on Baseball.* New York: Scribner, 1998.

Williams, Peter. "Every Religion Needs a Martyr: The Role of Matty, Gehrig, and Clemente in the National Faith." In *From Season to Season: Sports as American Religion.* Ed. Joseph L. Price, 99-112. Macon: Mercer University Press, 2001.

_____. *The Sports Immortals: Deifying the American Athlete.* Bowling Green OH: Bowling Green State University Popular Press, 1994.

Muscular Faith: Expressions and Histories

Abramowitz, Martin. "The Making of a Card Set: American Jews in America's Game." *Heritage: Newsletter of the American Jewish Historical Society* 1/2 (Fall/Winter 2003): 10-11.

Brown, Matthew Hay. "Promoting Christian Gospel to Ballplayers; Evangelical Group Spreads through All Levels of Pro Baseball." *Baltimore Sun*, 31 March 2006, A1.

Bundgaard, Axel. *Muscle and Manliness: The Rise of Sport in American Boarding Schools.* Syracuse: Syracuse University Press, 2005.

Burns, Roger A. *Preacher: Billy Sunday and Big-Time American Evangelism.* New York: W. W. Norton & Company, 1992.

Dravecky, Dave, with Mike Yorkey. *Called Up: Stories of Life and Faith from the Great Game of Baseball.* Grand Rapids: Zondervan, 2004.

Ephross, Peter. "Hall of Fame Celebrates Jewish Major Leaguers." *Canadian Jewish News* 34/36 (9 September 2004): 70.

Firstenberger, W. A. *In Rare Form: A Pictorial History of Baseball Evangelist Billy Sunday.* Iowa City: University of Iowa Press, 2005.

Gordon, Rabbi James. *Pray Ball! The Spiritual Insights of a Jewish Sports Fan.* Jerusalem: Gefen, 1999.

Greenberg, Hank, and Ira Berkow. *Hank Greenberg: The Story of My Life.* Benchmark Press, 2001.

Hohler, Bob. "Faith Binds Many of Sox—Evangelicals Give Sport a Sport a Spiritual Context." *Boston Globe*, 31 August 2005, A1.

Holmquist, David. "Will There Be Baseball in Heaven?" *Christianity Today* 38 (10 January 1994): 30-33.

Hubbard, Steve. *Faith in Sports: Athletes and Their Religion on and off the Field.* New York: Doubleday, 1998.

Jewish Sports News. Monthly newsletter featuring reports and articles on Jewish athletes at all levels of play.

John, Tommy and Sally, with Joe Musser. *The Tommy John Story.* Foreword by Tommy Lasorda. Old Tappan NJ: Fleming H. Revell Company, 1978.

Jones, Todd. "Religion Serves Great Purpose in Baseball." *The Sporting News,* 26 December 2002.

Kanter, Arnold B. *Is God a Cubs Fan?* Evanston IL: JRC Press, 1999.

Knickerbocker, Wendy. "Billy Sunday, the Baseball Evangelist." *Elysian Fields Quarterly* 21/3 (Fall 2004): 46-52.

Krattenmaker, Tom. "Does Proselytizing Cross the Line in Pro Sports?" *USA Today,* 7 November 2005, A13.

Leavy, Jane. *Sandy Koufax: A Lefty's Legacy.* New York; HarperCollins, 2002.

Ladd, Tony and Mathisen, James A. *Muscular Christianity: Evangelical Protestants and the Development of American Sport.* Grand Rapids: Baker Books, 1999.

Maass, Peter. "A Gathering Place for Faithful Fans: Orthodox Jews Can See Orioles Games, Satisfy Religious Needs." *Washington Post,* 5 May 1996, B1.

Peale, Norman Vincent. *Faith Made Them Champions.* Carmel NY: Guideposts Associates, Inc., 1954.

Pearlman, Jeff. "The Passion of J. D. Drew." *Sports Illustrated* 100/12 (22 March 2004): 52-55.

Pierce, Gregory F. Augustine, ed. *Diamond Presence: Twelve Stories of Finding God at the Old Ball Park.* Chicago: ACTA Publications, 2004.

Poland, Hugh. *Steal Away: Devotions for Baseball Fans.* Foreword by Mariano Rivera. Valley Forge PA: Judson Press, 2006.

Putney, Clifford. *Muscular Christianity: Manhood and Sports in Protestant America, 1880-1920.* Cambridge: Harvard University Press, 2001.

Sandul, Duane G. *When Faith Steals Home.* Plainfield NJ: Logos International, 1980.

Sharing the Victory. Magazine on Faith and Sport published nine times a year by the Fellowship of Christian Athletes.

Shields, Sherice L. "Players and Prayers." *Tallahassee Democrat,* 24 June 2001, D1,6.

Simonson, Ted, ed. *The Goal and the Glory: America's Athletes Speak Their Faith.* Intro. by Branch Rickey. Westwood NJ; Fleming H. Revell Company, 1962.

Sports Spectrum. Bi-monthly periodical featuring player testimonies and articles on muscular Christianity.

Springer, Steve. "Dodgers' Green Keeps the Faith." *Los Angeles Times,* 26 September 2001, D5.

Sunday, William A. "Billy." *The Sawdust Trail: Billy Sunday in His Own Words.* Iowa City: University of Iowa Press, 2005.

_____. "Why I Left Professional Baseball." *Young Men's Era* 19/20 (27 July 1893).

Website. Official website of Baseball Chapel: www.baseballchapel.org.

_____. Official website of Athletes in Action: www.aia.com/baseball.

_____. Articles and interviews related to Jewish ballplayers: www.JewishSports.com.

Fiction

Carpenter, Jacob M. "Top of the Ninth." *Aethlon: The Journal of Sport Literature* 22/2 (Spring 2005): 93-98.

Coover, Robert. *The Universal Baseball Association, Inc., J. Henry Waugh, Prop.* New York: Random House, 1968.

Craig, David. *Our Lady of the Outfield*. Oak Lawn IL: CMJ Marian Publisher, 1999.

Donohue, James F. *Spitballs and Holy Water*. New York: Avon, 1977.

Duncan, David James. *The Brothers K*. New York: Doubleday, 1992.

Greenberg, Eric Rolf. *The Celebrant*. Lincoln: University of Nebraska Press, 1983 [reprint].

Hedley, Leslie W. "The Day God Invented Baseball." In *Baseball and the Game of Life: Stories for the Thinking Fan*. Ed. Peter C. Bjarkman, 67-74. New York: Vintage Books, 1991.

Levine, Peter. *The Rabbi of Swat*. East Lansing: Michigan State University Press, 1999.

Mark Harris. *Bang the Drum Slowly*. New York: Knopf, 1956

Kinsella, W. P. *The Iowa Baseball Confederacy*. Toronto: Collins, 1986.

_____. "The Last Pennant Before Armageddon." In *The Thrill of the Grass*, 3-21. New York: Penguin, 1984.

_____. *Shoeless Joe*. New York: Houghton Mifflin, 1982.

Malamud, Bernard. *The Natural*. New York: Farrar, Strauss, and Giroux, 1952.

Memoirs

D'Antonio, Dave. *Invincible Summer: Traveling America in Search of Yesterday's Baseball Greats*. South Bend IN: Diamond Communications, Inc., 1997.

Fimrite, Ron, ed. *Birth of a Fan*. New York: Macmillan Publishing Company, 1993.

Goodwin, Doris Kearns. *Wait Till Next Year*. New York: Simon and Schuster, 1998.

Gould, Stephen Jay. *Triumph and Tragedy in Mudville: A Lifelong Passion for Baseball.* New York: W. W. Norton and Company, 2003.

Jolley, Marc A. *Safe at Home: A Memoir of God, Baseball, and Family.* Macon: Mercer University Press, 2005.

Lamb, David. *Stolen Season: A Journey through America and Baseball's Minor Leagues.* New York: Random House, 1991.

Lehmann-Haupt, Christopher. *Me and DimMaggio: A Baseball fan Goes in Search of His Gods.* New York: Simon and Schuster, 1986.

Lomax, James W. "Opening Day." *American Journal of Psychiatry* 161/2 (February 2004): 224-225.

Mayer, Robert. *Baseball and Men's Lives: The True Confessions of a Skinny-Marink.* New York: Delta, 1994.

Mungo, Raymond. *Confessions from Left Field: A Baseball Pilgrimage.* New York: E. P. Dutton, Inc., 1983.

Sheed, Wilfred. "Why Sports Matter." *Wilson Quarterly* (Winter 1995).

Stanton, Tom. *The Road to Cooperstown: A Father, Two Sons, and the Journey of a Lifetime.* New York: St. Martin's Press, 2003.

Swirsky, Seth. *Baseball Letters: A Fan's correspondence with His Heroes.* New York: Kodansha, 1996.

Index